378.196 OPP

David Warren Piper
Southampton Institute
East Park Terrace
Southampton SO14 0YN
Tel. 01703 319687
david.w.piper@solent.ac.uk

ST

556 78 31

Impacts of Study Abroad Programmes on Students and Graduates

The Higher Education Policy Series

Edited by Maurice Kogan

Higher Education Policy Series 11, volume 2

Impacts of Study Abroad Programmes on Students and Graduates

Susan Opper, Ulrich Teichler and Jerry Carlson

Preface by Barbara B. Burn, Ladislav Cerych and Alan Smith

Jessica Kingsley Publishers
London

Copyright © 1990 European Cultural Foundation

First published in the United Kingdom by
Jessica Kingsley Publishers
118 Pentonville Road
London N1 9JN

British Library Cataloguing in Publication Data
Opper, Susan
    Impacts of study abroad programmes on students and
    graduates. - Higher education policy series ; 11, v. 2.
    1. Educational relations
    I. Title II. Teichler, Ulrich III. Carlson, Jerry IV.
    Series
    370.196

    ISBN 1-85302-523-2
    ISSN 0954-3716

Printed and bound in Great Britain by
Biddles Ltd, Guildford and King's Lynn

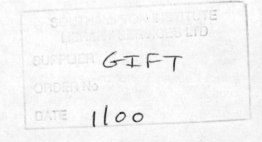

Content

Preface

Since the mid-1980's the European Institute of Education and Social Policy (Paris/Brussels) has been co-ordinating a major international research effort designed to analysze the structures and impacts of study abroad programmes offered by higher education institutions in four European countries (France, the Federal Republic of Germany, Sweden and the United Kingdom) and the USA.

The "Study Abroad Evaluation Project" has been carried out by a decentralized research team whose members were drawn from all five countries concerned and who represent a wide spectrum of academic disciplines and professional backgrounds in teaching, research and various administrative functions related to international co-operation in higher education.

The project received its main financial support from the Commission of the European Communities, the Federal Ministry of Education and Science in the Federal Republic of Germany, the European Cultural Foundation, the Council for National Academic Awards (UK), the Swedish National Board of Universities and Colleges and the United States Information Agency.

The Project's findings are published in two parts, Volume I being devoted to the study abroad programmes as such, and Volume II to their impact on students.

We hope that the report will not only provide some illuminating insights into this under-researched and increasingly important aspect of education, but also that it will help to stimulate more in-depth investigation of many issues which merit and require such further analysis. Full acknowledgements to the many persons and organizations who have made the present report possible are contained in the first chapter of Volume I.

Ladislav Cerych
Director
European Institute of
Education and Social Policy
Paris

Barbara B. Burn
Associate Provost
University of
Massachusetts
Amherst

Alan Smith
Director
Office for Cooperation in Education
Brussels

Chapter 1

Research Aims, Design and Methods

1.1   Research Aims

The Study Abroad Evaluation Project (SAEP) has had three main objectives.
First, in analysing a large number of study abroad programmes which promote
mobility between institutions of higher education in the United Kingdom, France,
the Federal Republic of Germany, Sweden and the United States, it has explored
a spectrum of "organised" study abroad programme models. Several of the following chapters are primarily descriptive, tracing the origins and underlying purposes of the study abroad programmes, their formal administrative, financial, and
academic structures, as well as major features of the higher education institutional
and national contexts. The reader will note that a common thread in this expose is
that the predominant characteristics and norms of the respective systems of higher education have an impact on the structure of the study abroad programmes
themselves. Also, as many of the study abroad programmes are affiliated with distinct areas of study, the particular features and requirements of the academic
disciplines have had their influence upon the shape of the study abroad programmes. Rounding out the descriptive analysis, we present a background sketch of the
participants: their academic achievements, extra-curricular activities and internationally-oriented interests, information on their living situations at home and
abroad, and highlights of their experiences abroad.

Extending beyond the aim to describe the diversity in programme models and
the experiences of their participants, the second aim is to evaluate the extent to
which study abroad programme outcomes can be judged "successful". The attention to outcomes covers not only programme administration and content, but
also the effects the programmes have on their participants. Regarding the evaluation of programme operations, the interest is in whether programmes succeed in
fulfilling their stated goals; in ensuring that the period abroad is given academic
credit toward the degree the students are pursuing at their home institutions of
higher education (also referred to as the "sending" institution). Are students able
to avoid having their study period abroad prolong the time it takes for them to
obtain their degrees? Do the programmes enable certain individuals to study
abroad, who otherwise might not have had the means to do so on their own?
Have the programmes run into funding difficulties? Have there been other problems, perhaps in the nature of co-operative links sought with partner institution(s)
abroad?

Pursuing indicators of programme "success" in the realm of student experiences, enquiries are made with varying degrees of specificity into whether study
abroad participants considered the period(s) abroad stimulating and generally
worth the investment of time and other resources. Did students run into problems

because of any aspects of programme organisation - or lack thereof? Did they feel the sojourn delivered or led to any academic gains; and if so, how would these be characterised? What impact did the experience abroad have in areas which are most commonly expected to be affected by a foreign sojourn: foreign language proficiency and knowledge of life in other countries? How, and with what strength of conviction, did programme participants alter formerly held beliefs and values as a result of their exposure to other cultures? Did students feel that study abroad would somehow be instrumental in what eventually happens to them as they enter the workforce?

The third objective for the research is explanatory in that we have explored potential causes for the nature and degree of success achieved by the programmes and their participants. The crux of the analysis is the question as to whether programme and student-related outcomes can be attributed to characteristics of the programmes as such. This analysis is based principally on the replies received from those mainly responsible for the programmes (called "programme directors") and from programme participants, as both groups have responded to a battery of questionnaires developed by the research team. The major patterns in the responses were derived predominantly through quantitative analysis, and further interpreted through more qualitative procedures and consultation of secondary sources.

For practical reasons, the report on the findings is divided into two volumes. The first focuses on the programmes per se, covering the contexts and origins of the programmes, the rationales and objectives which launched them, the means by which participants are recruited, selected, and funded; and of course the curricular provisions, modes of assessment and matters of academic recognition which are the primary justification for the study abroad programmes' existence. The first volume also examines factors which may explain the nature and degree of the programmes' success.

The second volume focuses primarily upon the study abroad programme participants. It highlights students' personal and educational backgrounds, their experiences during their sojourns, and it details programme "success" as measured by the perceived changes in participants' academically related achievement and their thinking concerning effective teaching and learning strategies. It documents as well the participants' foreign language proficiencies, knowledge and attitudes about the culture and society of their respective home and host countries, and participants' views about the utility of the study abroad experience in their work-related roles. In this process, the extent and nature of students' satisfaction with the academic and extra-curricular experiences of their sojourn is examined, as are the basic types of problems participants encounter. Finally, in similar fashion to the first volume on programmes, there is an examination of factors which may explain the observed changes in participants' abilities, values and attitudes which are apparently linked to their studies abroad. The major topics for Volume II and the structure of the analysis are shown in Diagram S1.

Diagram S1
Structure of the Analysis of the Outcomes of Study Abroad for Participants

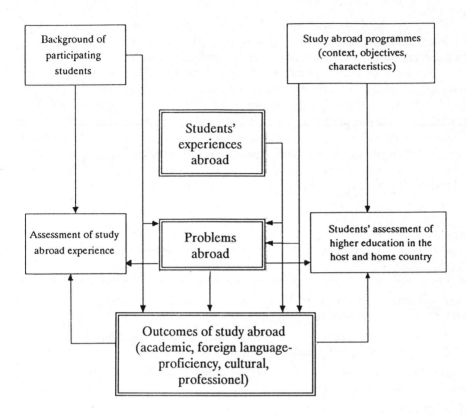

1.2　The Surveys

In the framework of the Study Abroad Evaluation Project, a multitude of surveys were conducted which aimed at exploring the respective themes of the project in more detail and which combined a larger set of issues related to study abroad than prior surveys in this areas had done. The analysis of the programmes was based predominantly on a written questionnaire sent to programme directors as well as subsequent interviews. In addition, written questionnaires addressed the institutional and, if applicable, the departmental context of the study abroad programmes.

Replies to two written questionnaires are the major source of analysis of the impacts of study abroad programmes upon their participants. All students who went abroad during the 1984-85 academic year in the programmes surveyed were sent a "Pre-Study Abroad Questionnaire" immediately prior to their departure. Students who replied to this survey were sent in 1985 the "Post-Study Abroad Questionnaire" approximately one month after they had returned to resume studies at their home institutions. Students who had remained abroad consecutively for more than one year received the questionnaire one year into their sojourn.

The longitudinal approach of asking the same students twice made it possible to observe changes in self-ratings of academic competence, foreign language proficiency, knowledge of their study abroad host country and the students' international interests. In addition, students were asked prior to their sojourn about their educational background, their motives and expectations regarding studies in general and study abroad in particular and about their ways of preparing themselves for the study abroad period. Additional questions upon return addressed life and study while abroad as well as experiences upon return, as, for example, issues of recognition regarding their achievements abroad. Finally, students were asked to compare teaching and learning at the host institution abroad to that at their home institution. An overview of the major topics of these questionnaires is provided in Table S1.

Table S1
Main Topics Addressed in the Pre-, Post- and Retrospective Student Questionnaires

---

Student background data (age, gender, nationality, parents' background, accommodation, leisure activities)

Students' educational history (including reasons for choosing home instution and field, academic achievement, abilities and accomplishments)

Students' international perspective (interest and attitudes towards events relating to own/ other countries, travel)

Students' decision to study abroad

Preparation for study abroad

Students' foreign language proficiency

Students' career goals

Students' academic and work placement experiences abroad

Degree of satisfaction with study abroad programme

A separate group of students, the 1983-84 cohort for the programmes under review, were sent a single questionnaire some months after their return in 1984 ("Retrospective Study Abroad Questionnaire"). This second group was asked nearly all of the questions which were put to the 1984-85 group. A comparison of findings of the retrospective and longitudinal questionnaires revealed differences which appeared to be more readily explained by uneven return rates than by other factors. Therefore, the replies to this questionnaire are not presented in this volume.

An additional set of questions was sent to students whose study abroad period also involved a practical work placement. An adapted version of the questionnaires was also devised for students going to *two* foreign countries under the auspices of a single study abroad programme. This applied to a select number of British, French, and German students only. In the case of a few American students spending their sojourns in Germany during 1984-85, a standardised "Language Proficiency Oral Interview" was conducted both before and after the study abroad period as a cross-check on the validity of students' self-appraisals of foreign language competence.

A "Comparison Group Questionnaire" was administered to a randomly selected group of students at two of the American sending institutions. The comparison group met the general criteria for inclusion in study abroad programmes (a 3.0 or better grade point average and sophomore status). Foreign language proficiency criteria were not used in selection of the comparison group. Nor were students who turned out to have had first hand experience in a foreign country systematically excluded from this sample.

From autumn 1985 until summer 1986, a "Questionnaire for Graduates" was administered to former students who, at some point before graduating during the period 1980-84, had participated in a study abroad programme. This enquiry provided information on the first stages of their professional careers and assessed the relevance of the study abroad experience primarily in this connection. Corresponding graduate interviews were conducted by telephone with former participants of the American programmes. Persons with previous study abroad experience, who had graduated five to twenty years prior, were interviewed for approximately thirty minutes each. The findings from the European and American graduate surveys were not systematically compared with those from the surveys of the 1983-84 and 1984-85 cohorts since we did not examine the degree to which the programmes themselves had changed over the corresponding years. The findings of telephone interviews are reported in a separate publication on the American study abroad programme.

It should be noted that for all of the student questionnaires - whether for the 1983-84, the 1985-86, or the graduate cohorts (see below) - British and Swedish students received the original English version of the questionnaire, and the French and German students the appropriate translated versions. Adaptations from one version to another were inevitable in questions which dealt with educational and occupational background. Also, the American version was modified in several respects, partly to allow a more detailed exploration of participants' cultural values. On a technical matter, in several items of the American questionnaire, 7-point Likert scales were used, whereas 5-point scales were used in the European questionnaires. Several items were worded differently in the American instrument as compared with the European, or contained a different number of items in the lists of pre-supplied potential responses.

These sub-variations reflect the researchers' sensitivity to the differing emphases and aims of the study abroad programmes which operate from sending institutions in the different parts of the world. This is also an indication that there were some significant differences in research philosophy between the American and European members of the research team; not to mention occasional technical difficulties in trans-Atlantic communication.

1.3 Procedures and Response Rates

The ways in which the questionnaires were distributed differed from country to country, owing in part to organisational conditions under which members of the research team and the programmes themselves were operating, as well as to certain regulations for data protection. Questionnaires to be answered by students were sent to them by their home institutions, thus preventing the research team from knowing the names and addresses of students without the students' consent. Along with the questionnaires, European students received envelopes in which to send their returns directly to members of the research team, ensuring that teaching or administrative staff at the home institutions would not see the responses. To enable a longitudinal analysis of study abroad from the students' perspective, the research team requested that persons who agreed to participate in this facet should disclose their names and addresses on the pre-departure questionnaire. During processing, this information was separated and stored apart form the main body of the questionnaire, to guarantee anonymity at all stages of the subsequent analysis.

Most of the data reported in this study refers to 82 study abroad programmes defined as a set of arrangements for sending students within a major field of study, or a group of students from a variety of fields, to an institution or institutions in another country. Of the 82 programmes:
- 22 were in the United Kingdom (home country);
- 14 in France;
- 26 in the Federal Republic of Germany;
- 8 in Sweden; and
- 12 were in the USA.

Programmes were selected which had received support in the framework of the "Joint Study Programmes" sponsored by the European Community (which preceded the current ERASMUS scheme), in the framework of the "Integrated Study Abroad" scheme administered by the German Academic Exchange Service (DAAD), as well as programmes partially funded through the "Internationalisation of Higher Education" grant administered by the Swedish National Board of Universities and Colleges. American programmes were established at those institutions which actively participated in the establishment of the research project. Finally, some programmes were included which were established by the partner institutions of those institutions selected according to the above stated criteria.

As far as students' responses are concerned, a total of 890 students replied to the Pre-Study Abroad Questionnaire. This is approximately 57 percent of all participants in the programmes surveyed, a return rate which is higher than the 40 percent traditionally considered quite favourable where students are asked to disclose their names and addresses for later distribution of a follow-up questionnaire. Our return rate is especially satisfactory given the length of the questionnaire (more than 20 pages).

Diagram S 2
Written Questionnaire Surveys and Interviews conducted with participants in Study Abroad Programmes

---

"Pre-Study Abroad Questionnaire"

First Interview with participants 1984/85	N = 890
1984	(UK: 145, F: 110, D: 232, S: 45,
	US: 358)

"Post-Study Abroad Questionnaire"

Second Interview with participants 1984/85	N = 439
1985	(UK: 60, F: 46, D: 154,
	S: 38, US: 141)

"Retrospective Study Abroad Questionnaire"

Interview with participants 1983/84	N = 416
1984	(UK: 107, F: 55, D: 133, S: 11,
	US: 110)

"Study Abroad and Career"
(Questionnaire for Graduates)

Interview of former participants:	N = 458
Graduates of the years 1980-84	(UK: 194, F: 83, D: 115, S: 66)

1985/86

"Interviews conducted with former participants in Study Abroad Programmes"

Telephone interviews conducted with	N = 77
a selection of former participants: Graduates 1966-81	(US: 77)

1986

Of the total 890 participants who replied to the Pre-Study Abroad Question-naire, 439 (49%) responded to the Post-Study Abroad Questionnaire as well. Thus responses to both questionnaires were available for 28 percent of the entire 1984-85 student cohort we attempted to survey. We estimate that approximately 20 percent of the 890 students were "lost" for reasons related to administrative problems in distributing the second questionnaire; for example, because some of the original respondents decided not to go abroad after all, or because the follow-up questionnaires were sent to addresses which were no longer valid and for which there were no forwarding addresses. In addition, approximately 30 percent of the students who received the Post-Study Abroad Questionnaire did not respond. Some of them intended to go abroad at the time of the first survey but actually did not go.

The return rates differ substantially by country. The highest were those of Swedish participants, 65 percent of whom returned the first questionnaire, and of those receiving the second questionnaire, 84 percent replied. The overall return from the German participants - rates of 75 and 66 percent - was almost equally high, whereas American (55 and 39%), British (48 and 41%) and French students (46 and 42%) were somewhat less co-operative. As already mentioned, similar questionnaires were sent to American students not participating in the study abroad programmes analysed. Of the 820 sent a questionnaire, 43 percent re-sponded, and among those who received the second questionnaire the response rate was 51 percent.

The response rate for those who went abroad in 1983-84, and who were sent the Retrospective Study Abroad Questionnaire, was about 45 percent. A total of 416 students replied. The analysis in this volume is consistently based on the 1984-85 data set (the 439 replies), with the obvious exception of the alumni data.

The European graduate questionnaire was sent to approximately 1,200 former participants in 50 (of 70) of the European programmes. The selection was based almost exclusively upon the availability of current addresses. The actual return rate on this survey was nearly 50 percent, but it was subsequently discovered that se-veral people had graduated earlier or later than the defined target date, and their responses had to be excluded. The final number of valid returns came to 458.

For the corresponding survey of the American study abroad programme grad-uates, a random sample was taken from a group which had graduated five to twenty years prior to the evaluation. A letter was sent to 158 of these people, re-questing their co-operation in a telephone interview. Altogether, 101 persons (65%) replied positively, and 77 were interviewed.

1.4   Data Processing and Analysis

Most of the questions asked of students and European graduates were "closed"; that is they provided respondents with categories to be marked if applicable in their situation. Replies to the "open" questions in the student and graduate questionnaires were summarised by a subgroup of the research team and processed alpha-numerically on the computer. Photocopies of the results were distributed to all members of the research team.

Data processing and statistical analysis took place at the Gesamthochschule Kassel with the help of SPSS programmes on TR440 Siemens BS2000 computers and IBM AT personal computers, and at the University of California at Riverside on a SAS-VAX 2 computer.

All coded and quantifiable data were made available to members of the research team in the form of basic frequency distributions, percentages, arithmetic mean scores and basic significance tests, cross-tabulations according to home country and field of study. For example, the aggregate value of replies to rating scales, where 1 = "very important" and 5 = "not important at all", are presented in arithmetic means. Pearson correlation coefficients have been used as measures of association. Supplemental analyses were tailor-made to the requests of the various authors in the current report.

Multi-dimensional scales were subjected to factor analysis, whereby promax rotation was used in each case, with the number of factors extracted based on their Eigenvalues, Scree plots, and examination of the percent of variance each factor contributed to the total variance. The results served to establish indices, which, for diverse reasons (i.e. slight differences in the factor structure of replies before and after the study abroad period), do not always strictly rely on the factor structure thus derived.

Although the many variables used were not interval measurements, and although the Likert scales used in many items of the questionnaires provide data that may not follow a normal distribution curve, parametric tests were employed that have turned out to be robust and thus appropriate to use for such data. The parametric procedures employed were T-tests, Pearson product-moment correlations, analyses of variance, multivariate analyses of variance, regression analysis, and factor analysis. Nominal data were analysed by means of chi-square tests with strength of association represented by Kendall's tau.

To simplify the procedures and presentation of results, significance tests and other more detailed accounts of the statistical measures employed are not included in the report on results. While this may frustrate the more technically oriented reader, the report could not remain at a readable length if the complexity and extent of the data were documented so conscientiously. And, too, the readership addressed is not limited to specialists in statistical methodology.

The 0.05 level of statistical significance was adopted for the programme data; the 0.01 level for students and graduate data. However, at many points, a simpler procedure was followed. For example, when pre-post changes on a 5-point Likert scale turned out to be significant in a certain series of tests - ranging between 0.13 and 0.15 - changes of a magnitude of 0.2 were reported to be significant. Average changes of 0.3 for students of a given country and field of study were also reported, although statistical measurements might not have supported this as being significant in all cases due to different absolute numbers of students by country or by field of study.

In conclusion, reference is again made to the concern for data protection. In citing the programme directors, students, and graduates, the members of the research team who drafted chapters of this report originally identified the citations by using a prescribed system of code numbers. These notations were then deleted in the final version of the manuscript, so the data source could not readily be identified by the reader. Similarly, the proper names of higher education institutions, cities, and any other descriptions which would enable sources to be identified were either deleted or replaced by notations such as "University X" in "City Y".

1.5   Conceptual Background and Limitation of the Project

Any research of this kind is influenced to a considerable extent by previous concepts, methods, and other available literature on the topics under consideration. In order to draw systematically from the appropriate legacy, a review of the research literature and other factual accounts was conducted, to tap:
- historical developments in international academic exchange and study abroad programming in Western Europe and the USA;
- accounts of existing support schemes aiming to facilitate mobility and study abroad programmes in particular;
- the findings and methodology of surveys and other research on academic mobility, study abroad programmes, and additional international dimensions of higher education;
- the methodological approaches and findings of research on topics relevant to the foci of the present evaluation (e.g. assessment of academic achievement in higher education, of foreign language learning and proficiency; formation and change in personal and cultural values);
- concepts and methods of evaluation research;
- multivariate and multi-level analyses, especially statistical analyses appropriate to the current research design.

Some of the detailed studies led to separate publications during the course of the overall research endeavour:
- Asa Briggs and Barbara B. Burn analysed trends and traditions in international academic mobility in higher education, focussing on the origin and context of increasing efforts over the last two decades in Western Europe and the United States to promote study abroad through organised programmes[1];

---

[1]   Briggs, A. and Burn, B. *Study Abroad: A European And An American Perspective*. Paris: European Institute of Education and Social Policy, 1985 (Organisation and Impact of Study Abroad, No. 1).

- Dieter Danckwortt compiled an overview of concepts, methods and results of surveys on study abroad conducted at various places in the Federal Republic of Germany[2];
- Fritz Dalichow and Ulrich Teichler conducted a questionnaire survey on academic recognition of study abroad, which covered all programmes supported through the EC's "Joint Study Programme" scheme during 1976-1983[3];
- Two bibliographies were compiled on study abroad: one by Britta Baron and Peter Bachmann on West European publications[4]; the other by Henry Weaver on American publications[5].

It should be added here that additional information on the research methodologies and findings of the study are provided in separate reports on the USA programmes and participants[6] as well as on the reports published in German.[7] A separate report on the American experience will be published in 1990.

The present research is in many ways the first of its kind. While considerable descriptive literature exists on study abroad which involves the participation of American and West European students, it is rare that any of the existing sources document a systematically analytical enquiry into whether study abroad makes any difference in its participants' behaviours and performance; and if so, whether the influence can be attributable to study abroad programme characteristics per se. The current research has been an all-embracing, exploratory study to open up the research field. The statistical design for treatment of the findings is one reflection of this effort. The more consistent use of a comparative approach, taking into consideration the different disciplines and systems of higher education as they influence expectations and arrangements for study abroad, is also an important element.

---

2   Danckwortt, D., *Auslandsstudium als Gegenstand der Forschung - eine Literaturübersicht.* Kassel: Wissenschaftliches Zentrum für Berufs- und Hochschulforschung an der Gesamthochschule Kassel, 1984 (Werkstattberichte, No. 11).

3   Dalichow, F. and Teichler, U. Recognition of Study Abroad in the European Community, *Higher Education in the European Community.* Luxembourg: Office for Publications of the European Communities, 1986.

4   Baron, B. and Bachmann, P. Study Abroad in Western Europe: A Bibliography, *European Journal of Education,* Vol. 22, No. 1, 1987.

5   Weaver, H. D. *Research on U.S. Students Abroad: A Bibliography with Abstracts.* Education Abroad Program: University of California, 1989

6   Forthcoming in 1989.

7   Teichler, U., Smith, A. and Steube, W.: *Auslandsstudienprogramme im Vergleich.* Bad Honnef: Bock, 1988 (Schriftenreihe Studien zu Bildung und Wissenschaft, No. 68, edited by Bundesminister für Bildung und Wissenschaft); Teichler, U. and Opper, S.: *Erträge des Auslandsstudiums für Studierende und Absolventen.* Bad Honnef: Bock, 1988 (Schriftenreihe Studien zu Bildung und Wissenschaft, No. 69, edited by Bundesminister für Bildung und Wissenschaft).

Due to the considerable breadth of the research focus and to resource constraints, we were forced to make certain compromises with the research methodology. We could not devise a series of unique investigative approaches to look
into all areas central to the intended analysis. Consequently, for a portion of the
survey, we drew pragmatically from existing expertise and employed slightly
adapted versions of research instruments which had been tested and employed in
other contexts. This is particularly the case for portions of our study where we
attempted to obtain a reading on the study abroad participants' foreign language
competence, attitudes and values, and cultural learning. (All of this is described
fully in the chapters which follow.) Also, as mentioned above, we had to work with
a sample based on what was available in terms of study abroad programme
models. This is not strictly a statistical probability sample. Finally, as already discussed, we used variables (for certain study abroad programme characteristics,
participant behaviours and experiences etc.) for statistical analysis instead of ana-
lyzing case studies across all thematic areas.

1.6   Financial Support And Members Of The Research Team

The primary sponsors of the project are as follows:
The European Cultural Foundation (Amsterdam), the Federal Ministry of Ed-
ucation and Science (Bonn), the Swedish National Board of Universities and
Colleges (UHA, Stockholm), the Council for National Academic Awards
(CNAA, London) and the United States Information Agency (USIA, Wash-
ington, D.C.).

Additional financial and other support for the project's organisational infras-
tructure were provided by:
The German Academic Exchange Service (DAAD, Bonn), the National Association of Foreign Student Affairs (NAFSA, USA), the Council for International Educational Exchange (CIEE, USA), and the Institute of International
Education (IIE, New York).

This decentralised research effort benefited further from personnel and other
resources made available by:
The European Institute of Education and Social Policy (Paris), the Office for
Co-operation in Education/Erasmus Bureau (Brussels), the Centre for Research on Higher Education and Work (Kassel), the Netherlands Institute for
Advanced Study in the Humanities and Social Sciences (NIAS, Wassenaar), the
University of Massachusetts at Amherst, the University of California, the University of Colorado at Boulder, Kalamazoo College, and the University of Upp-
sala (Sweden).

The project was conducted by a decentralised, international team, the composition of which is indicated below. The group brought together a mix of professional backgrounds in administration, teaching and research in higher education,

international education, and managing study abroad programmes. The team included representatives from all the countries from which the study abroad programmes were drawn, in order to ensure that the various orientations in higher education and in the rationale(s) for study abroad would be adequately represented in the research design and ensuing analysis. It was important to ensure as well that, on the part of the research team, there would be expertise in all languages in which the investigation was conducted. Development of the research instruments and drafts of the various chapters in the report were the subject of in-depth and continual discussions among all members of the team.

Overall co-ordination of the project has been the responsibility of: Ladislav Cerych (European Institute of Education and Social Policy), Barbara B. Burn (University of Massachusetts/Amherst), and Alan Smith (Office for Co-operation in Education/ERASMUS Bureau). Co-ordinators of the survey methodology and data analysis were: Jerry Carlson (University of California) and Ulrich Teichler (Centre for Research on Higher Education and Work, Gesamthochschule-Universitat Kassel). Britta Baron (Office for Co-operation in Education/DAAD) and Susan Opper (University of Uppsala/European Institute of Education and Social Policy) served as the principal research staff members in preparing the project's reports on the European side. Barbara B. Burn and Jerry Carlson assumed similar responsibility on the American side. Susan Opper and Ulrich Teichler co-ordinated the finalisation of the two-volume report on the project's findings.

The decentralised surveys were conducted in the UK by David Warren Piper and Robert Murray (Centre for Staff Development in Higher Education, University of London Institute of Education); in France by Ladislav Cerych and Denyse Saab; in the Federal Republic of Germany by Ulrich Teichler and Wolfgang Steube; in Sweden by Susan Opper; and in the USA by Barbara B. Burn and Jerry Carlson.

Many additional people have been involved in the conceptualisation and design of the evaluation, in conducting interviews, and in analysing and interpreting the findings: William H. Allaway (University of California), Elinor G. Barber (Institute of International Education), Jean Delaney (University of Colorado/Boulder) Joe Fugate (Kalamazoo College), Denis Kallen (European Institute of Education and Social Policy), Maryelise Lamet (University of Massachusetts/Amherst), Pat Martin (University of Pennsylvania), Roderick Paton (Buckinghamshire College of Higher Education), John Useem (Professor Emeritus, Michigan State University), and Henry Weaver (University of California).

Assistance in data processing and statistical analysis was provided by: Wolfgang Steube, Harald Schomburg and Friedhelm Maiworm (Gesamthochschule Kassel) and David Yachimovicz (University of California).

Others spent time as research assistants and word processing specialists: Helga Cassidy, Kristin Gagelmann, and Heidi Winter (Gesamthochschule Kassel), Maria Gonzales (Office for Co-operation in Education/Erasmus Bureau) and Danny Milman (University of California).

The complexity of the overall project structure, covering as it did researchers, sponsors and higher education institutions in several different countries, has naturally given rise to a number of difficulties. However, it is strongly felt that these have been more than offset by the manifest benefits which have accrued to the project in terms of familiarity with national systems, linguistic competence across several languages, diversity of disciplinary approaches, sharing of resources and the general group dynamics of an internationally based team.

Chapter 2

The Participants

2.1 Introduction

The academic, linguistic, cultural and professional effects of the programmes detailed in following chapters are derived from comparisons of relevant aspects in the students' personal, academic, and social backgrounds with their post-study abroad accounts of proficiencies and sojourn-related experiences in the corresponding areas. The research team could measure the effects of the sojourn most objectively with the group of students who were abroad in 1984-85 as they responded to a questionnaire *before and after* their sojourn. This is in contrast to the 1983-84 group which answered the questionnaire only retrospectively.

The background sketch on the 1984-85 participants is taken primarily from information they provided in their Pre-Study Abroad Questionnaires. Some portions of this profile sketch are supplemented with programme directors' descriptions of the type of student who generally participates in their programmes. The students' and programme directors' reports are comparable, but they do not match exactly. This is partly because the programmes vary in size in terms of student numbers, and the programme directors' replies are not weighted accordingly; partly because approximately thirty percent of the 1984-85 group of participants did not respond to the Pre-Study Abroad Questionnaire.

The number of students who filled out both Pre- and Post-Study Abroad Questionnaires was 439. This, our target group, differs in its distribution by country and field of study affiliations - although not excessively - from the *entire* population of 890 who replied to the Pre-Study Abroad Questionnaire (and it is this larger group which forms the basis for the analysis in chapter 5 of volume 1, which is otherwise similar to the analysis in this chapter). The major differences in the group of 439 compared with the group of 890 are reported elsewhere in this chapter.

Within the target group of students, there are:
- 154 (35.1%) from German institutions of higher education;
- 141 (32.1%) from American institutions;
- 60 (13.7%) from the UK;
- 46 (10.5%) from institutions in France; and
- 38 (8.7%) from Sweden.

Thus, over two-thirds (68%) of the students are at institutions in Europe, of which:
- 25.3% are enrolled in Business Studies;
- 11.4% in Law;
- 10.3% in Natural Sciences;

- 6.4% in Engineering; and
- 5.2% in Foreign Languages.

Over a third of the 439 students are recorded as participants in the study abroad programmes which serve "various" fields. For these students, the major field of concentration could not be identified. Most of the American students fall within this category, although not necessarily because they had gone abroad without declaring a major. Some of the concentrations the American students had chosen were not as restricted to single fields of study as is more commonly the case in European degree programmes. Because the field of study could not be identified for a substantial proportion of the American students, further tables in this volume which present the results by field of study refer only to the European students.

2.2   Age and Sex of Participants

Most of the students are in their early twenties, as can be seen from Table S2. Only ten percent of the participants are 25 years old and older, among them 22.9 percent of the Swedes and 17.4 percent of the Germans.

Table S2
Age of Study Abroad Participants in 1984, by Home Country
(in percentage of students)

| Age of participants | Home country | | | | | |
	UK	F	D	S	US	Total
19 years and younger	7.8	33.3	1.5	-	5.0	6.9
20-22 years	80.4	62.2	39.4	25.7	87.9	62.8
23-24 years	5.9	2.2	41.7	51.4	2.1	19.9
25-28 years	3.9	-	17.4	20.0	2.1	8.7
29 years and older	2.0	2.2	-	2.9	2.9	1.7
Total	100	100	100	100	100	100
(N)	(51)	(45)	(132)	(35)	(140)	(403)

Source: Pre-Study Abroad Questionnaire SAEP D 1 (D 111)

The average age of the study abroad participants corresponds with the age structure of the general student population in the respective countries in that the majority of American, British and French students are 22 years old or younger, and a substantial share of German and Swedish students are older, in their mid-twenties. However, the relatively small proportion of students over the age of 25 in the study abroad programmes is somewhat in contrast to the share of students older than 25 in the student population at large. To illustrate, 12.5 percent of British students in 1982 were over 24, and the corresponding share of the 1984-85 British study abroad participants is 5.9 percent. In France, 41.2 percent of the students overall were older than 22 in 1983/84, whereas only 4.4 percent of the French study abroad participants fell within this age category. In Germany in 1982/83, 42.2 percent of all students were older than 24, whereas only 17.4 percent of the German study abroad participants in 1984-85 were of that age. In autumn 1983, 59 percent of all Swedish students were older than 24, compared with the 22.9 percent shown in Table S2. Finally, about a third of American college and university students were 25 years and older in 1983, which is in contrast to the 5 percent shown in the Table.[1] It does appear that some impediment reduces the participation rate of relatively older students in the programmes under review. As noted for the 1983-84 participants in the corresponding chapter of Volume I, the obstacle may well be the responsibility for a family which is taken on by students in their late twenties and older.

As Table S3 shows, the Business and Foreign Language (European) students in the 1984-85 group are relatively young, whereas students in Natural Sciences, Law and particularly Engineering are older. This distribution reflects primarily the differences in timing of the period abroad within the respective degree programmes.

Table S3
Age of European Study Abroad Participants in 1984, by Field of Study
(in percentage of students)

	Field of study				
	Business	Engi-	Natural		Foreign
Age of participants	studies	neering	sciences	Law	languages
19 years and younger	13.0	3.7	2.4	2.3	20.0
20-22 years	52.2	18.5	52.4	61.4	70.0
23-24 years	22.8	59.3	40.5	31.8	5.0
25-28 years	12.0	14.8	4.8	4.5	-
29 years and older	-	3.7	-	-	5.0
Total	100	100	100	100	100
(N)	(92)	(27)	(42)	(44)	(20)

Source: Pre-Study Abroad Questionnaire SAEP D 1 (D 111)

---

[1] For the age distribution of the total student population in each of the five countries, see: Department of Education and Science. Statistical Bulletin 1/85 London: January 1985, Table 6; Ministère de l'Education Nationale, Service de l'Informatique de la Gestion et des Statistiques. Tableaux statistiques. *Principaux résultats concernant l'enseignement supérieur 1983/84.* Paris: Spetembre 1984, p. 31; Bundesminister für Bildung und Wissenschaften. *Grund- und Strukturdaten 1984/85.* Bonn: 1985, pp. 142-143; Swedish Institute. *Higher Education in Sweden, Fact Sheets on Sweden.* Stockholm: October, 1985; Office of Educational Research and Improvement, U.S. Department of Education, Center for Statistics. *Digest of Education Statistics 1985-1986.* Washington D.C.:U.S. Government Printing Office 1986, P. 106.

On average, there is an almost even split in the male/female ratio for the 1984-85 group of participants, although, as evident in Table S4, the actual percentages vary from one country to the next. A particularly high proportion of females is found in the American portion of the sample.

Table S4
Share of Female among Study Abroad Participants, by Home Country and Field of Study (in percentage of students)

Country/Field	Percentage female
United Kingdom	60.0
France	54.3
Germany	32.5
Sweden	36.8
United States	72.3
Total	51.7
Business studies	41.4
Engineering	14.3
Natural sciences	28.9
Law	40.0
Foreign languages	100.0

Source: Pre-Study Abroad Questionnaire SAEP D 2 (D 112)

These findings might at first glance suggest that women are over-represented in study abroad programmes at sending institutions in the UK and the USA, and under-represented in the German and Swedish programmes. Yet if a cross-check is made with the distribution by field of study, one sees that a very high proportion of the German and Swedish students surveyed are enrolled in fields traditionally dominated by males. In addition, a very large share of the American participants are in fields traditionally dominated by females. Only in the case of the UK is the share of females in the study abroad group higher in comparison with the total student population, if the distribution is controlled for field of study.

2.3　Students' International Experience and Previous Connections Abroad

In many cases, by conscious programme design, the study abroad group contains a much smaller portion of foreign nationals as compared with the general student body at each of the sending institutions. On average, less than three percent of the 1984-85 participants were registered as students of foreign nationality at their home institutions. In the French and British programmes, the proportion with foreign citizenship was higher (10.9% and 8.5%, respectively).

Study abroad programme participants have had substantial international exposure through their families. For example, a high proportion of their fathers, mothers, brothers and sisters lived abroad for extended periods of time. Nearly half the European students reported that immediate family members (fathers: 31.5%; mothers: 24.4%; and siblings: 24%) had spent more than three consecutive months abroad. The proportion of students whose fathers and/or mothers lived abroad is higher amongst the French (48%) and the British (40%) than amongst the Swedish (32%), American (31%), and German (28%) participants. The degree of internationality in terms of family members spending lengthy periods abroad is particularly above average in the families of students in Business Studies and Law.

The majority of students themselves have had international experience prior to the study abroad programme. As Tables S5 and S6 show, two-thirds of the European students report to have spent a period of at least one month abroad after the age of fifteen and prior to their participation in the study abroad programme.[2] The French students are above average with respect to the amount of time they have previously spent in other countries. In considering the distribution by field of study, we discover a comparatively higher previous international exposure for the Engineering and Law students.

The enquiry about previous international experience was worded somewhat differently in the questionnaires addressed to the American students. About two thirds (62%) of this group had previously spent time abroad, which can be viewed in relation to the 55 percent of the American comparison group which had done so.

The amount of time spent abroad by European students since the age of fifteen is shown in Tables S7 and S8.

To summarise the major messages of these four tables, tourism is cited most frequently as the reason for the students' previous visits abroad. More remarkable, perhaps, is the finding that as many as one out of four European study abroad participants had already lived or worked abroad for a long period of time, either in the eventual host country for the study abroad programme evaluated here, or in other countries. A greater proportion had attended a foreign school or university for longer than one month. While tourist visits had more frequently been to other countries than the eventual study abroad host country, the periods of living/working or attending school/university more often took place in the host country. The latter two kinds of experience may harbour more binding and intensive forms of contact with a foreign country than tourist visits. The average length of time spent living/working or attending school/university is, at any rate, longer than the average amount of time the students spent in tourist visits. This previous non-tourist association with other countries might be pointing to a significant

---

2   The way the relevant question was worded in the Pre-Study Abroad Questionnaire, however, students could have included a period of pre-study abroad language tuition as part of their international experience prior to departing on their study abroad programme as such.

pattern of influence upon students' motivation to participate in study abroad at the higher education level.

2.4   Family and Social Background

The social background of the participants is captured very generally in descriptions of the educational and occupational backgrounds of their parents. The proportion of study abroad participants' parents who completed higher education is shown in Table S9. The percentage is by far the highest for the American participants. This difference is not surprising, given the larger overall share of the higher education-trained adult population in the USA as compared with Europe.

Solely within the European portion of the target group there are higher percentages of French students whose fathers and mothers are college-trained (45.5 and 26.7%), although the percentage of Swedish students whose mothers completed higher education is even larger (28.9 %) than the French. The German students least frequently reported their mothers had completed higher education (13.0 %).

Table S9
Proportion of SAP Students' Parents Who Completed Higher Education, by Home Country (in percentage of students)

Parents who completed	Home country					
higher education	UK	F	D	S	US	Total
Fathers	28.1	45.5	35.9	31.6	82.6	50.2
Mothers	17.5	26.7	13.0	28.9	63.1	32.1

Source: Pre-Study Abroad Questionnaire SAEP D 7 (D 120-121)

The occupational status of the parents cannot be compared directly across all five countries since the significance of occupational categories differs and the questionnaire instruments were designed accordingly. For this reason, only a general distinction is made between "high status" or comparatively "lower status" occupations. Using these categories, 63.4 percent of the fathers and 30.9 percent of the mothers of study abroad students are in highly qualified and high status occupations, as is shown in Table S10.

In comparison with available statistics on the social background of students in the respective countries, we note that students whose fathers are in high-status occupations are clearly more dominant among the study abroad participants in some of the countries surveyed:

- Whereas about 38 percent of all German students' fathers are in such high-status occupations[3], the corresponding share among the study abroad participants is 53.2 percent.
- About 47 percent of all French students' fathers are classified as being in highly qualified and prestige occupations[4], as compared to 71.7 percent among the study abroad participants.

Table S10
Proportion of SAP-Students' Parents in Highly Qualified Occupations*, by
Home Country (in percentage of students)

	UK	F	D	S	Total EUR	US	Total
			Home country				
Fathers	53.3	71.7	53.2	50.0	55.7	80.2	63.4
Mothers	30.0	43.5	13.0	39.5	24.5	44.6	30.9

*   In the version of the questionnaire which was distributed to British, Swedish and US students: "senior managers/top administrators and senior civil servants, professions in higher education, education professions in other than higher education sector, health professions (i.e. doctors, dentists, veterinary surgeons and other senior level health professions), writers, artists, athletes and kindred professions, engineers, natural scientists, other liberal professions (e.g. independant accountants, etc.)"; in the French version of the questionnaire: "patron de l'industrie et du commerce, profession libérale, cadre supérieur, professeur d'université, cadre moyen, professeur de l'enseignement secondaire ou instituteur"; in the German version of the questionnaire: "Manager, höherer Verwaltungsangestellter bzw. Staatsbeamter, Hochschullehrer, Wissenschaftler, Schullehrer, Arzt, Zahnarzt, Apotheker usw., Schriftsteller, Künstler, Sportler o.ä., Ingenieur, Naturwissenschaftler, andere hochqualifizierte Berufe"

Source: Pre-Study Abroad Questionnaire SAEP D 8 (D 122-125)

For the American students, no comparable data are available. It seems likely, though, to that the percentage of study abroad participants' fathers in high-status occupations is higher than among the university student population at large.

For the British students, one cannot come to any valid conclusion. Over half (59%) the students in higher education in the UK have fathers in highly qualified

---

3   *Das soziale Bild der Studentenschaft in der Bundesrepublik Deutschland. Ergebnisse der 10. Sozialerhebung des Deutschen Studenwerks im Sommersemester 1982.* Bundesminister für Bildung und Wissenschaft, Bonn 1983. Bild 2.17. The figure quoted refers to the total number of students at universities, assimilated institutions and Fachhochschulen. The following occupational categories were included: Angestellter in gehobener Position, Beamter des höheren Dienstes, gröÄere Selbständige, mittlere Selbständige.

4   Ministère de l'Education Nationale, Service de l'Informatique de Gestion et des Statistiques. *Statistiques des étudiants inscrits dans les établissements universitaires 1983-84.* Paris: 1984. This includes the students at French universities whose fathers belong to the following occupational categories: industriels (with more than 6 employees), moyens et gros commerçants, professions libérales et cadres supérieurs, cadres moyens.

occupations.[5] This is less than the corresponding share (66.9 %) among all British students who replied to the Pre-Study Abroad Questionnaire, but greater than the corresponding share (53.3 %) among the students who replied to the Pre- and the Post-Study Abroad Questionnaires, i.e. the target group for this volume. Obviously, many British students of higher social background did not reply to the second questionnaire.

The Swedish study abroad participants provide a noteworthy contrast. The 50 percent among them whose fathers are in highly qualified occupations is lower than the overall average of 68 percent among the entire group of 25-34 years olds in post-secondary studies in Sweden.

Further information provided by programme directors confirms that the above results are not unique to the 1984-85 group. In the majority of French, German and American study abroad programmes, students do tend to come from particular segments of society (higher social background as defined by financial and educational parameters), whereas this happens in fewer of the Swedish and British programmes.

2.5   Students' Living Situation at Home

In examining the educational and occupational backgrounds of participants' parents, we are exploring the link between participation in study abroad and the students' general style of life, or perhaps more explicitly, their material living conditions. We can extend this examination to other aspects of the students' living situation in their home country, thereby enabling a slightly different type of comparison (in chapter 3), between the conditions experienced by students prior to study abroad and those they encountered during their sojourns.

The proportion of students who were living with a partner at the time they responded to the Pre-Study Abroad Questionnaire (6.0 %) was very low. The percentage of students with their own children was even lower (2.3%).

The distance between the students' parents' residence and the home university/college which the students attended in the sending country is a particularly interesting feature, as the data in this respect indicate once more that the study abroad participants are clearly mobile. For over half (54.4%) of these students, the distance between their parents' residence and their home institution of higher education was more than 100 km. Only 28.9 percent studied at an institution in the immediate vicinity (i.e. within a 50 km radius) of their parents' residence. Many British students (68.3 %) in particular were pursuing higher education at a distance of more than 100 km from their parents' home; the lowest share could be observed among German students (44.2 %).

---

5   Fulton, O. (ed). *Access to Higher Education, Research into Higher Education Monographs.* (Guildford: Society for Research into Higher Education, 1983). This figure takes into account all full time students at British institutions of higher education born in the years 1961/62. It includes both the upper classes on a 6 point scale, which were entitled "professional etc. occupations" and "intermediate occupations". Amongst students at polytechnics the proportion of fathers in this category is still lower, namely 46 percent.

Prior to their study abroad, nearly half (47.2 %) the students lived in apartments or houses, and just over a third (39.1%) lived in university dormitories or halls of residence. Under ten percent were living in a private room with another family. Living in a residence hall was most common among the British students (70.0% did so, as compared with 44.7% of the Swedes, 38.6% of the Americans, 29.7% of the Germans and 25% of the French). Living in an apartment or a house most characterised the French (61.4% of them had this type of arrangement, in comparison with 52.9% of the Americans, 52.6% of the Swedes, 45.3% of the Germans, and 25.0% of the British students). Generally in these findings, one cannot discern any specific characteristics for the study abroad participants in contrast to the overall higher education student body in each of the five countries. However, the variations in the study abroad group from one country to the next will figure in the later analysis of this group's social integration during the sojourn and the extent to which they could cope with their new living environments abroad.

In their extra-curricular activities prior to departing for study abroad, the participants were also clearly "mobile." They ranked travelling in second place - along with participating in sports - in their response to a pre-supplied list of possible leisure time activities. The list also included performing in music or arts; joining social, political or religious organisations; working (giving private lessons, working as a graduate assistant etc.); visiting museums; attending concerts or the theatre; attending (spectator) sports events; reading literature other than coursework and watching television. Students overall ranked reading and watching TV as their most frequent activities. The Americans and Swedes had invested less time in travelling, in comparison with students from the other countries.

Roughly a third of the study abroad participants had interrupted their educational careers for a significant length of time. The proportion of the Swedish and German groups which had spent a relatively long period in other activities was rather high, whereas the proportion was very low for the British, American and French students. Out of the eight alternatives they could have identified in answering this portion of the questionnaire, three were most applicable:

- *military service*, which applied predominantly to German and Swedish males;
- *employment*, in which the British and Swedish students had spent time in comparatively greater proportions;
- *vocational training*, with a few exceptions found exclusively among the German students. Almost a third of the German study abroad participants had such training. As these students were most prevalent among those taking Business Studies degree courses at the Fachhochschulen, the vocational training background is probably related to some of the access routes connected with these particular institutions.

On the whole, the average length of time spent in previous vocational training had been nearly two years. This is longer than the average period of time for each of the other two activities.

2.6   Choice of Academic Concentration and Institution

In choosing *an academic concentration, a field of study*, the strongest criterion for most of the study abroad participants had been their "general interest in the subject area", followed by their interest in the profession to which the field of study related. As Table S11 shows, interest in the subject area is more strongly emphasized by the American than by the European students. Students from Anglo Saxon countries attached somewhat less weight to the related profession(s) in choosing a field than did students in the other countries.

Among the Europeans, students in Joint Study Programmes identified study abroad possibilities as the second most compelling rationale for their having chosen their field of study. For the Europeans participating in other forms of study abroad, the anticipated opportunity to study abroad was ranked in sixth place as a motivating factor. This difference might be explained by the fact that for many Joint Study Programmes, study abroad is considered an integral - and in many cases, mandatory - curricular component of the overall degree programme, and it is widely announced in this regard.[6]

Table S11
Motives for Choosing a Field of Study, by Home Country (in arithmetic means)*

| | | Home | country | | | Total | | | |
Rank	Motive	UK	F	D	S	EUR	US	Total	(N)
(1)	General interest in the subject area	1.9	1.8	1.6	1.5	1.7	1.3	1.6	(435)
(2)	Interest in vocational area(s) or direction(s) to which the field relates	2.5	1.8	1.7	1.6	1.9	2.1	1.9	(428)
(3)	Career prospects	2.3	2.0	2.5	2.6	2.4	2.6	2.4	(427)
(4)	Personal strength in the subject area(s)	2.5	2.7	2.4	2.3	2.5	1.9	2.3	(431)
(5)	The field offered study abroad possibilities	2.1	1.9	2.5	3.7	2.5	.	.	(294)
(6)	Strength of the institution in the subject areas(s)	2.7	2.6	3.0	3.2	2.9	2.7	2.8	(424)
(7)	The field was recommended	3.7	3.8	3.9	4.3	3.9	4.0	3.9	(418)
(8)	No particular reason	4.6	5.0	4.8	4.6	4.7	4.6	4.7	(254)

*   Students were requested to rate the importance of each aspect on a scale from 1 = "very important" to 5 = "not at all important"
Source: Pre-Study Abroad Questionnaire SAEP D 20 (D 215-222)

---

[6]   The item dealing with the importance of study abroad pssibilities to the students' choice of field (and institution of higher education) was not incorporated into the questionnaire sent to American students. The reason for this omission was that, unlike the situation in a number of European degree programmes, study abroad is rarely built into or excluded from American degree programmes.

As might be expected, when the European students are examined by their fields of study (see Table S12), Business, Engineering and Law students stand out for the emphasis they place on professional and career goals for studying abroad. Natural Science and Foreign Language students strongly emphasize their interest in the subject area. For the Business and Foreign Language students, the study abroad possibilities embodied a much more important aspect in the choice of field than it did for the students in Law, Engineering and Natural Sciences. This can be explained - as already discussed in the first volume of this study - by the fact that study abroad in many cases is a very central element of Business and Foreign Language fields, whereas for the others this has customarily not been the case.

Table S12
European Students' Motives for Choosing a Field of Study, by Field of Study (in arithmetic means)*

		Field of study				
Rank	Motive	Business studies	Engi-neering	Natural sciences	Law	Foreign languages
(1)	General interest in the subject area	1.8	1.7	1.4	1.9	1.3
(2)	Interest in vocational area(s) or direction(s) to which the field relates	1.7	1.8	2.2	1.8	2.1
(3)	Career prospects	1.9	2.3	3.0	2.3	2.8
(4)	Personal strength in the subject area(s)	2.7	2.6	2.0	2.6	2.3
(5)	The field offered study abroad possibilities	1.7	3.2	3.5	2.7	1.9
(6)	Strength of the institution in the subject area(s)	2.5	2.4	3.7	3.2	2.8
(7)	The field was recommended	3.6	4.0	4.1	3.9	3.6
(8)	No particular reason	4.7	5.0	4.7	4.7	4.6

* Students were requested to rate the importance of each aspect on a scale from 1 = "very important" to 5 = "not at all important"
Source: Pre-Study Abroad Questionnaire SAEP D 20 (D 215-222)

The strength of students' convictions in choosing their institution of higher education (the sending institution) appeared to be less pronounced than their motivation level in selecting a field of study. The average rating for the most important reason for choosing the institution was 2.4, and for choosing a field was 1.6 (on a scale of 1 = "very important" to 5 = "not at all important").

The variation in students' reasons for choosing a home institution are more dramatic when viewed by field of study than by home country; consequently, Table S13 shows only the former. The major findings by home country can be summarised as follows:

- For the American students, the geographical location of the higher education institution played the most important role (a mean of 2.2 as compared with the Europeans' 2.8 to 3.6).
- The strength of the institution in the given subject area was comparatively less important for the Germans and Swedes than for students from the other countries (2.6 and 2.7, respectively, as compared with 2.0 to 2.3). British and Swedish students stressed the importance of institutional prestige much less than students from the other countries (3.3 and 3.2 for the British and Swedish students, respectively, as compared with 2.4 to 2.7 for the others).
- Only among the British group had a considerable number of students settled for the institution in which they enrolled because they had not been admitted to the one of their first choice.

Table S13
European Students' Motives for Choosing Home Institution, by Field of Study
(in arithmetic means)*

		Field of study						
Rank	Motive	Business studies	Engi-neering	Natural sciences	Law	Foreign languages	Total**	(N)
(1)	Strength of the institution in certain subject areas	2.2	2.0	2.7	2.8	2.2	2.4	(287)
(2)	The institution offered study abroad possibilities	1.7	3.3	3.5	2.8	2.2	2.6	(289)
(3)	The institution offered the particular study abroad programme	2.0	3.5	3.7	2.9	2.9	2.8	(284)
(4)	General prestige of the institution	2.8	2.6	3.2	2.8	3.4	2.9	(286)
(5)	Area in which the institution is located	3.7	3.8	3.0	3.1	2.7	3.3	(288)
(6)	Proximity of the institution (e.g. to work, family etc.)	3.7	4.2	2.6	2.9	3.1	3.3	(289)
(7)	Chance, no special reason						4.0	(237)
(8)	Not admitted to another institution	4.4	4.5	4.6	4.5	4.1	4.4	(229)

*   Students were requested to rate the importance of each aspect on a scale from 1 = "very important" to 5 = "not at all important"
**   Also including other fields of study
Source: Pre-Study Abroad Questionnaire SAEP D 19 (D 174-212)

In the questionnaires mailed to the European students, the section which listed potential motives for choosing an institution drew a distinction between study abroad in *general*, and study abroad through the *particular* programmes encompassed by the current evaluation. These two were identified as the second and third most important reasons for which the European participants had sought to study at their respective institutions. As Table S14 demonstrates, the major difference can be observed between participants in Joint Study Programmes, for whom the general prospect of study abroad had been the most important reason for choice of institution, and participants in all other programmes who ranked such a possibility fifth out of eight possible motives for choice of institution.

Table S14
Importance Placed on Study Abroad Possibilities in Choosing Field of Study and Institution by Participants of Joint Study Programmes and by Participants of Other European Study Abroad Programmes

	Joint Study Programmes		Other study abroad programmes	
	Arithmetic mean*	Rank**	Arithmetic mean**	Rank**
Importance in choice of major field of study: "This field offered study abroad possibilities"	2.0	2	3.3	6
Importance in choice of home institution: "You knew the institution offered study abroad possibilities"	2.0	1	3.7	5
Importance in choice of home institution: "The institution offered the particular study abroad programme (SAP) in which you wanted to enrol"	2.3	3	3.8	6

*   Students were requested to rate the importance of each aspect on a scale from 1 = "very important" to 5 = "not at all important"
**   Among 8 categories each
Source: Pre-Study Abroad Questionnaire SAEP D 19 and 20 (D 177, 211 and 218)

Examining European students' responses by field of study, the Business Studies and Foreign Language students put more emphasis on the importance of study abroad opportunities for their choice of institution than did students in Law, Engineering and Natural Sciences. Business students stressed the importance of the particular study abroad programme, in addition to the general prospect of studying abroad; whereas Foreign Language students seemed to have been primarily interested in the general prospect. This undoubtedly reflects awareness of the very specific programmes for Business students, e.g. European Business Studies, which have been initiated in recent years.

Immediately prior to going abroad, students were asked about the weight they attached to potential benefits of the studies abroad (on a scale of 1 = "very important" to 5 = "not at all important"). The desire to use or improve a foreign language and to live in or make acquaintances from another country clearly come in first place across the board (see Table S15).

Table S15
Motives for Studying Abroad, by Home Country (in arithmetic means)*

		Home country					
Rank	Motive	UK	F	D	S	US	Total
(1)	Desire to use/improve a foreign language**	1.2	1.2	1.2	1.3	1.1	1.1
(2)	Desire to live in/make acquaintances from another country	1.5	1.3	1.4	1.4	1.3	1.4
(3)	Desire to enhance the understanding of the particular SAP host country	2.2	1.8	1.9	2.4	1.5	1.8
(4)	Expectation that the SAP would improve career prospects	1.9	1.6	1.8	2.1	2.4	2.0
(5)	Desire to travel (e.g. SAP offered convenient/cheap means of going abroad)	1.7	2.7	2.8	1.9	1.8	2.3
(6)	Desire to gain another perspective on the home country	3.1	2.6	2.7	2.5	1.8	2.4
(7)	Desire to become acquainted with teaching methods other than those adopted at the home institution	3.6	2.2	2.6	3.2	3.2	2.9
(8)	Desire for break from usual surroundings	3.2	2.7	2.8	2.7	3.9	3.2
(9)	Desire to become acquainted with subject matter not offered at home institution	3.5	3.5	3.2	3.7	3.4	3.4
(10)	Expectation to get better marks/examination results after return from SAP	3.2	2.6	4.1	4.2	4.5	4.0
(11)	SAP afforded opportunity to establish ties with family/ethnic heritage	4.7	4.7	4.3	4.5	3.9	4.3
(12)	Other friends were going	4.5	4.4	4.4	4.5	4.5	4.4
(13)	No special reasons (e.g. it was required for the degree programme)***	4.1	4.8	4.6	4.9	.	4.6

* Students were requested to rate the importance of each aspect on a scale from 1 = "very important" to 5 = "not at all important"
** Does not include UK students going to US and US students going to UK
*** Not included in list of items in US version of the questionnaire
Source: Pre-Study Abroad Questionnaire SAEP D 31 (D 333-347)

Looking at the four most strongly motivating factors for study abroad, it is obvious that students' overwhelming interest was to experience a foreign setting. They wanted to confront the challenge this implied for their personal and professional development. More restricted academic motives (for example, to improve marks

Table S16
Motives of European Students for Studying Abroad, by Field of Study
(in arithmetic means)*

		Field of study				
Rank	Motive	Business studies	Engi- neering	Natural sciences	Law	Foreign languages
(1)	Desire to use/improve a foreign language	1.1	1.3	1.7	1.2	1.1
(2)	Desire to live in/make acquaintances from another country	1.4	1.2	1.5	1.4	1.5
(3)	Desire to enhance the under-standing of the particular SAP host country	1.9	2.2	2.4	1.9	1.5
(4)	Expectation that the SAP would improve career prospects	1.4	1.9	2.4	1.6	2.4
(5)	Desire to travel (e.g. SAP offered convenient/cheap means of going abroad)	2.8	2.2	2.4	2.7	2.0
(6)	Desire to gain another perspective on the home country	2.7	3.0	2.8	2.6	2.8
(7)	Desire to become acquainted with teaching methods other than those adopted at the home institution	2.7	3.1	2.7	3.1	3.0
(8)	Desire for break from usual surroundings	3.0	3.0	2.6	2.5	3.0
(9)	Desire to become acquainted with subject matter not offered at home institution	3.3	3.9	3.3	3.4	3.1
(10)	Expectation to get better marks/examination results after return from SAP	3.8	4.2	4.0	3.9	2.0
(11)	SAP afforded opportunity to establish ties with family/ethnic heritage	4.4	4.7	4.5	4.2	4.8
(12)	Other friends were going	4.4	4.8	4.5	4.4	4.0
(13)	No special reasons (e.g. it was required for the degree programme)	4.3	5.0	4.8	5.0	3.6

*   Students were requested to rate the importance of each aspect on a scale from 1 = "very important" to 5 = "not at all important"
Source: Pre-Study Abroad Questionnaire SAEP D 31 (D 333-347)

or examination results) were secondary. Students attached least importance to what might be termed more "casual" motives for going on a particular pro-gramme, for example, to join other friends who were going. This implies that they had indeed made a conscious decision to study abroad and that they had certain expectations about its benefits.

Travelling around in different countries was most important for students from the UK, the USA and Sweden. The French students stand out for a moderately strong expectation that they would receive better marks or examination results after a study abroad experience (2.6), a consideration which is of lesser concern for students in all other countries (3.2 to 4.5). Finally, Swedish and British students show comparatively weaker interest in furthering their understanding of the prospective host country.

As regards field of study (see Table S16), Foreign Language and Business students wished most strongly to use or improve their foreign language skills. This same motive was least frequently reported by Natural Science students. It is also hardly surprising that Foreign Language students most frequently expected their study abroad period would impact favourably upon their marks and examination results (2.0 as compared to 3.3 to 4.2 in other fields), since study abroad is so obviously linked to the characteristics of their field of concentration.

In examining these results, one should keep in mind that the standardised questionnaires provided little opportunity for students to indicate how the various motives may have been interlinked. For example, in looking for ways by which to enhance foreign language competence, a student could obviously be hoping by the same process to strengthen his or her career chances.

Chapter 3

Students' Experience Abroad

3.1   Purpose and Information Base for the Chapter

The purpose of this chapter is to describe what happened to students as they participated in the study abroad programmes, for obvious reasons, looking most closely at their activities and impressions during the actual time spent in their host countries. This account in combination with the profile sketch of the previous chapter helps to interpret the various effects of the study abroad programmes which are analysed toward the latter part of this volume.

The information in this chapter complements that in chapter 5 of the first volume, which allows more room for the directors' interpretations of experiences they observe students have while on their programmes and draws extensively on the results of the Pre-Study Abroad Questionnaire. In the sections which follow, the studyabroad programme experience is presented primarily from the student perspective, from responses to the Post-Study Abroad Questionnaire which: described the living and study conditions abroad and, where relevant, the work placement; which pointed out the primary differences between the learning environment at the host and the home institutions; and assessed the extent to which the study abroad participants managed to become integrated within the academic and surrounding communities in their respective host countries. The questionnaire asked about activities apart from academic studies which filled students' time abroad, about the information sources they tapped in getting to know about their host countries, and the people whom students considered had most shaped the character of their overall experiences abroad. Students were encouraged to take stock of problems encountered while in the host country or as a consequence of the time spent away from home (e.g. prolongation of their overall degree course), and to assess the overall value of the sojourn. The underlying assumption in designing the questionnaire was that the composite, the totality, of the academic as well as extra-curricular experiences had to be considered in evaluating the overall effect of the study abroad period. Thus, the interrelationships between the several different types of experiences students had is a crucial element in the analysis.

3.2   Pre-Sojourn Preparation

Students who enroll in organised study abroad programmes are obviously not expected to enter the host country and the new educational settings cold, without any form of preparation. What was striking from the programme directors' testimony was that even in these programmes, where academic and administrative staff are so much more involved than in students' independent ventures studying in another country, students are nevertheless prepared for their sojourn to a large degree by their peers. The most frequent procedure (in 84% of the programmes) is to put the group about to go abroad in contact with those who have just returned from the same programme. In a majority (61%) of the programmes, students at the partner institution abroad also have some input into the preparation of study abroad participants. For both types of peer preparation, its nature is categorised generally as "individual advice".

There is also preparation through foreign language instruction. In 55 percent of the programmes, students are required to take a certain amount of foreign language instruction prior to departing from their home institutions; 54 percent of the programmes require foreign language study upon students' arrival at the host institution.[1]

It is also quite common that students are given a quantity of printed material to familiarise them with the host country. This is at hand in 54 percent of the programmes, especially the French, British and American sending institutions. Over half the programmes also furnish an orientation to study patterns and teaching methods to be encountered at the partner institution(s).

The role these various measures played in the totality of the European students' preparation for study abroad during 1984/5 (as reported by the students) is illustrated in Table S17[2]. The methods are categorised somewhat differently from the ones commented upon by programme directors, but in the student responses, it is clear that conferring with study abroad returnees, on average, comprised a relatively significant part of the preparatory phase - although to a far lesser degree for the Swedish students.

In general, mandatory foreign language courses and preparatory courses related to the academic content of the study abroad programme made up a greater part of the preparation for students from the UK and France than from Germany or Sweden. What is striking about the latter group is the limited extent to which any of the methods listed figure in the students' preparation. Where Swedes did prepare for the sojourn, they did so independently more than because of specific programme requirements. The thoroughness of their independent initiatives was nevertheless surpassed by the Germans.

With the exception of the German students, the data when viewed by home country suggest a somewhat complementary function of mandatory and optional foreign language courses. When the courses are not required, students invest more extensively in foreign language preparation on an independent basis. If students prepare more thoroughly through mandatory courses, they are less prone to study foreign language on their own. This is less pronounced when the students are viewed by field of study, with the exception of students in Foreign Languages. The latter prepared more thoroughly through mandatory methods, even apart from foreign language courses, than students in other fields. Evidently, for the

---

[1] A negligible portion of the programmes (less than 10%) report that there are also academic course requirements that must be fulfilled explicitly as preparation for the study period abroad.

[2] The question did not appear in the American version of the pre-departure questionnaire.

Engineering and Natural Science students, less effort had gone into preparing explicitly for study abroad.

Table S17
European Students' Preparation for Study Abroad, by Home Country and Field of Study (in arithmetic means)*

Method of preparation	Home country				Field of study					
	UK	F	D	S	Bus	Eng	NatSc	Law	Lang	Total***
Talking with returnees from earlier SAPs**	2.4	2.1	2.4	3.2	2.4	2.8	2.2	2.6	2.3	2.5
Mandatory courses related to academic content of SAP	2.3	1.9	2.8	4.7	2.3	3.7	4.0	2.5	1.1	2.7
Mandatory foreign language courses	1.9	1.7	2.9	5.0	2.3	3.2	3.8	2.7	1.2	2.8
Talking with students and staff in SAP host country	3.2	2.0	3.3	4.1	2.8	3.5	4.0	2.9	3.6	3.1
Independent reading/ optional courses about society etc. of SAP host country	3.7	3.1	3.0	3.9	3.3	3.6	3.6	3.0	2.9	3.3
Independent study/ optional courses in foreign languages	4.0	4.0	2.8	3.7	3.4	3.0	3.7	2.8	4.0	3.3
Independent study/ optional courses related to academic content of SAP	3.8	3.7	2.9	3.6	3.5	3.8	2.9	2.7	3.3	3.3
Mandatory orientation/ guidance sessions on social etc. aspects of SAP country	3.3	3.1	3.6	4.7	3.4	4.3	3.9	4.1	2.8	3.6
(N)	(59)	(44)	(143)	(35)	(101)	(26)	(42)	(49)	(22)	(281)

```
*       Scale from 1 = "very thoroughly" to 5 = "not at all"
**      The sequence of the categories does not correspond to the questionnaire but rather to a
        rank order according to replies
***     Also including other fields of study
Source:   Post-Study Abroad Questionnaire SAEP D 35 (D 373-380)
```

All the practical arrangements that have to be made constitute a different type of preparation. This includes lining up insurance coverage, registering with civil authorities, arranging accommodation etc. Students are assisted in these activities by their programme directors or other staff on the sending and/or receiving sides. It is common that American students can turn to a resident director sent from the home institution, or an appointed contact person at the host institution.

Arranging for students' living accommodation in the host community has become a fairly standard feature of study abroad programme design, although this does not mean that arrangements are imposed upon students. In all French programmes, eighty percent of the German, and some two-thirds of the American, rooms for the study abroad participants are regularly reserved in the host institution's residence halls. In about a quarter to a third of the programmes, this dormitory accommodation is encouraged, but, in the others, it is essentially a fallback position in the eventuality that students are not able to find alternative solutions. In fact, forty percent of the American programmes recommend, for the sake of greater cultural immersion, that their students seek other types of accommodation such as living with local families.

The presence or absence of dormitory arrangements shows no distinctive pattern by programme type. It is generally not any different for unilateral, in contrast to bilateral or multilateral, programmes. Furthermore, it appears to be only slightly related to in-country traditions, as can be seen in Table S18. The Table shows that the majority of the study abroad participants did live in dormitories and for large portions of the French and Swedes, this represented a different living arrangement than the custom at home. This was not so much the case for students from the other countries, although in many cases, the actual conditions of dormitory life abroad were certainly different from such life at home and some of the Europeans obviously had difficulties in the USA. One British student noted in response to the questionnaire that "producing academic work of quality that I was satisfied with while sharing a dormitory with a first-year American student was one of the most difficult things I had to do abroad". This was a response echoed by several German students. More than anything else, this may have been a function of the differences in age between the incoming students from abroad and their American dorm-mates.

Table S18
Percentage of Students Living in Dormitories Before and During the Study Abroad Period

Country	Before SAP	During SAP	
	Home Country	Home Country	Host country
UK	70	78	71
F	25	70	43
D	30	45	79
S	45	89	83
US	39	55	47

Source: Pre-Study Abroad Questionnaire SAEP D 11 (D 132) and Post-Study Abroad
            Questionnaire SAEP F 1 (F 113).

The second most prevalent mode of accommodation (notably, for nearly a quarter of all American and German study abroad participants) was an apartment or house. In contrast to the situation for students from all the other countries, about a fifth of the Americans were accommodated as boarders in private homes. A tenth of the German participants lived in this manner while abroad, and a fifth noted "other" types of arrangements than those listed in the questionnaire.

3.3 Immersion in the Culture Abroad

The majority of study abroad participants were in the host country for an academic year, a rather substantial length of time. They were more often than not fully registered at the host institution, while at the same time also fully registered at home. Regardless of their formal registration status, the majority of the students studied alongside their peers at the host institution in all the lectures, seminars and project groups. Not too surprising then, when students were asked about their primary channels of information about their host countries, they recalled extensive communication with host country natives (see Table S19). Asking host nationals about their country was notably pronounced among the Americans,

Table S19
Methods Used Abroad for Information About the Host Country, by Home Country (in arithmetic means)*

	Home country					
Method of information	UK	F	D	S	US	Total
Talking with host country nationals**	1.8	1.9	1.8	1.7	1.3	1.6
Host country newspapers	2.6	2.2	2.2	2.3	2.2	2.2
Host country radio programmes	2.4	1.8	2.4	2.4	2.2	2.3
Host country magazines	2.9	2.4	2.7	3.2	2.3	2.6
Talking with fellow nationals	2.6	2.5	3.0	3.3	2.2	2.7
Host country television	3.2	1.9	3.0	2.8	2.8	2.8
Lectures	3.2	3.3	3.5	3.7	2.8	3.2
Host country fiction books	3.5	3.1	3.4	3.4	3.4	3.4
Host country non-fiction books	3.6	3.4	3.3	3.8	3.4	3.4
Other media	3.6	3.6	3.6	3.9	3.3	3.5
Host country professional journals and books	3.8	2.7	3.1	3.6	3.9	3.5
Discussion groups	4.1	2.4	4.0	4.5	3.3	3.6

*   Scale from 1 = "extensively" to 5 = "not at all"
**   The sequence of categories does not correspond to the questionnaire but rather to a rank order according to replies
Source: Post-Study Abroad Questionnaire SAEP F 17 (F 351-362)

whose responses interestingly also indicated they had conferred comparatively more extensively with fellow Americans abroad, to become more knowledgeable about the host country.

The table points out that students did not perceive that professional journals and academic literature, lectures or discussion groups had been a source of information about the host country as much as newspapers, magazines and radio programmes. The Americans and French departed somewhat from this average pattern, however, in that both obtained comparatively more information from discussion groups, the Americans compared with all the other national groups got more from lectures, and the French more from professional journals and books.

A slightly different aspect is the issue of who or which sources were most influential in what might be called "shaping the quality" of the study abroad participants' experiences. This was something that host institution students and others (in the host country) outside the academic community had apparently accomplished more than any others (see Table S20).

Table S20
Importance of Certain Social Contacts in Shaping the Overall Experience Abroad, by Home Country (in arithmetic means)*

Type of Contact**	Home country					
	UK	F	D	S	US	Total
Students of SAP host country	2.0	1.7	1.8	1.8	1.8	1.8
Other people from SAP host country outside university	2.2	2.4	2.1	3.0	1.8	2.1
Students from other foreign countries	2.4	1.9	2.4	2.0	2.4	2.3
Students from home country	2.8	2.3	2.7	2.7	2.2	2.5
Teaching staff of SAP host country	3.1	2.2	2.6	2.9	2.8	2.7
Other people from home country	3.9	3.4	3.5	3.9	3.7	3.6
Teaching staff from home country	4.4	3.2	4.0	4.6	4.3	4.0
Administrators from home country	4.5	3.4	4.6	4.3	3.6	4.0

*   Scale from 1 = "very important" to 5 = "not at all important"
**   The sequence of categories does not correspond to the questionnaire but rather to a rank order according to replies
Source: Post-Study Abroad Questionnaire SAEP F 16 (F 342-350)

Several additional points should be brought out with respect to the types of exposure implied in Table S20, which would be fundamental to an evaluation of programme design. One concerns the American situation. In addition to the direct and spontaneous contacts with host country nationals, the American students usually interact with someone from the home institution or some other liaison person at the host institution. In terms of the students' own perceptions of who most shaped their overall experiences abroad, there are a few significant differences between the American students and those from the other countries in the extent to which they perceived host students and teaching staff as influential. In fact, the Americans attached greater importance to these two groups of contacts in the host country than the British did. Further, especially the French but also the German students rated the importance of teaching staff and others (not students) from their home countries higher than the Americans did. Most striking of all is the greater importance Americans attached to contacts outside the academic community in the host country. This especially exceeded the influence attributed by the Swedes to such contact.

The unsurprising link between accommodation arrangements and the type of social contacts which most shaped study abroad participants' experiences is found in responses that students housed in dormitories abroad, more frequently than any of the others, felt their peers in the host country were important influences. The impact of students from other foreign countries was felt second most strongly. By comparison, study abroad participants who had lived in apartments tended slightly less to identify students in the host country as having been the most fundamental in shaping the sojourn experience. For these participants, the influence of host country students was felt to be about the same as that of other contacts outside the academic community.

The most pronounced pattern to emerge was that students who had boarded in private homes, more frequently than students who lived in dorms or apartments, reported that contacts outside the higher education institution in their host countries had been important in shaping the sojourn experience. Students who had lived in private homes mentioned much less often that students of the home and host countries had been important in this respect. Thus, it does appear that students more likely find their peers in the host country leave strong imprints upon the study abroad experience if the study abroad participants are housed in dormitories. Contacts with others outside the higher education institution, to the extent that these persons could be central in moulding the overall experience of the sojourn, is more likely to result from accommodation in an apartment and even more so when students board in private homes.

An overview of participants' extra-curricular activities abroad (Table S21) lends further insight into the context for their social encounters and channels of information about the host country. A list of eleven activities was pre-supplied in the Post-Study Abroad Questionnaire, and, in responding, students indicated they most often spent free time discussing and exchanging views with friends, going to parties, playing chess and the like. Almost as frequently, they travelled, attended museums, concerts, theatre and the cinema.

The question which immediately comes to mind is to what extent students spent their free time abroad differently from at home.[3] The greatest difference is apparently in employment alongside studies. The contrast was most considerable

---

[3] It is possible to make only an approximate comparison, since some of the key items were categorised differently from the pre-departure questionnaire in the follow-up version. This had been necessary because of the number of respondents who in pre-departure situation specified frequent involvement in activities "other" than those specifically mentioned in the supplied list.

Table S21
Frequency of Participation in Selected Extra-curricular Activities Before and During the Study Abroad Period, by Home Country (in arithmetic means)*

Type of activity		UK	F	D	S	US	Total
		Home country					
Travelling	Before	2.3	2.2	2.3	2.9	3.0	2.6
	During	2.3	2.3	2.2	2.1	1.4	2.0
Participating in sports	Before	3.0	2.5	2.5	2.7	2.6	2.6
	During	3.5	2.4	2.4	2.3	3.3	2.8
Attending museums, theater, concerts, cinema	Before	3.1	2.7	2.9	3.1	2.5	2.8
	During	2.1	1.7	2.0	2.0	1.7	1.9
Working (i.e. employment during academic year)	Before	4.5	3.7	3.0	4.0	2.9	3.3
	During	3.7	4.2	4.6	4.8	4.5	4.4
Participating in clubs	Before	3.2	4.2	3.4	3.6	3.3	3.4
	During	3.8	3.9	3.8	4.2	4.0	3.9
Performing in music, arts etc.	Before	3.9	3.6	3.6	3.8	3.7	3.7
	During	4.2	4.5	4.0	4.2	4.3	4.2
Attending sports events	Before	4.1	4.2	4.2	4.0	3.5	3.9
	During	4.1	3.9	4.3	4.0	4.0	4.1
"Other" in % of respondents	Before	1	22	23	24	.	14
	During	**	**	**	**	**	**
Reading literature other than coursework, watching TV	Before	2.2	1.7	2.2	2.4	2.4	2.2
	During	**	**	**	**	**	**
Being with friends, going to parties, playing chess etc.	Before	**	**	**	**	**	**
	During	1.9	1.5	1.9	1.9	1.5	1.7
Reading literature other than coursework	Before	**	**	**	**	**	**
	During	2.8	2.2	2.6	3.3	2.0	2.5
Watching television	Before	**	**	**	**	**	**
	During	3.6	2.5	3.5	3.7	3.6	3.5
Hobby, craftwork (e.g. photography)	Before	**	**	**	**	**	**
	During	3.7	4.1	3.6	4.0	3.0	3.5

*   Scale from 1 = "very frequently" to 5 = "never"
**   Categories not presented as such in this questionnaire
Source: Pre-Study Abroad Questionnaire SAEP D 12 (D 133-142) and Post-Study Abroad
           Questionnaire SAEP F 14 (F 326-338)

for the Americans and Germans, although, for all except the British, the study period abroad involved far less - in fact, virtually no - employment. Among the reasons for this may be the constraint of regulations which prohibit temporary employment of foreign nationals who have entered a country for the purposes of study.

The second area where there was a marked difference in leisure time activities abroad was in museum, theatre, concert and cinema attendance. In this case, the contrast in lifestyle - between habits at home and abroad - was slightly less for the Americans, and greatest for the British and French. But across the board, students while abroad were engaged in these activities far more frequently than they had been at home. It is also striking how much more the Americans and Swedes travelled while abroad, and how the American students' participation in sports dropped approximately the same amount that their museum and concert attendance increased while abroad. The differences between the home and host situation with respect to the frequency of involvement in sports were not as dramatic for students from the other four countries. Concerning participation in clubs and taking part in musical performances or art exhibitions, the pattern is very much the same for all five groups.

3.4   The Academic Context of the Programme

As the term implies, the central activity for a study abroad programme is indeed the academic study. Even for students who carried out a work placement abroad, this was never done without a period of academic study (abroad) as well. Moreover, as will be discussed in a later section, the work placement experiences were confined to slightly less than a quarter of the students in the target group for this portion of the evaluation.

The majority of students reported generally that the period abroad provided the chance to take courses which were different in content from those available at home, and to experience teaching methods not practised at home; thus, essentially "broadening" their academic and cultural backgrounds. Many study abroad participants had the flexibility abroad to take a number of courses which were not directly related to the field of primary study they had established at home (see Table S22).

It was particularly the British and Swedish students who reported they had studied new topics abroad, the French and Germans who mentioned exposure to different instructional methods and learning modes, and the Americans and Germans who broadened their academic and cultural backgrounds. A tenth of the students indicated they had changed their specialisation while abroad, however, and less than a fifth had developed a new specialisation. The Americans illustrate this situation. While three-quarters had "broadened their backgrounds," not a single one had developed a (new) specialisation through the study abroad. Meanwhile, among the comparison group of American students who did not participate in study abroad, nearly a quarter changed their major field of study during the corresponding ("junior") year. A contrast is shown by the considerable number of Swedes who developed new areas of specialisation abroad, in spite of the fact that most participated in study abroad during the final stages of their respective degree programmes which meant they had firmly established a specialisation at home. The areas of specialisation acquired during study abroad presumably supplemented, rather than replaced, the specialisations declared earlier in Sweden. Though less pronounced, a similar pattern is visible among the British students.

Table S22
Type of Activities for Academic Enhancement During the Period Abroad, by Home Country (in percentage of students)*

Type of academic enhancement**	Home country					
	UK	F	D	S	US	Total
Take courses involving content/ topics not available at home	85.5	55.8	64.8	85.7	66.2	68.8
Take courses involving teaching methods not available at home	52.7	76.7	69.0	31.4	54.7	59.7
Take courses to broaden academic/ cultural background	45.5	23.3	63.4	42.9	74.8	59.0
Take language courses in SAP host country language***	30.9	11.6	16.6	17.1	54.7	30.7
Utilize laboratories or other facilities not available at home	10.9	27.9	35.9	25.7	11.5	22.8
Take language courses in other language than of SAP host country	9.1	30.2	24.8	2.9	18.0	19.2
Develop new area of specialization	30.9	16.3	22.1	40.0	0.0	16.8
Change an earlier chosen specialization	1.8	0.0	15.2	11.4	12.9	10.8
(N)	(55)	(43)	(145)	(35)	(139)	(417)

*   Multiple reply was possible
**   The sequence of categories does not correspond to the questionnaire but rather to a rank order according to replies
***   Other than intensive foreign language programme arranged as part of SAP
Source: Post-Study Abroad Questionnaire SAEP F 7 (F 173-180)

There were also differences among the groups of study abroad participants insofar as their involvement in foreign language courses abroad, i.e. courses over and above any arranged formally as "intensive language instruction" by the programme in order to bring students' proficiency level to a point where they could participate in regular host institution courses. A third of the British and over half the American students took courses in the language of their host country as part of their regular courseload at the host institution. A quarter of the Germans and a third of the French studied courses in languages other than those of their respective host countries.

3.5 Comparison of Academic Learning Climate at Home and Host Institutions

The type of academic and work placement which the programmes had formally set up was reported earlier in the documentation of findings from the question-naire and interview survey of the directors. But how did students perceive the set-ting abroad, in contrast to what they were accustomed to at home? And did their depictions of the academic setting abroad corroborate their statements in another section of the questionnaire (reported above) that many of them had experienced teaching and learning modes during the sojourn which were different from those they mainly encountered at home?

Because of the degree of study abroad participants' immersion in the host in-stitution academic environment, the researchers assumed these students would be able to make qualified comparative assessments of the host and home institution climates. Consequently, students were asked to rate the extent to which certain features were strongly - or not at all - emphasised at their host institutions and at their home institutions. The format in the questionnaire encouraged comparison in the process of responding, as the ratings for host institution were to be made alongside ratings for the home, in that order, on the same horizontal line for each of the thirty-six features covered. In listing these features, account had been taken of available research into acquired qualities attributed to educational contexts.[4] The features brought four general areas of the higher education context into fo-cus:

Orientation of course content: degree of emphasis on:
- aspects in the cognitive domain (acquiring facts, learning equations and for-mulae and understanding theories, concepts and paradigms);
- differentiated thinking (through interdisciplinary approaches, obtaining views from different schools of thought, providing European, intercultural or inter-national comparative perspectives); and
- developing applied knowledge and personal skills for practical problem solving.

Instructional styles and learning modes:
- "Instructor dominated" seminars and lectures in the sense that the instructor was viewed as the main source of information, assigned all the reading, fre-quently monitored students' achievement; versus
- A learning climate which assigned greater priority to students' active par-ticipation, taking the initiative, and cultivating critical thinking skills. This could be pitched on an individual level, through independent work or having students choose areas of study within a more general field. It could also be invoked on a group basis, for example, by encouraging students' active participation in class discussion, and other means by which students led the academic interactions.

---

[4] Bloom, B.S. *Taxonomy of Educational Objectives: The Classification of Educational Goals.* New York: David McKay and Co., Inc., 1964; Sandberger, J.-U. and Lind, G. The Outcomes of Uni-versity Education: Some Empirical Findings on Aims and Expectations in the Federal Republic of Germany, *Higher Education* 8 (1979).

Predominant learning resources called upon: libraries, laboratories, foreign language publications, etc.

Methods of assessing student performance: overall degree of emphasis on grades and more specifically the use made of oral examinations, written essay exams, multiple choice texts, and written papers submitted as independent work or as the product of group effort.

Students' responses are summarised in Table S23a-c. This complex Table provides information on:

- how higher education in the individual countries is perceived by incoming students from all the other countries (i.e. the left column in each grouping of three columns per country, in the Table);
- how students perceived higher education in their home institution (middle column in each grouping of three); and
- how students who were sent from any one country perceived higher education abroad; in this case, "abroad" is a combination of the various host countries (right column in each grouping of three).

Examining the columns of the Table permits two kinds of comparison. One is the extent to which students of a certain country experienced a different learning climate abroad as compared to the learning climate at home (comparison of middle and right columns). The second is the extent to which the learning climate in a certain country is perceived similarly or differently by all the incoming students, as compared with the way students from that country characterise it (left and middle columns).

As the research team aggregated these responses, an implicit assumption was made that identifiable national "modes" of higher education would be reflected through the learning climate of the individual institutions. As will be shown in the following analysis, this assumption was upheld. It is worthwhile to analyse, as well, whether the "cultures" of the disciplines played as strong - or, in some few cases, stronger - roles. Table S24 provides information on how the learning climate abroad and at home is perceived by all (European) students in each field of study. One should bear in mind that the ratings by field in Table S24 refer in each instance to the arithmetic mean of students' ratings from four different countries.

A comparison of the left columns for each of the five countries in Table S23a-c shows, for one, that the British institutions reportedly emphasise written communication skills and rather active student initiative. These institutions are weakest in having students use foreign language publications and in utilising oral examinations as a form of student assessment. (Multiple choice tests hardly exist in any of the four European countries.)

Incoming study abroad participants perceive that the French institutions stress teachers as the main source of information, lectures as a predominant form of instruction, and written essay examinations as a prevalent mode of assessing students' performance. Overall, the French institutions also place relatively strong emphasis on grades (i.e. marks). On the other hand, out-of-class communication between students and teaching staff and having students develop their own points of view are least emphasised.

German institutions reportedly give strong credence to students' independent work, their using the library, and producing written papers as a basis for assessment of their learning. There is a pronounced theoretical orientation to the curriculum, and for the times students meet their professors, a decided emphasis on professors lecturing. There is minimal emphasis on having instructors regularly monitor students' achievement through frequent tests or keeping track of class

Table S23a

Features of Academic Learning Climate at Study Abroad Participants' Host and Home Institutions, Assessed for Extent of Emphasis by Incoming and Outgoing (Home) Students, by Country (in arithmetic means)*

	UK inst. viewed by		UK outgoing view on host inst.	F inst. viewed by		F outgoing view on host inst
	in-coming	out-going		in-coming	out-going	
Orientation of course content						
Acquiring facts	2.7	3.2	2.6	2.4	1.7	2.1
Understanding theory, concepts	2.2	2.1	2.8	2.8	2.0	2.0
Develop applied knowledge	2.5	2.5	3.4	3.2	2.5	2.5
Methodology of inquiry	2.7	3.2	3.5	3.1	2.8	2.8
Views different schools thought	3.0	2.6	3.5	3.4	3.0	2.9
Comparative perspectives	2.8	2.8	3.0	2.7	2.8	2.7
Interdisciplinary approaches	3.0	2.6	3.6	3.4	2.7	2.7
Acad. credit, practical experience	2.9	3.4	3.6	3.5	3.0	2.9
High quality courses	2.5	2.2	2.6	2.7	1.9	2.2
Learning resources						
Library	1.6	1.9	3.1	3.3	2.8	1.4
Laboratory facilities	3.1	3.5	3.7	3.5	3.0	3.0
Foreign language publications	3.4	3.2	2.9	3.0	2.6	2.9
Instructional/learning modes						
Lectures	2.4	2.0	2.1	1.7	2.0	2.5
Seminars	2.3	2.2	3.6	3.3	2.6	2.2
Tutorials	2.4	2.7	3.9	3.2	3.7	2.5
Group study/projects	2.9	3.3	3.6	3.4	2.6	2.6
Individual study/projects	2.4	2.3	2.9	2.3	2.5	2.4
Laboratory work	3.4	3.8	4.0	3.7	3.6	3.5
Teacher-assigned texts	2.2	2.1	3.0	3.1	2.9	1.7
Regular class attendance	2.4	2.5	2.7	2.3	2.3	2.6
Teachers as main info source	2.8	3.1	2.8	2.0	2.7	3.2
Tchrs regulrly monitor students	2.6	2.4	3.1	2.6	2.5	2.7
Adherence to deadlines	2.5	1.9	2.3	2.5	2.1	2.3
Tchr/Students talk out of class	2.1	2.1	4.0	3.8	3.5	1.8
Students choose study areas	2.5	2.6	2.8	3.3	2.6	2.3
Students active class discussion	2.2	2.1	2.6	3.2	2.7	1.9
Stud. challenge each other acad.ly	3.0	2.9	3.0	3.4	2.9	2.8
Students develop own views	2.5	2.2	3.1	3.6	2.5	2.2
Project work/written papers	1.8	1.9	2.6	2.5	1.9	1.9
Independent work	2.1	2.1	2.6	2.9	2.4	2.3
Writing/communication skills	2.2	2.0	2.6	2.3	2.1	1.9
Assessment						
Overall emphasis on grades	2.5	2.1	2.1	2.2	1.8	2.3
Oral examinations	3.3	3.3	2.9	2.4	2.4	1.9
Written essay examinations	1.6	1.5	2.4	1.7	1.5	1.6
Multiple choice tests	4.3	4.7	4.2	4.3	4.1	4.2
Evaluation of written papers	2.0	2.3	2.9	2.5	1.8	2.0

* Scale from 1 = "strongly emphasized" to 5 = "not at all emphasized"

Table S23b
Features of Academic Learning Climate at Study Abroad Participants' Host and Home Institutions, Assessed for Extent of Emphasis by Incoming and Outgoing (Home) Students, by Country (in arithmetic means)*

	D inst. viewed by		D outgoing view on host inst.	S inst. viewed by		S outgoing view on host inst
	in-coming	out-going		in-coming	out-going	
Orientation of course content						
Acquiring facts	2.8	2.4	2.3	2.7	2.5	2.4
Understanding theory, concepts	2.3	1.8	2.5	1.7	1.8	2.5
Develop applied knowledge	3.0	3.0	2.2	3.4	2.6	3.0
Methodology of inquiry	2.8	2.6	2.7	2.6	3.0	3.2
Views different schools thought	2.9	2.7	3.4	1.5	3.5	3.5
Comparative perspectives	2.4	2.9	3.0	1.5	3.8	3.8
Interdisciplinary approaches	3.4	3.2	3.1	2.7	3.4	3.4
Acad. credit, practical experience	3.3	3.2	2.8	3.8	3.4	3.7
High quality courses	2.6	2.2	2.5	1.7	2.4	2.5
Learning resources						
Library	2.2	2.1	2.4	2.8	3.7	2.1
Laboratory facilities	3.1	3.5	3.2	2.4	2.7	3.1
Foreign language publications	2.4	2.7	3.5	1.0	2.0	4.7
Instructional/learning modes						
Lectures	2.3	2.6	1.9	2.0	2.0	2.2
Seminars	2.4	2.8	2.6	2.3	3.2	3.7
Tutorials	3.4	3.3	2.9	3.5	3.6	3.6
Group study/projects	2.7	3.2	2.7	2.0	3.1	3.9
Individual study/projects	2.5	2.9	2.7	2.2	3.0	2.2
Laboratory work	3.5	3.2	3.4	2.4	2.4	3.2
Teacher-assigned texts	3.0	2.7	2.6	2.2	2.4	2.4
Regular class attendance	3.7	3.9	1.6	2.5	3.0	3.0
Teachers as main info source	3.2	2.2	2.0	2.7	2.6	2.8
Tchrs regulrly monitor students	4.0	3.3	1.8	3.3	3.5	3.1
Adherence to deadlines	3.1	2.0	2.2	3.0	3.0	2.2
Tchr/Students talk out of class	3.6	3.5	2.5	1.5	3.2	3.4
Students choose study areas	2.7	2.4	2.8	3.2	3.4	2.3
Students active class discussion	2.5	2.8	2.6	1.3	3.0	3.6
Stud. challenge each other acad.ly	2.9	3.0	3.0	2.0	3.2	3.3
Students develop own views	2.6	2.8	3.0	2.5	3.1	3.3
Project work/written papers	2.4	2.6	2.2	2.3	2.6	2.0
Independent work	2.1	1.9	2.5	2.2	2.8	2.3
Writing/communication skills	2.6	2.5	2.6	2.2	3.0	2.7
Assessment						
Overall emphasis on grades	3.2	2.3	2.0	4.0	2.8	1.8
Oral examinations	2.5	2.8	3.1	2.4	4.0	3.6
Written essay examinations	2.6	2.6	1.6	1.8	3.1	2.2
Multiple choice tests	4.5	3.7	3.8	4.2	4.6	4.3
Evaluation of written papers	2.2	2.8	2.1	2.2	3.2	2.8

* Scale from 1 = "strongly emphasized" to 5 = "not at all emphasized"
Source: Post-Study Abroad Questionnaire SAEP F 8, 9, 10 (F 213-324)

Table S23c
Features of Academic Learning Climate at Study Abroad Participants' Host and Home Institutions, Assessed for Extent of Emphasis by Incoming and Outgoing (Home) Students, by Country (in arithmetic means)*

	US institutions viewed by		Outgoing US Students view on host inst.
	incoming students	outgoing students	
Orientation of course content			
Acquiring facts	2.1	2.0	2.9
Understanding theory, concepts	2.1	1.8	2.3
Develop applied knowledge	2.1	2.6	3.3
Methodology of inquiry	2.7	2.5	2.8
Views different schools thought	3.0	2.4	2.6
Comparative perspectives	3.5	3.1	2.1
Interdisciplinary approaches	3.1	2.7	3.4
Acad. credit, practical experience	2.8	2.7	3.4
High quality courses	2.2	1.9	2.7
Learning resources			
Library	2.0	2.3	2.6
Laboratory facilities	2.6	2.4	3.1
Foreign language publications	4.2	4.0	2.4
Instructional/learning modes			
Lectures	1.9	1.4	2.0
Seminars	3.0	3.0	2.5
Tutorials	3.6	3.1	2.8
Group study/projects	3.1	3.4	3.2
Individual study/projects	2.1	2.4	2.4
Laboratory work	2.4	2.7	3.2
Teacher-assigned texts	1.8	1.4	3.0
Regular class attendance	1.9	2.0	3.3
Teachers as main info source	2.1	2.4	2.5
Tchrs regulrly monitor students	1.9	2.3	3.7
Adherence to deadlines	2.0	1.8	3.1
Tchr/Students talk out of class	2.0	2.3	3.4
Students choose study areas	2.1	2.3	3.1
Students active class discussion	2.5	2.3	2.8
Students challenge each other acadamicly	2.6	2.7	3.1
Students develop own views	2.7	2.4	3.0
Project work/written papers	1.9	1.9	2.2
Independent work	2.1	2.5	2.2
Writing/communication skills	2.8	2.2	2.2
Assessment			
Overall emphasis on grades	1.5	1.6	3.2
Oral examinations	3.0	4.3	2.4
Written essay examinations	1.9	1.8	1.9
Multiple choice tests	2.9	2.7	4.5
Evaluation of written papers	2.2	1.8	2.0

* Scale from 1 = "strongly emphasized" to 5 = "not at all emphasized"
Source: Post-Study Abroad Questionnaire SAEP F 8, 9, 10 (F 213-324)

Table S 24
Features of Academic Learning Climate at Study Abroad Participants' Host and Home Institutions, Assessed for Extent of Emphasis by Outgoing (Home) European Students, by Field of Study (in arithmetic means)*

	Business studies		Engineering		Natural sciences		Law		Foreign languages	
	View on home inst.	View on host inst.	View on home inst.	View on host inst.	View on home inst.	View on host inst.	View on home inst.	View on host inst.	View on home inst.	View on host inst.
Orientation of course content										
Acquiring facts (including learning equations and formulae, where applicable)	2.3	2.8	2.4	2.0	2.5	2.1	2.3	1.7	2.8	2.7
Understanding theories, concepts paradigms	1.9	2.5	1.8	2.1	1.5	2.2	1.7	2.9	2.6	3.0
Development of applied knowledge and personal skills for practical problemsolving and/or future employment opportunities (e.g. computer, urban planning)	2.5	2.1	2.2	2.8	2.7	2.6	2.8	2.9	3.3	3.7
Methodology of inquiry in discipline areas, field methods	2.7	2.8	3.0	2.9	2.9	2.7	2.8	3.1	3.5	3.8
Providing views from different schools of thought	2.8	3.2	3.3	3.7	3.4	3.6	2.4	3.5	2.8	3.4
Providing comparative (e.g. international/European, inter-cultural) perspectives	2.5	2.6	3.7	3.6	4.0	3.9	2.9	2.9	2.7	3.0
Interdisciplinary approaches	2.7	3.0	3.3	3.5	3.2	3.3	3.3	3.3	3.0	2.9
Academic credit given for applied/practical experience	2.9	2.6	3.3	3.5	3.3	3.1	3.8	3.8	3.6	3.3
High standard, quality courses	2.1	2.8	2.4	2.2	2.4	2.5	2.1	2.4	1.9	2.2

continued Table S 24

	Business studies		Engineering		Natural sciences		Law		Foreign languages	
	View on home inst.	View on host inst.	View on home inst.	View on host inst.	View on home inst.	View on host inst.	View on home inst.	View on host inst.	View on home inst.	View on host inst.
Learning resources										
Use of the library as a learning resource	2.3	2.2	3.0	3.0	2.8	1.9	1.9	2.9	2.0	2.7
Use of laboratory facilities as a learning resource	3.6	3.5	2.4	2.6	2.4	2.7	4.4	4.1	3.0	3.1
Using publications in foreign language(s)	2.8	3.1	2.8	3.7	2.3	3.6	3.6	3.8	1.8	2.2
Instructional style and learning modes										
Lectures	2.3	2.2	2.3	1.7	2.1	2.1	1.8	2.6	2.0	2.4
Seminars	2.5	2.6	3.1	3.3	3.0	3.1	3.0	2.7	2.5	3.5
Tutorials	3.6	3.5	3.1	3.4	3.3	2.9	2.4	3.3	3.1	3.2
Group projects or other forms of independent study	2.8	2.3	2.6	3.1	3.6	3.5	3.6	3.8	3.2	3.3
Individual projects or other forms of independent study	2.6	2.7	2.7	2.8	2.7	2.0	3.5	2.9	2.3	2.4
Laboratory work	3.5	3.9	2.5	2.8	2.4	2.4	4.3	4.1	3.4	3.8
Instructor-assigned text books/ reading lists	2.4	2.4	2.8	3.2	3.0	2.4	2.8	2.6	2.2	2.2
Regular class attendance	3.2	2.3	3.7	2.6	3.3	2.3	3.6	1.5	2.0	2.2
Teachers as the main source of information	2.3	2.9	2.4	2.3	2.3	2.4	2.8	1.9	2.9	2.7
Instructors regularly monitoring students' achievement	2.9	2.7	3.2	2.6	3.2	2.4	3.4	1.7	2.2	2.3
Adherence to deadlines	1.9	2.6	2.4	2.2	2.7	2.0	1.9	2.1	1.9	2.0
Out of class communication between students and teaching staff	3.1	2.6	3.1	3.6	3.1	2.7	3.5	3.3	3.0	2.3
Students' freedom to choose specific areas of study within general fields	2.4	2.6	2.5	2.8	2.5	2.4	2.7	3.2	3.0	2.3

continued Table S 24

	Business studies		Engineering		Natural sciences		Law		Foreign languages	
	View on home inst.	View on host inst.	View on home inst.	View on host inst.	View on home inst.	View on host inst.	View on home inst.	View on host inst.	View on home inst.	View on host inst.
Instructional style and learning modes										
Active participation in class discussions	2.8	2.3	3.2	3.7	2.5	2.9	2.5	2.6	2.1	2.1
Students stimulating and challenging each other academically	3.1	3.1	3.0	3.3	2.8	3.0	2.9	3.1	3.1	2.8
Students developing their own points of view	2.8	2.6	3.2	3.6	2.8	3.3	2.5	3.6	2.1	2.3
Students written papers and project work	2.4	1.8	2.3	2.4	2.7	2.1	2.5	3.1	1.5	2.0
Independent work	2.2	2.4	2.6	2.6	2.4	2.1	2.0	3.1	1.7	2.3
Writing and communication skills	2.2	2.5	3.1	2.8	2.9	2.8	2.1	2.4	1.9	1.8
Assessment										
General:										
Degree of emphasis on grades	2.0	2.5	2.2	2.1	2.6	1.6	2.1	1.7	1.9	2.3
Methods:										
Oral examinations	2.9	3.1	3.7	3.3	3.0	4.0	3.0	2.8	2.3	1.8
Written examinations	2.0	1.8	2.4	2.2	2.9	1.7	1.9	1.5	1.7	2.2
Multiple choice tests	3.9	3.9	4.4	4.5	4.2	4.1	4.0	4.4	4.3	4.2
Evaluation of papers submitted (written) independently or as product of group work	2.5	2.1	3.0	2.8	3.1	2.3	2.3	2.5	2.1	2.4

* Scale from 1 = "strongly emphasized" to 5 = "not at all emphasized" (question: "According to your experience, to what extent are each of the following emphasized at your host institution, as compared with your home institution?")

Source: Post-Study Abroad Questionnaire SAEP F 8, 9, 10 (F 213-324)

attendance; and there is little interaction out-of-class between students and teaching staff.

The USA is seen to give great weight to lecture classes, to instructor-assigned texts and reading lists, regular class attendance and instructors' regularly monitoring students' achievement (through written essay exams); at the same time, students work together on projects, write papers and must make frequent use of the library. Students are quite preoccupied with working for good grades. Features which are less prevalent in the American institutions are tutorials as a form of instruction, the use of foreign language publications, and cultivation of international, comparative perspectives.

The Swedish universities are in a somewhat special situation since they are the host for the smallest number of students. This has consequences for the statistical computation of the means. There is also a different inherent basis for comparison, since there is not as wide a spread in the home institution affiliation, which is the point of departure for students assessing the Swedish institutions as hosts. Because - as will be discussed below - some similarities exist between the perceptions of incoming students to each country and students of that country, one can look at how the Swedish students perceive the learning climate in Sweden, compared with how students from the other countries perceive *their* home institutions. This contrasting analysis shows that Swedish institutions seem least to stimulate students' active participation (in choice of study areas, class discussion, developing their own points of view, independent work, writing/communication skills). Somewhat surprisingly, adherence to deadlines and teacher monitoring are not strong features, either. Little emphasis is placed on assessment by written examinations, evaluation of written papers; and altogether the emphasis on grades is perceived to be low. Swedish students find reading foreign language publications is emphasised at their institutions.

Given the differences in duration of students' firsthand experience of their home versus their host institutions, and also that the mix of institutions was not identical across all five countries - the aggregate ratings of the German institutions, for example, refer to universities, Fachhochschulen, and Gesamthochschulen - it is remarkable that there are far more perceived similarities between the home and the host institutions than differences. Also, the ratings of incoming students to a country essentially corroborate the perceptions of the same country's home students in assessing the emphases in higher education in that country. The difference between the two groups' ratings is 0.5 or less (on a scale where 1 = "strongly emphasised"), for the vast majority of features. The Swedish situation is the most exceptional due to the statistical consequences mentioned earlier.

Where the most pronounced differences between home and host institutions were registered - for 7 of the 36 features - 6 of these were in the area of instructional styles and learning modes. For three of the features, the differences which students detected between their home and host institutions stood out more when comparing the ratings by the students' home country affiliation than by their field of study affiliation. These three are: tutorials, instructor-assigned texts and reading lists, out-of-class communication between students and teaching staff. Two additional features - emphasis on attending class regularly, and on having students write papers and/or do project work - are practices where the variation seems greater from one field 'of study to another. For the sixth - instructors regularly monitoring students' achievement - it is not obvious whether the variation is greater by country or field. Regarding the seventh feature - emphasis on theories, concepts and paradigms - differences are more evident when students of one country describe their various host institutions, rather than in the comparisons of home and host institutions made by students all in one field.

The observation that, on average, it is the country slightly more than field of study which lies behind the differences students perceive between their home and host institutions strengthens the argument for study abroad if the objective is to expose participants to an academic context which is not the same as the one at home. At the same time, it does not appear that students in this survey would be extremely disoriented abroad, since it is the similarity between home and host institutions which prevails, more than the dissimilarities. Undoubtedly, a good deal of the concerted effort of programme directors lies behind the students' perceptions of similarity between the sending and receiving institutions.

Focussing on the more obvious differences in students' perception of the academic climate at home and abroad has highlighted matters of instructional style, learning modes and resources and assessment practices, more than the orientation of course content. This is a notable finding in itself, suggestive that patterns in instructional style and the like are more easily recognisable and categorised than the presumably more intricate and abstract features of course content and orientation. Ratings for the latter tend to cluster in the "neutral 3" range of the scale. It is also likely that, in reality, the orientation of courses at the level of the first higher education degree does tend to be highly similar across most institutions in Western countries.

Nevertheless, some slight variations in emphasis can be detected. Courses at French institutions are comparatively less theoretical than in the other countries. Acquiring facts is comparatively more emphasised in the French and American courses. Development of applied knowledge is relatively strong at British and American institutions. International, European and inter-cultural perspectives are less prevalent in the USA, strong in Germany and Sweden. Finally, high standards in course quality are reported for all institutions, but the USA is rated as particularly strong in this respect.

Diagrams S3-6 provide the opportunity to view the degree of consistency in the way that students discern the emphases at their host institution as a function of the students' perception of contrast with the conditions they experienced at home. In the F-US-D triangle of Diagram S4, the American students' average rating of the emphasis on tutorials at home is 3.1, which is stronger than the Germans' rating of this feature at their home institutions, 3.3. But the Americans who went to Germany perceived the emphasis on tutorials in that host country was stronger than at home. The Americans also sensed the emphasis on tutorials was stronger in France, as did the German students who went to France.

Diagram S 3
Study Abroad Participants' Assessments of Emphasis on Understanding
Theories, Concepts, Paradigms at Host and Home Institutions; Home-Host
Institution Pairs by Country (in arithmetic means)*

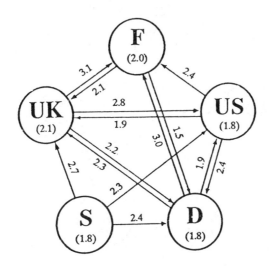

* Scale from 1 = "strongly emphasized" to 5 = "not at all emphasized"

  Assessment of home country is presented in circles, those of the host country to the
  arrows, whereby the direction of the arrows represents the home ---> host relationship.

Source: Post-Study Abroad Questionnaire SAEP F 8, 9, 10 (F213-324)

One of the more logically consistent findings is illustrated in Diagram S5, in the
UK-US-D triangle. The British students who went to Germany on average assessed the emphasis on out-of-class communication between students and teachers at their host institutions at a low 4.3 This could appear strange in relation to
the Americans' assessment of the same feature at a higher 3.2, given that the
British and American points of departure are so similar (2.1 and 2.3, respectively,
in assessing their home institutions). The discrepancies appear to be explained by
the British students' significantly lower assessment of the American situation, implying that the British home rating of 2.1 is far stronger than its 0.2 point difference from the Americans' rating.

Impacts of Study Abroad Programmes

Diagram S 4
Study Abroad Participants' Assessments of Emphasis on Tutorials at Host
and Home Institutions; Home-Host Institution Pairs by Country
(in arithmetic means)*

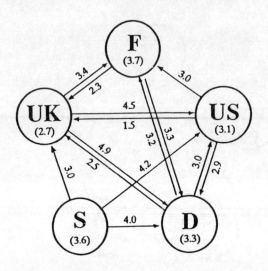

Diagram S 5
Study Abroad Participants' Assessments of Emphasis on Out-of-Class
Communication between Students and Teaching Staff at Host and Home
Institutions; Home-Host Institution Pairs by Country (in arithmetic means)*

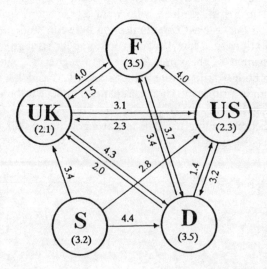

Diagram S 6
Study Abroad Participants' Assessments of Emphasis on Instructor-Assigned Text Books/Reading Lists at Host and Home Institutions; Home-Host Institution Pairs by Country (in arithmetic means)*

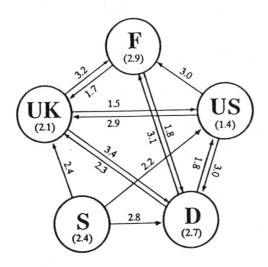

3.6   Work Placement Abroad

As reported previously, a number of the study abroad programmes examined here supplement a phase of study abroad with a work placement in the host country. This applies to a portion of the British, French and German programmes promoted by the European Community through the "Joint Study Programme" scheme. Thus, of the 439 students who answered the Pre-Study Abroad and Post Study Abroad questionnaires, 102 also answered a Work Placement Supplement both before and after they went abroad. Of these, 92 were in Business Studies, and the remaining ten in Engineering, Natural Sciences or Foreign Languages. Because of this distribution, an overall statistical summary of participants' assessments of the benefits and pitfalls of study abroad, comparing the group with work placement and the group without, would have the responses from Business Studies students overshadowing other fields. Even the general description of the work placement situation, below, is heavily influenced by conditions encountered by the Business Studies students. It is nevertheless included because it raises some issues of more generalizable concern.

Of all the participants from whom there is information on the practical phase, 68 came from German universities, 22 from British and 12 from French. Because of the small number of students involved, the following summary of findings generally does not differentiate according to students' country of origin or their host country. When,exceptionally, results are presented by country, this is done as elsewhere in this volume, noting differences by country of origin more frequently than by host country.

For nearly all (94%) respondents, the work placement abroad was mandatory. It was nine months or longer for sixty percent of the respondents; no more than two months for almost a third of the students. Nearly half (47%) the respondents overall had a 3-6 months phase of practical experience in the home country as well, and most completed this before going abroad.

Locating a suitable work placement was problematic for about half the students. On the whole, students themselves were fairly involved in this search, though for half the respondents, the host institution was primarily responsible for making the arrangements. Only a fifth of the students mentioned the home institution in this capacity, and some of the respondents had been left entirely on their own to make the arrangements. Half the respondents reported they had been able to choose among two or more possible placement sites.

Since for the majority (74%) of respondents the practical phase abroad came after the period of study at the host university, it is not surprising the students seldom reported they had received preparation for work placement while still at the home institution. Preparatory courses for the work placement abroad were more frequently held at the host institution, yet only about a fifth of the respondents had taken any of these. As was evident for the study phase abroad, the most frequent form of preparation for the work placement was talking to former participants. At the end of the work placement, respondents were neither effusive in their praise nor unduly critical about the preparation they had received.

Most (85%) of the respondents had their work placement in industrial or private service enterprises. A scant two percent had been in public administration, and 13 percent in other organisations. Slightly less than half (44%) had been in organisations with less than 100 employees; a further third (37%) in organisations with up to 1,000 employees; about a fifth (19%) in even larger ones.

For the most part, students had not been hampered by financial difficulties during work placement. For three-quarters of the respondents, expenses incurred during the practical phase abroad were covered by remuneration from the employing organisation. Slightly more than a tenth of the respondents received student stipends or loans during work placement. In some cases, the students or their parents had to bear the greater part of the expenses.

A good number (76%) of the students had found it necessary to move their residence for the practical phase since the employing organisation was not located near the university they had attended in the host country. Most of the students rented a room or an apartment while on work placement. There appeared to have been few problems in connection with this, or with other issues such as securing a work permit, obtaining the relevant visa or health or social insurance.

As far as supervision during the work placement was concerned, 16 percent of the respondents reported regular contact with someone in this capacity from the actual employing organisation. More common, however, (for 45% of the respondents) was that someone only occasionally checked on the students' progress; 28 percent responded that no one was officially designated to look after them. Whatever the system, students seemed very satisfied with the nature of supervision. Responding on a scale from 1= "very satisfied" to 5= "very unsatisfied," they gave an average rating of 2.1, and only 17 percent expressed dissatisfaction (4 or 5 on the scale) with the supervision.

In contrast, the students were not in the least impressed by their universities' styles of supervision. Nearly half (43%) of the students received at least one visit from representatives of the host university. A quarter of the respondents were visited by representatives of their home university. On the same five-point scale, the degree of respondents' satisfaction with the way the host university looked after them averaged 3.3; 47 percent of the students expressed dissatisfaction. Similarly, the rating in respect of the home university was 3.4; 42 percent expressed dissatisfaction. Among the latter were 36 percent of the German respondents and half the French and British.

Students nevertheless reported few if any difficulties with the practical phase abroad. Average values on a scale from 1= "very great difficulties" to 5= "no difficulties at all" were:
- 4.3 in respect of difficulties with colleagues at the place of work;
- 3.9 in respect of contacts with colleagues outside working hours; and
- 4.3 in relations with students from the host country who were also on the work placement (two-thirds of the students participating in work placement replied to this question).

Moreover, only six percent of the respondents reported language problems to such an extent that, in their view, what they could gain from the practical phase was adversely affected. Most of the students were satisfied with their degree of integration into the employing organisation. On the five-point scale (1= "very satisfied" to 5= "not satisfied at all"), the average value was 1.9; 12 percent were very dissatisfied.

As Table S25 shows, assessment practices varied in measuring what students gained from the work placements. It is nevertheless apparent that the predominant form of assessment was something in writing (a substantial project report or a shorter written assessment - or both), generated by the students. Students were by and large accountable to both home and host institutions.

Two-thirds of the respondents felt the work placement abroad had been more valuable than simply a period of studies would have been in the host country. Some representative comments from British students in Business Studies follow:

"The work placement was an outstanding opportunity to gain real mastery of the foreign language - much better than during the study phase abroad."

"I would have preferred to spend the whole year in the practical phase rather than at the university. My foreign language level is not good enough really to profit from lectures at universities abroad. This meant that I wasted time. In respect of culture, mentality, language, I learnt much more during the practical phase."

Table S25
**Types of Formal Work Required to Do During or Immediately After the Work
Placement** (percentage of students participating in work placement abroad)

Type of Formal Work	Required by Only home institution	Required by Only host institution	Both	Not required	Total	(N)
Written assessment or evaluation	31.9	34.1	22.0	12.1	100.0	(91)
Oral assessment or evaluation of the placement	30.8	9.9	-	59.3	100.0	(91)
Substantive project report	14.3	8.8	26.4	50.5	100.0	(91)
Written test on knowledge/ skills acquired	-	-	-	-	-	(91)
Oral test on knowledge/ skills acquired	4.4	-	-	95.6	100.0	(91)

Source: Post-Study Abroad Work Placement Questionnaire SAEP FP 20 (F 1113-1124)

A third of the respondents rated the study and work placement abroad equally.
This is clearly in contrast to expectations before the stay abroad. At that time,
only 23 percent of the respondents indicated they had greater expectations about
the practical phase than the studies abroad, while 65 percent had equally great expectations about both. In many cases, respondents pointed out that the impact of
the work placement depended heavily on external circumstances:

"One reason why the practical phase was of greater value was the fact of being in another place with no German students present. This decisively encouraged both my mastery of the language and my independence. I had
much more contact with the inhabitants of the host country." (German student in Business Studies)

Among respondents who had participated in a practical phase at home as well, 46
percent regarded the practical experiences abroad as more valuable. It was also 46
percent who ranked the value of work placement at home and abroad equally,
whereas only 8 percent gave a higher rating to the practical phase at home.

Table S26 attempts to compare respondents' *original expectations* about the
practical phase abroad (expressed before they departed from the home country)
with students' assessments of the *results* as experienced after they had returned
from the sojourn. Only a limited comparison can be made since the form of the
questions was slightly different in the Pre- and Post-Study Abroad Work Placement Supplement questionnaires. Before study abroad, students were asked to list
their five most important reasons for seeking work placement experience abroad.
In the follow-up questionnaire, students described the benefits of the work placement by rating each of several pre-supplied categories on a five-point scale. These
are shown in the righthand column of the Table (ratings of 1 and 2 are added together).

Table S 26
Effects of Work Placement Abroad Most Strongly Desired Before the Sojourn and Strongly Realized According to Students' Assessment Upon Return
(in percentage of participating students)

	Desired*		Realized**	
	Percentage	Rank	Percentage	Rank
Prepare you for internationally oriented job tasks in your home country	60	(1)	68	(5)
Give you an opportunity of learning and using the language of the host country in non-academic context	55	(2)	90	(1)
Help to acquaint you with management techniques	48	(3)	66	(7)
Enhance your prospects of obtaining a job involving interesting assignments	47	(4)	65	(1)
Improve your chances of finding a job abroad after completing your studies	41	(5)	74	(4)
Give you a chance to get to know people and their way of life in the host country outside higher education circles	35	(6)	85	(2)
Increase your ability to work independently	33	(7)	67	(6)
Give you an insight into industrial relations (employer - employee relations) in a country other than your own	26	(8)	85	(3)
Acquaint you with different orientations available within your intended career field	22	(9)	52	(9)
Give you a better chance of earning a higher income on completion of your studies	16	(10)	42	(10)
Help you choose an area of specialization within your subject field	15	(11)	42	(12)
Enhance your performance in your academic studies	8	(12)	21	(12)

* Named as one of the 5 most important reasons (question: "Why were you interested in having the opportunity of carrying out a work placement abroad?")
** 1 or 2 on a scale from 1 = "very strong effect" to 5 = "no effect at all" (question: " What effects do you feel the work placement which you have carried out abroad had had for you?")
Source: Pre-Study Abroad Work Placement Questionnaire SAEP DW 11 (D 636-647) and Post-Study Abroad Work Placement Questionnaire SAEP FW 24 (F 1128-1139)

In retrospect, students perceived a wide range of benefits from the work experience. It cannot be discounted, however, that a similarly wide range in students' expectations might have been displayed if the question had been phrased in the same way in the Pre-Study-Abroad Questionnaire as in the follow-up. One should also note the categories in the Post-Study Abroad Questionnaire refer to learning processes and acquired knowledge which could be useful to further university study and/or later in a career. Since students answered the second questionnaire while still completing studies at their home university, they were probably able to judge the worth of the work placement more accurately in terms of its utility in the academic context as compared with its future value to a career.

The greatest benefits of work placement were felt to be learning and practising the host country language, becoming acquainted with people in the host country outside the university environment, and experiencing employer-employee relations. The majority of respondents also considered that the practical phase had enhanced their capacity for independent work and given them insight into management techniques in another country, as well as a better idea of what they might encounter in a future career.

The ranking of expectations before the practical phase abroad and the retrospective assessment of perceived effects differed significantly only on one point. Before students went abroad, their expectation level was generally high about the value of the practical experience for increasing understanding of management techniques; relatively low in terms of gaining insight into employer-employee relations. Afterwards, the order was reversed. Clearly, the experiences during the practical phase abroad were more strongly related to the situation of employees below management level than was expected or even desired in advance.

Before going abroad, students' expectations about the work placement were especially associated with thoughts about the likely *nature* of their professional activities after graduation. At the end of the sojourn, students emphasised more the probability that the foreign work experience could improve their prospects of simply *finding* a job. Also before they went abroad, students thought the practical work experience could boost their chances of obtaining a job in another country or being accepted for a job that had at least some internationally oriented activities. After the sojourn, however, this expectation no longer stood out so strongly, in comparison with several other career related expectations. The same was true of students' expectations about the influence their practical phase abroad would have on their access to an "interesting" career. Finally, a number of respondents to the Post-Study Abroad Questionnaire thought that work placement might somehow improve their prospects of a higher income in their subsequent career. All of these expectations seem rather realistic, judging from the findings of the survey of European graduates, reported in Chapter 7.

At the end of the practical phase abroad, five percent of the respondents had already been offered more long-term employment at the same site. A further five percent reported that negotiations of this nature were underway, and forty percent thought such a job might be possible even though they had no concrete plans in this connection.

It was very striking that, before their sojourn, few if any of the students foresaw the work placement would impact favourably upon their study habits once they had returned to their home institutions. After the study and work placement abroad, a fifth of the students perceived such an effect, and 42 percent were convinced that the practical phase abroad had helped them choose a specialisation in their studies (see Table S26). In addition, they recognised the value of the work experience abroad to help them understand the relation between theory and practice:

"I regard the practical phase as the core of my training, and without it I would not have the reference to practice which is so important to me." (German student in Business Studies)

Three-quarters of the students reported the work placement abroad had influenced their plans for a future profession. Most frequently, the period abroad helped confirm and strengthen earlier decisions (34%), although it also contributed to replacing vague aims with concrete plans (19%) or correcting earlier plans (14%) about the type of career to pursue.

The students mostly thought the timing and duration of the work placements abroad were appropriate and that the assignments had been varied, interesting, challenging, and had encouraged independent work. About half the students' positive assessments related to the flexible and open atmosphere they experienced at the workplace, the independence encouraged of trainees, and the amount of responsibility they were given. Criticism of the work placements stressed absence of the same:

"I did not like the long and boring jobs on the computer, the boring donkey work."(German students in Business Studies)

"The practical phase was good as a whole, but, as often happens with practical phases for students, there was too little for the students to do, and that meant boredom." (British student in Business Studies)

The second most frequent theme in students' narrative comments about their work placements abroad concerned communication with fellow employees and supervisors. Here too, there were twice as many positive as negative statements. Some of the criticism related to unpleasant treatment of foreigners:

"What displeased me most was the way foreigners were treated; there seemed to be a preconceived idea that if you weren't good at expressing yourself in the language, this indicated a lack of intelligence and talent." (British student in Business Studies, on work placement in Germany)

Other negative comments referred to working conditions such as placement in rooms without windows, having to start work as early as 8 in the morning, low pay or no leave. Still, only few students offered suggestions for what the university could do to make the work placements abroad more rewarding. The proposals which were made related more to the choice in types of placements offered, rather than the way in which students were supervised during such a period. And one student insisted:

"You have to approach the practical phase in a positive frame of mind. When you see people who look as if they have an interesting job to do, or who have a great deal to do, you should go up to them, ask if you can help, observe what they do. Then you will learn a great deal more about the firm. You will be given work that is more demanding, more interesting and more stimulating; and hopefully you will end up becoming indispensable!" (British student in Business Studies)

3.7   The Return Home

Students returned to their respective home countries, mostly to resume studies at the same institutions as before; although for 11%, study abroad was the final segment in their degree programme, so they returned home to graduate. Nearly all (95%) the students who had chosen a field of study or a major prior to going abroad returned home to the same field and did not admit even to considering any possible changes. However, a third of the students conceded they would have liked to remain at the partner institution abroad to complete their overall degree programme there. This was especially true of the French; and by field was reported by the majority of Foreign Language, Law and Natural Sciences students. Anticipated financial difficulties and the regulations of one or both of the institutions involved in the study abroad programme militated against finishing the degree programme at the study abroad host institution.

Table S27
Extent to Which Study Abroad Participants Felt Integrated into the Academic Life of the Home and Host Institutions, by Home Country
(in arithmetic means)*

| | Home country | | | | | |
	UK	F	D	S	US	Total
Extent of integration into academic life of host institution for SAP	2.9	1.7	2.3	2.5	2.8	2.5
Extent of integration into academic life of home institution, prior to study abroad	2.1	2.1	2.4	2.1	2.1	2.2
Extent of integration into academic life at home institution, after study abroad	2.1	2.1	2.3	2.7	2.0	2.2
(N)	(51)	(28)	(121)	(28)	(134)	(362)

*   Scale from 1 = "to a great extent" to 5 = "not at all" (Question: "To what extent did/do
    you feel integrated into the academic life of your home (host) institution?")
Source: Post-Study Abroad Questionnaire SAEP F 35 and 36 (F 813-815)

In few of the countries were re-integration measures provided (by the home institution) nor - if provided - ulitised by more than a marginal portion of returnees. At the same time, most of the returnees did not feel terribly disoriented, and in fact sensed little or no difference between the degree of their integration into academic life at their respective home institutions after the sojourn, as compared with before (see Table S27). The Swedes were the major exception. They admitted feeling significantly less integrated after the sojourn, compared not only with how they felt before departing for study abroad, but also with how they felt during studies at the host institution. The French had also felt significantly more integrated into academic life at the host institution, but when they returned home,

they sensed they were part of the academic community just as they had been before they left. Finally, the Germans registered no difference in the extent to which
they felt integrated within the academic community abroad and at home; prior to,
during and after the sojourn.

Another form of integration concerns the amount of academic recognition
granted for studies carried out at the host institution. At the time they answered
the Post-Study Abroad Questionnaire, some of the students were unsure about
this, but nearly two-thirds anticipated the entire programme would be granted full
credit toward their degree at the home institution. In France, Sweden and the
USA, approximately three-quarters of the study abroad returnees expected to receive credit for the entire programme. By field (European students only), this
characterised a similarly high proportion of students in Engineering and Foreign
Languages. Leaving aside the students who had requested to receive credit for
only a portion - or for none - of their study abroad, problems to the extent that
students wanted more credit than the amount granted were greatest among the
British and German groups; and by field, among the Business Studies and Law
students. In each case, nearly a third of the study abroad participants had received
credit for only part or for none of the work carried out abroad. Nevertheless, the
overwhelming majority of students did not see that their study abroad was likely
to prolong the total duration of their studies in higher education by more than one
semester or term. Among those who thought prolongation of more than one
semester likely, the British and German students were slightly more prevalent. By
field, there was clearly a greater proportion of Law students who faced this
prospect, as is shown in table S28.

Table S28
**Possible Prolongation of Studies in Higher Education Due to Study Abroad
Period, by Home Country and Field of Study** (in percentage of students)

Extent of prolon-gation likely	Home country					Field of study					
	UK	F	D	S	US	Bus	Eng	NatSc	Law	Lang	Total*
None	69	82	36	57	56	69	50	57	21	78	53
Prolongation up to 1 semester	-	-	39	23	23	13	33	25	36	9	23
Prolongation more than 1 semester	26	18	23	17	20	18	17	9	38	4	22
Not known	5	-	2	3	1	-	-	9	4	-	2
Total	100	100	100	100	100	100	100	100	100	100	100
(N)	(57)	(33)	(131)	(35)	(138)	(78)	(24)	(44)	(47)	(23)	(394)

*   Also including other fields of study
Source: Post-Study Abroad Questionnaire SAEP F 41 (F 819)

3.8   Overall Assessment of the Study Abroad

Most of the students were satisfied with the support and counselling they received from the host university during their stay abroad. About 90 percent of the respondents reported support in:
- general organisational and practical arrangements (registering with authorities, insurance etc.);
- searching for apartments and other questions of accommodation;
- academic matters (where applicable, including matters related to work placement);
- cultural and social opportunities.

About 70 percent indicated that the programme had explicitly helped them learn the language and become more knowledgeable about the host country, had served as a broker in making contacts even outside the academic community, and had provided assistance in other personal matters. About half the respondents reported they had received support or counselling related to personal finances and help in understanding the university system of the host country.

Interestingly, students' assessments were most reserved with respect to satisfaction with academic matters: 52 percent indicated satisfaction by marking the first or second category on a 1-5 scale, where 1= "very satisfied" and 5= "not at all satisfied". In contrast, 71 percent expressed satisfaction with cultural and leisure activities arranged or facilitated by the programme.

While students were predominantly positive in their assessment of the way they were looked after during their study abroad, this does not downplay the fact that a fifth of all respondents stipulated they were unsatisfied with the academic support or lack thereof. Also about a fifth of the respondents found the help with accommodation inadequate. It was seldom asserted that no support was given; rather, these students expected more effort to be made, or effort that produced a more suitable final result.

Overall, British and German students expressed less satisfaction about the way they were looked after during their study abroad than the students from the other three countries. As regards accommodation and social contacts abroad, notably British students going to France and the USA were less frequently satisfied, whereas criticism regarding financial support abroad was more frequently voiced by British students going to Germany and France. In addition, several German students going to the United Kingdom expressed dissatisfaction regarding financial support abroad. Foreign language students were far more satisfied with the way they were looked after abroad than students in all other fields.

A similar picture emerges from the answers to the question to what extent the students during their stay abroad had difficulties with various aspects of learning and living abroad. In all aspects, only a minority reported great difficulties, as shown in Table S29. It appears there were few problems related to contacts with host country nationals, the lifestyle abroad, diet, weather, etc. But it cannot be overlooked that a considerable number of problems were mentioned. In academic matters, a quarter of the respondents stated they had serious problems (values 1 or 2 on the scale from 1= "very great difficulties" to 5= "no difficulties at all") because of the differences between host and home institution teaching methods and patterns of learning. Fifteen percent reported great problems in academic counselling. It was more seldom that problems were reported as a function of the academic level of the courses or with learning in a foreign language.

Table S 29
Problems Faced by Students during Their Study Abroad Period, by Home Country (percentage)*

| Type of Problems | Home country | | | | | |
	UK	F	D	S	US	Total
Too much contact with people from other country**	37.7	33.3	23.0	16.6	33.3	28.6
Differnces in teaching/learning methods (between home and host institutions	37.9	16.3	22.4	5.3	25.9	23.4
Administrative matters	31.0	22.3	14.9	7.9	26.5	20.9
Readiness on part of teaching staff to meet and/or help foreign students	37.9	6.5	10.3	5.4	16.6	15.2
Guidance concerning academic program	20.7	6.8	5.3	13.2	26.1	15.0
Not enough time available for travel	11.9	21.7	25.5	10.5	3.6	15.0
Accommodation	15.5	17.3	18.2	7.9	7.9	13.6
Finding a place to concentrate on studies, outside the classrooms	15.5	-	19.4	2.6	8.8	12.1
Financial matters	21.4	24.3	11.6	5.2	8.7	12.9
Interaction among/with host country students	17.2	8.7	7.8	2.6	16.7	11.6
Differences in class or student project group size	34.8	4.5	2.1	-	6.6	10.0
Academic level of courses	19.3	-	7.8	5.4	-	8.6
Climate, food, health etc.	5.2	10.8	5.2	2.6	14.4	8.5
Taking courses/examitations in a foreign language	16.3	6.7	5.3	-	8.7	7.3
Guidance concerning nonacademic matters	10.5	4.5	4.0	8.1	9.8	7.0
Lifestyles of nationals in host country	5.2	6.5	3.9	-	10.1	6.0
Communication in a foreign language outside the classroom	4.0	2.2	8.6	-	2.7	4.8
Not enough contact with people from your own country	3.6	6.6	3.3	-	0.7	2.6

*   Scores 1 or 2 on a scale from 1 = "very serious problems" to 5 = "no problems at all"
** The sequence of categories does not correspond to the questionnaire but rather to the rank order according to replies.

Source: Post-Study Abroad Questionnaire SAEP F22 (F613-630)

A considerable number of students (21%) experienced difficulties with administrative matters as well, but the item most frequently (29%) rated as a problem was actually that the study abroad participants felt they had "too much" contact with people from their own country. This shows that many students would have preferred to concentrate even more on learning and living immersed in the host country.

And again, it was apparent that the habits and expectations which students had formed in their home countries greatly influenced whether they felt they had problems during the stay abroad. Thus, for example, many British students complained about large class enrollments abroad, instructors' lack of readiness to join in with foreign students, and the differences between teaching methods at home and at the host university.

Understandably there is a somewhat different focus on problems in the returnees' responses to open-ended questions about their most aggravating experiences, as distinct from their ranking, as above, the order of severity of presupplied lists of problems. When students were asked to write about their worst and most difficult experiences abroad, little mention was made of "too much contact" with people from their own countries. Rather, academic and linguistic hurdles most often stood out in the students' recollections of difficulties. And among the worst things that had befallen them were illnesses, administrative frustrations ("Having to deal with the German banks and the bureaucracy of the registrar's office at the university!" "Having to figure out the maze of health insurance in the USA"), having to cope with lack of money or other financial problems (some of which stemmed from fluctuations in exchange rates), being treated unkindly, or having things stolen. Students usually insisted, however, that these few instances had not overpowered the beneficial effects of the study period abroad.

It had been difficult for students to wait out the initial period of minimal contacts with people in their new environment: "It was as if one had to live in a closed vase for four months," said one of the French students. Of course, students had to conquer feelings of homesickness at the outset, but in retrospect, they focussed more on difficulties in getting over the barrier of being a "strange foreigner," the work it took to become accepted among natives, accepted as an individual, "what I am - not only following the crows like a dog", to cite an American student who had been in Sweden. It had been difficult to summon courage to join in conversation with huge groups of people from the host country (British student in Natural Sciences who studied in France); to come to terms with the embarrassment of speaking with a foreign accent (French student in Business Studies who went to the UK) or with the difficulties in making oneself understood sufficiently well when it mattered so much in the academic context:

> "It was painful not being able to communicate will enough with others in my research project just at the time our group had to re-define the objectives for our work." (French student in Engineering who studied in Germany)

The academic challenges are taken up in greater detail in a following chapter.

In sum, the following assessment by a German Business Studies student who had gone to the UK is quite characteristic:

> "The whole year abroad was strictly speaking a hurdle or difficulty in my life which had to be overcome and mastered. There were no particularly striking problems. One problem which was, however, continually present, at least in the first six months, was that of inner solitude or social isolation. With an eye to improving my linguistic competence I kept contact with the other three Germans who were with me there to a minimum (I scarcely knew them before the study abroad period) and concentrated on the local population. Although I knew a number of people, I didn't really become closely acquainted with anyone. Only as time went on did friendships develop which were then maintained afterwards (after my return)."

Thus, positive experiences during the study abroad outweighed negative ones and students manifested strong satisfaction in overall terms with the study abroad: 89 percent declared themselves satisfied; the average value was 1.6 on the scale from 1= "very satisfied" to 5= "very dissatisfied". The British group showed the least proportion (74%) of satisfied students, and among all the fields of study (European students only), the proportion was least among respondents in Business Studies (79%). Conversely, students of Foreign Languages and Natural Sciences most frequently reported overall satisfaction with the study abroad and felt most strongly integrated into the host institution.

As far as the entire group of respondents was concerned, the average response to a question about degree of integration felt at the host institution was 2.5 on a scale from 1= "felt integrated to a very great degree" to 5= "did not feel integrated at all" (see Table S27). Slightly over a fifth had felt "not much" or "not at all" integrated. The French students gave by far the strongest impression of fitting right in at their host institutions. It is probably significant that, as documented in Chapter 6, the French students also on the whole assessed higher education in their respective host countries more positively than higher education in France. Where integration problems had occurred, these were foremost among the British and American students. It may be significant that these were students who in their home countries experienced relatively frequent contact between teachers and pupils, and were accustomed to being able to participate in extra-curricular activities as part of university life.

Nevertheless, almost all students judged the stay abroad had been worthwhile, by far because of the social contacts, taking a break in the routine at home to travel and get to know another country and its people. They cited, for example:
- "making friends for life with people from a variety of backgrounds, cultures and with different experiences";
- "visiting very different cities in Europe";
- "having the cultural facilities of Paris at my doorstep";
- "being part of the closeness of family life in another country and constantly being met with a lot of differences in opinion";
- "getting to know big city life";

- "spending Christmas in New York";
- "integrating into another culture and realising that one was at home in it";
- "getting engaged";
- "just generally experiencing a lot more personal freedom";
- "finally achieving an ambition to drive coast to coast, camping in the Rockies, and learning to fence".

Academic experiences were cited second most frequently on the whole, and were often items of rather specific detail: "the opportunity to take two courses I wouldn't have been able to study at my home institution," "getting a 15/20 for a criminal law oral examination," "learning so much about computer science," or "studying feminist theory, taught by an exceptionally inspiring woman." Nonetheless, many comments had a broader scope and pointed to the advantages of discovering whole new areas in a field of study, feeling one's view of life change under the influence of the broadened (academic) experiental base through study abroad, "really enjoying my work and producing essays that I was pleased with," and taking up different approaches to learning, which for many a study abroad participant meant working more directly with instructors in tutorials, seminars, or out-of-class discussions.

Mastery of a foreign language was also high on the list of benefits:
- "My oral French improved to the extent that I was able to speak and think in French without having to translate to and from English";
- "I was thrilled at being mistaken for a German, after having had a conversation with a German native."

Students also appreciated the time abroad because of the different angle it had given them on themselves and on life in their home countries:
- "I developed more appreciation for my family and more awareness and sensibility toward other people's needs";
- "I learned a lot more about myself, and how to take care of myself";
- "I have become different, less rigid in my view about my own country".

Finally, many students expected the study abroad would impact favourably upon their career prospects.

A rather serious postscript should be added. Students frequently complained that their home institutions too infrequently incorporated returnees' observations and reflections into the overall evaluation of the programmes and the preparation of new groups of students. Over a third of the respondents - and particularly the Swedes - had made no report whatsoever at their home universities about their study abroad experiences. For those who did report back, the Germans did so mainly by sending small written assessments to their programme directors. The French reported back to their programme directors and contributed to preparation sessions of the next generation of participants. American students reported back mainly by answering questionnaires.

Chapter 4

Academic Effects of Study Abroad

4.1 Hypothetical Model and Design of the Survey

Universities and other institutions of higher education would no doubt hesitate to endorse study abroad if the prognosis were weak about its academic outcomes. Indeed, the formal goals of the programmes reviewed here and the stated priorities of their directors leave little room to question that the academic outcomes are the main factors used to gauge programme success.

This emphasis stands alongside the outlook of programme participants, for whom academic benefits of study abroad are not singularly overpowering. As shown in Chapter 2, students are strongly drawn to the cross-cultural comparative experiences and the stimulus to think and act outside established routines which day-to-day living in a foreign academic context affords. Immersion in the language environment is among the most highly prized of students' reasons for going abroad. Students tended less to specify other academic motives among their foremost priorities. Also, while Chapter 3 documented participants' perceptions of distinctive differences at their host as compared with their home institutions, the differences did not appear so extreme as to imply that study abroad was a fundamentally different academic experience than the habitual one at home. Nevertheless, study abroad could conceivably hinder a student from attaining the same level of academic achievement as at home. For many, the foreign study adds a challenge of understanding lectures and seminars, producing papers and examinations in a foreign language; and deciphering other clues on how to behave in an unfamiliar educational system. In some cases more than others, study abroad forces students to cope with noticeable disjunctions in the course of study begun at home. Added to this are the unavoidable distractions of the extra-curricular setting abroad.

The fact that students recognise differences between their home and host institutions is in itself an academic impact. Less visible effects of the foreign exposure could be solidification of viewpoints and learning styles previously held, perhaps even new-found appreciation for the way things are organised at the home institution. Study abroad could bring students to articulate some of the views they had previously held silent, and could give them reasons to practice many other new behaviours as well. The current chapter therefore attempts to assess the changes in students' *academic abilities and accomplishments* which occurred over the study period abroad, as well as the change in students' *thinking about what is important for their intellectual development,* whether or not these changes carried over to overt behaviours.

In preparing the evaluation of academic impacts, the research team consulted existing literature on empirically manifested aims and expectations about the out-

Table S 30
Dimensions of Academic Abilities and Learning Styles Addressed in Questions Regarding Competences and Importance Placed on Before and After the Study Abroad Period*

Dimension of abilities/learning styles	Categories provided in questions regarding competencies	regarding importance placed
Knowledge	Knowledge related to the field of study	Learning facts
	Knowledge of research (in the student's field of study conducted abroad)	Familiarity with different schools of thought
	Knowledge of other cultures, countries, international/European affairs	Obtaining comparative (e.g. international) perspectives
	Comparative perspectives	Obtaining knowledge from different disciplines (e.g. inter-disciplinary approach)
	Approaches from other disciplines	
Intellectual/abstract thinking	Tackling abstract problems	
	Working with theories	Understanding theories
	Coping with ambiguity	Systematic thinking
	Formulating hypotheses and using them in analyses	Examining relationships between observations/hypotheses/facts/concepts
	Quick understanding	
	Imagination	
Independent/critical thought	Developing a point of view	Developing a point of view
	Articulating one's own thoughts and views	Freedom to choose one's own areas of study
		Independent work (e.g. writing papers, project work)
Application	Figuring out what is most significant to learn	Applying knowledge to practical areas
	Applying theories or abstract knowledge to practical issues	Methodology (research methodology, computer programming etc.)

continued table S 30

Dimension of abilities/learning styles	Categories provided in questions regarding competencies	regarding importance placed
	Choosing tasks commensurate with one's abilities	Utilizing publications in foreign languages
	Working continuously, rather than leaving all to the last minute	Regular class attendance
	Discipline in learning (not easy to become distracted from studies	Obtaining regular feedback from teachers
	Assuming a heavy workload	Studying to get good marks on examinations
Work technics	Working successfully under time pressure	Taking on a heavy workload
	Accepting criticism as a stimulus for further learning	Selecting demanding courses
	Good memory	Regarding teachers as the main source of information
	Planning and following through accordingly	
Learning-related social skills	Cooperating with others in academic work	Aktive participation in class discussion
	Motivating other people	Out-of-class discussion between students and teaching staff

* Hypothetical structures underlying the categories provided in questions SAEP D 24, F 23 and F 47

puts of tertiary education.[1] The researchers took account of the stated goals of the programmes under review and examined findings of participant surveys previously administered in several European and American study abroad programmes. On this basis, the team identified academic abilities and learning styles which were potentially germane to the study abroad situation. These were formed into the hypothetical model shown in Table S30.

Survey questions based on this model asked for:

1. *Students' perceptions of their academic abilities and accomplishments* (left portion of Table S30). Changes in these were measured by comparing students' responses to two identical lists of abilities and accomplishments, the one presented in the Pre-Study Abroad Questionnaire, the other in the Post-Study Abroad Questionnaire.

[1] For example, Sandberger, J-U & Lind, G. The outcomes of University Education: Some Empirical Findings on Aims and Expectations in the Federal Republic of Germany. *Higher Education 8 (1979)*: 179-203; see also Teichler, U. et al. *Hochschule - Studium - Berufsvorstellungen*. Bad Honnef: Bock 1987.

2. *Students' ratings, retrospectively and in a general sense, of their academic progress during study abroad,* compared to the level they expect they would have achieved during a comparable period at home. These ratings are more global assessments of the combined impact of the changes in discrete abilities and accomplishments referred to above.

3. *Students' views on the type of academic training necessary for their intellectual development* (right portion of Table S30). Even though students were asked about the views they held before and after study abroad, students reported on both retrospectively, in the Post-Study Abroad Questionnaire.

4. *A comparative evaluation of home and host institutions, solicited through open-ended questions.* On the basis of their experiences in the study abroad host country, students were requested to describe the teaching, learning and assessment characteristics which they especially liked or appreciated in their *home* institution, as well as the characteristics of the home institution about which they were most critical. Also, although it could not have been foreseen with certainty, a portion of the students' responses to the questions "What is the worst/best thing that happened to you while abroad?" "What was the most difficult thing you successfully accomplished while you were abroad?" provided further details on academic triumphs and challenges of the study abroad situation.

4.2   Changes In Academic Abilities And Accomplishments

The Pre- and Post-Study Abroad Questionnaires contained an identical list of twenty-four possible abilities and accomplishments. Students were requested to rate themselves on each feature, using a five-point scale (1 = "very strong" to 5 = "very weak"). A similar request was given at the same points in time to the American comparison group. To test how the abilities which had been identified hypothetically corresponded with students' actual responses, two separate factor analyses were conducted, the one based on students' replies concerning the pre-study abroad situation; the other on abilities post-sojourn. As there were only five items in the hypothetical model which did not cluster into domains extracted from the factor analysis,[2] the items in these domains form the basis of most of the analysis of students' academic abilities and accomplishments (see Table S31).

Already at the first point of assessment, students saw themselves as relatively strong in most of the abilities listed. Study abroad participants and non-participants alike perceived their strengths lay in the domains denoted "work pressure" and "views and perspectives." Students were comparatively weaker in the

---

2   The five items were knowledge of the student's chosen field of study, knowledge of research abroad in that field of study, knowledge of other cultures, coping with ambiguity and figuring out what is most significant to learn.

domains of "work discipline" and "international/comparative perspectives;" with abilities in the remaining two domains falling between these two extremes.

In regard to individual abilities, the students were strongest just prior to departure in their:
- imagination;
- quick understanding;
- ability to develop a personal point of view; and
- ability to articulate a view.

The British students did not rate themselves as highly as students from other countries on most of the above.

On the whole, students also felt strong in their abilities to:
- assume heavy workloads;
- work under pressure; and
- work co-operatively with others.

The French rated themselves comparatively weaker in these three abilities.
On average, students felt least competent in:
- theoretical respects: tackling abstract problems, formulating hypotheses, and applying theories to practical issues (again, the British students rated themselves lower);
- work discipline: in withstanding distractions and working steadily to avoid leaving everything to the last minute;
- motivating others; and
- developing comparative perspectives.

Focussing on the post-sojourn period, the arithmetic averages throughout the "total" column of Table S31 show a slightly perceptible change in the direction of stronger levels of ability after study abroad. With the exception of "developing comparative perspectives," however, the overall change appears so slight that the pattern of relatively stronger vs. weaker abilities as seen in the pre-departure situation is preserved. Students were still strongest in the "work pressure" and "views and perspectives" domains. This makes it difficult to attribute changes in ability unequivocibly to study abroad. In principle, other factors could have been more influential; for example, the extent to which students matured over the period in question.

Yet, the obvious strengthening of students' skills in comparative analysis, and the increase in their familiarity with research internationally in their field (additional data to that related to domains of the factor analysis, see Table S32), point to the singular influence of study abroad. These results are reinforced by the difference discovered between the American study abroad and comparison groups, and by the results of a more detailed examination of the post-sojourn changes within the study abroad group, examining results by the customary breakdown into categories of home country and field of study.

A determination of potentially significant statistical differences between the study abroad and comparison groups was made on the American portion of the

Table S31
Students' Abilities and Accomplishments in Higher Education Before and After the Study Abroad Period, by Home Country and Field of Study (in arithmetic means)*

		Home country					Field of study					
		UK	F	D	S	US	Bus	Eng	NatSc	Law	Lang	Total**
Theories and methods*												
Good memory	Before	2.7	2.1	2.6	2.6	2.0	2.4	2.7	2.8	2.2	2.6	2.3
	After	2.6	2.2	2.6	2.4	2.1	2.5	2.5	2.8	2.3	2.6	2.4
Applying theories or abstract knowledge to practical issues	Before	3.0	2.7	2.6	2.6	2.3	2.6	2.5	2.6	2.6	3.0	2.6
	After	2.5	2.6	2.5	2.3	2.1	2.5	2.4	2.6	2.5	2.9	2.4
Quick understanding	Before	2.6	2.2	2.3	2.3	2.0	2.2	2.2	2.3	2.3	2.7	2.2
	After	2.5	2.1	2.1	1.9	1.9	2.0	2.2	2.1	2.2	2.4	2.1
Tackling abstact problems, working with theories	Before	3.1	2.8	2.7	2.7	2.4	3.0	2.8	2.4	2.7	3.0	2.7
	After	2.9	2.8	2.6	2.3	2.4	2.8	2.5	2.2	2.7	3.1	2.6
Formulating hypotheses and using them in analysis	Before	3.5	2.7	3.0	3.0	2.6	3.1	2.9	2.8	2.9	3.4	2.9
	After	3.0	2.6	2.7	2.6	2.6	2.7	2.5	2.7	2.6	3.1	2.7
Views and perspectives												
Understanding approaches from several disciplines	Before	2.6	2.3	2.7	2.3	2.1	2.5	2.2	2.6	2.7	2.6	2.4
	After	2.4	2.3	2.4	2.2	2.0	2.3	2.2	2.3	2.5	2.7	2.3
Accepting criticism as a stimulus for further learning	Before	2.7	2.4	2.4	2.8	2.1	2.4	2.7	2.6	2.2	2.7	2.4
	After	2.5	2.7	2.2	2.6	2.1	2.4	2.6	2.1	2.2	2.6	2.3
Developing your own point of view	Before	2.6	2.3	2.3	2.4	2.0	2.3	2.4	2.7	2.3	2.4	2.2
	After	2.2	2.3	2.2	2.3	1.8	2.2	2.5	2.1	2.4	2.3	2.1
Articulating your own thoughts/views	Before	2.7	2.5	2.3	2.7	2.0	2.3	2.4	2.8	2.3	2.5	2.3
	After	2.4	2.6	2.2	2.6	2.0	2.3	2.3	2.5	2.3	2.5	2.2
Imagination	Before	2.6	2.5	2.1	2.2	2.1	2.3	2.2	2.3	2.2	2.4	2.2
	After	2.3	2.3	2.0	2.2	1.9	2.1	2.0	2.1	2.2	2.3	2.1
Choosing tasks commensurate with your abilities	Before	2.5	2.3	2.3	2.6	2.1	2.3	2.5	2.6	2.3	2.3	2.3
	After	2.3	2.2	2.3	2.3	2.0	2.2	2.2	2.4	2.4	2.1	2.2

continued table S31

		Home country					Field of study					
		UK	F	D	S	US	Bus	Eng	NatSc	Law	Lang	Total
Interactive learning												
Cooperating with others in academic work	Before	2.4	2.6	2.3	2.4	2.0	2.3	2.4	2.4	2.5	2.2	2.2
	After	2.2	2.5	2.2	2.1	2.0	2.2	2.4	2.2	2.2	2.1	2.1
Motivating other people	Before	3.1	2.9	2.6	2.6	2.3	2.6	2.5	2.9	2.9	3.0	2.6
	After	2.6	2.7	2.4	2.4	2.3	2.5	2.3	2.6	2.4	2.6	2.4
Work discipline												
Working continuously (e.g. rather than leaving everything to the last minute)	Before	2.7	2.7	2.8	2.6	2.6	2.8	2.8	2.8	2.5	2.5	2.7
	After	2.6	2.8	2.7	2.5	2.5	2.8	2.3	2.9	2.3	2.6	2.6
Discipline in learning (e.g. not easily distracted from your studies)	Before	2.9	2.6	2.8	2.6	2.4	2.7	2.5	3.0	2.5	2.6	2.6
	After	2.9	2.7	2.7	2.4	2.6	2.9	2.3	2.9	2.4	2.7	2.7
Planning and following through accordingly	Before	2.5	2.7	2.4	2.6	2.0	2.5	2.6	2.6	2.4	2.2	2.4
	After	2.3	3.1	2.2	2.3	2.2	2.4	2.3	2.4	2.3	2.5	2.3
Work under pressure												
Assuming heavy workload	Before	2.4	2.5	2.2	2.1	2.0	2.3	2.1	2.3	2.2	2.5	2.2
	After	2.3	2.3	2.1	2.1	2.0	2.1	2.1	2.2	2.0	2.6	2.1
Working under time pressure	Before	2.0	2.5	2.3	2.1	2.0	2.3	2.0	2.3	2.2	2.5	2.2
	After	1.9	2.5	2.1	1.9	1.9	2.1	2.0	2.1	2.1	2.6	2.0
International/comparative perspectives												
Developing comparative perspectives	Before	2.9	2.6	3.0	2.7	2.0	2.8	2.5	3.3	2.9	2.9	2.6
	After	2.5	2.4	2.6	2.5	1.9	2.5	2.5	2.6	2.5	2.6	2.3

*   Scale from 1 = "very strong" to 5 = "very weak" (question: "How would you assess your current abilities and accomplishments, within the framework of your studies in higher education? Please indicate whether you see yourself as being strong or weak in each of the following")

**   Also including other fields of study

***   The categories and sequence of items do not correspond to the questionnaire but rather to the results of a factor analysis conducted on the replies

Source: Pre-Study Abroad Questionnaire SAEP D 24 (D 228-251) and Post-Study Abroad Questionnaire SAEP F 23 (F 632-655)

data. Results indicated that both groups viewed themselves as very capable academically, but the self-ratings of the study abroad group were higher - before and
after study abroad - on two of the extracted dimensions: "theories and methods"
and "views and perspectives."[3]

Among the study abroad participants from all five countries, the Swedish and
British students were most changed after their foreign sojourns. The Germans
came next. There was significant change for all three groups in a feature noted to
be particularly weak prior to departure: the ability to formulate hypotheses and
use them in analysis. In addition, the Swedes emerged stronger in applying theories to practical issues, tackling abstract problems, and in quick understanding, as
well as planning their work (choosing tasks commensurate with their abilities,
following through accordingly, and cooperating with others in academic work.
The British similarly rated themselves higher in applying theories to practical issues and working with others; they also felt stronger in imagination, in developing
their own points of view and articulating their thoughts. Note that the German
students after study abroad felt they were stronger in understanding approaches
from several disciplines.

The small amount of change registered by American study abroad participants
compared with participants from the other countries is quite striking. Also, the
Americans and the French distinguished themselves as the only groups to perceive
weakening of abilities over the study period abroad. Both perceived they were
weaker in planning and following through; the French also in accepting criticism
as a stimulus for further learning; and the Americans in resisting distraction from
their studies.

Scanning the right half of Table S31 for differences by field (Europeans only),
the Engineering and Natural Science students perceived the greatest amount of
change in their own ability after study abroad. Engineering students felt stronger
in abstract, theoretical and comparative respects (tackling abstract problems and
formulating hypotheses for use in analysis, developing comparative perspectives)
and in work habits (choosing tasks commensurate with their abilities, working
continuously, planning and following through). Natural Science students showed
most pervasive change in the "views and perspectives" domain. They had become
stronger in understanding approaches from several disciplines, in accepting criticism as a stimulus for further learning, developing and articulating their own
views, and obtaining comparative/international perspectives.

For students in the other fields, fewer changes were apparent, apart from
strengthened abilities in formulating hypotheses and developing comparative perspectives. The Law students felt in addition they had become better at working
with and motivating others. The latter was also a noted change for the Foreign
Language students, as was "quick understanding." The least amount of change was
shown by the study abroad participants in Business Studies.

---

3   This analysis was conducted on a factor analysis run independently on only the American data,
    from which only four domains were extracted. The first two nevertheless corresponded to the
    first two domains resulting from the factor analysis of the entire five-country data set.

Table S32
Students Knowledge of Research in Their Field of Study Before and After the Study Abroad Period, by Home Country and Field of Study (in arithmetic means)*

		Home country					Field of study					
		UK	F	D	S	US	Bus	Eng	Nat	Law	Lang	Tot**
Students' knowledge of research	Before	3.8	2.9	3.7	3.5	3.6	3.5	3.5	3.7	3.7	3.3	3.6
in their field abroad	After	2.8	3.0	3.3	2.9	3.2	3.3	2.9	2.8	3.2	2.8	3.1

* Scale from 1 = "very strong" to 5 = "very weak"
** Also including other fields of study
Source: Pre-Study Abroad Questionnaire SAEP D 24 (250) and Post-Study Abroad Questionnaire SAEP F 23 (F 654)

Inspection of the student groups by home country to get a sense of the range in perceived abilities between the weakest and strongest student before study abroad compared with after, shows the range is wider in the various abilities before study abroad than after. In other words, the groups of students seemed to have become more alike in strength of academic abilities and accomplishments; or, more accurately, in their perceptions about their abilities and accomplishments. This is evident for all abilities except in the domain of work discipline (i.e. working continuously, planning and following through, and working under time pressure).

Of course, not all students sent from one country studied in the same host country abroad. Consequently, the results were examined by home-host country pairs. Noticeable differences emerged in the number and types of abilities which were stronger at the conclusion of study abroad. Overall, the magnitude of change was most considerably above average for the German students who went to the USA, although the magnitude of change was also quite high among the British students who went to the USA, and the Swedes who went to the UK. Compared with these, the change was slightly less pronounced among the Swedes who went to Germany, the Americans who went to the UK, and weaker - although still above average in many of the abilities - for Americans who went to France or Germany, and the German and French students who went to the UK. Since there were so few students who went to Sweden, these were excluded from the home-host country analysis.

The findings from this stage of the analysis- namely that fewest improvements were seen by students studying abroad in France- is noteworthy and may relate to the outcomes additionally reported in Chapter 6, that students have a relatively lower opinion of higher education in France. Indeed, the results immediately above do not show the Joint Study Programme partner countries in a leading position. It may be that the integrated nature of their courses in offsetting the sharpness of contrast between the home and host institutions also has an effect on the way that students perceive the evolution of their academic abilities and accomplishments, compared with students in the other types of programmes.

All groups cited explicitly in the above analysis by home-host country pairs shared two outcomes in common; they showed greater than average increase in strength of capacity to accept criticism as a stimulus for further learning and in ability to develop a personal point of view. Furthermore, students from sending institutions in Europe (including those students who went to the USA) all felt stronger after their foreign study in:
- cooperating with others in academic work;
- applying theories to practical issues;
- knowledge of their respective subject areas;
- choosing tasks commensurate with their abilities;
- coping with ambiguity; and
- understanding approaches from several disciplines.

4.3 Changes in Views about Thinking and Learning Styles

4.3.1 Changes in View Greater than Changes in Abilities

In the Post-Study Abroad Questionnaire, students recorded the importance that they attached to certain thinking and learning styles (see righthand portion of Table S30) by rating each item in a list of twenty-one (on a five-point scale, 1= "very important" to 5= "not important at all"). In responding, they were to recall the disposition of their views before study abroad on one scale and note current views on another.

As in the case of the abilities pre- and post-sojourn, two factor analyses were conducted on the degree of importance students attached, before and after study abroad, to the various thinking and learning styles. Results showed commonality with the factor structure for the abilities and accomplishments. Given this, the domains of Table S33 mostly follow those of Table S31. The exception is "work discipline" which was not extracted as a separate factor in the analysis of students' views.[4]

The changes in students' views about what was important for their intellectual development was more marked after study abroad than the change in their abilities. Compared with the differences between students' pre- and post-sojourn assessments of abilities, the differences in view were more numerous and of greater magnitude. The pre- and post differences in view averaged roughly three times greater magnitude than the differences in abilities.

Domains showing the greatest number of significant changes in view were "international comparative perspectives" and "views and perspectives." Looking at the values attributed to the individual aspects, one finds - unlike the situation for the abilities - the greatest changes in view were mostly where students had been comparatively weaker before they went abroad, i.e. in their views about the importance of:
- international comparative perspectives;
- research methodology;
- out-of-class communication between teachers and students;
- obtaining regular feedback from teachers;
- familiarity with different schools of thought;
- examining relationships between observations, hypotheses, facts, concepts; and
- obtaining knowledge from different disciplines.

Conversely, the changes were not as substantial in views about the importance of:
- understanding theories;
- systematic thinking; and
- regular class attendance.

---

[4] Aspects from the hypothetical model which did not show up in the major domains extracted through factor analysis of the students' responses to indicate views on thinking and learning styles were the importance of: learning facts, freedom to choose one's own areas of study, independent work (e.g. writing papers, project work), utilising publications in foreign languages, studying to get good marks on examinations.

Table S33

Importance of Certain Modes of Thinking and Learning for Students' Intellectual Development and Learning Before and After the Study Abroad Period, by Home Country and Field of Study (in arithmetic means)*

		Home country					Field of study					Total**
		UK	F	D	S	US	Bus	Eng	NatSc	Law	Lang	
Theories and methods*												
Understanding theories	Before	2.2	2.2	2.1	1.7	2.0	2.3	1.5	1.8	2.1	2.9	2.1
	After	1.9	2.2	2.1	1.7	1.8	2.3	1.6	1.6	2.0	2.7	1.9
Applying knowledge to practical areas	Before	2.6	2.4	2.6	2.0	2.1	2.4	2.0	2.5	2.9	2.9	2.4
	After	2.0	2.0	1.9	1.9	1.7	1.6	1.9	2.0	2.2	2.4	1.8
Systematic thinking	Before	2.3	2.8	2.0	1.8	2.4	2.2	1.7	1.9	2.3	2.8	2.2
	After	2.1	2.4	1.8	1.7	2.1	1.9	1.6	1.7	1.8	2.7	2.0
Methodology (research methodology, computer programming etc.)	Before	3.4	2.4	3.2	2.7	3.0	2.9	2.2	3.0	3.5	3.8	3.0
	After	3.0	2.3	2.7	2.4	2.7	2.4	2.0	2.5	3.3	3.6	2.7
Views and perspectives												
Familiarity with different schools of thought	Before	2.7	3.0	2.9	2.9	2.6	2.8	3.0	3.0	2.8	3.1	2.8
	After	2.4	2.5	2.6	2.6	1.7	2.5	2.4	2.7	2.6	2.7	2.2
Examining relations between observations/hypotheses/facts/concepts	Before	2.8	2.7	3.0	2.6	2.5	2.9	2.8	2.9	3.0	3.1	2.7
	After	2.5	2.4	2.7	2.4	2.1	2.6	2.7	2.6	2.8	2.9	2.4
Obtaining knowledge from different disciplines (interdisciplinary approach)	Before	2.9	2.3	2.8	2.6	2.7	2.7	2.6	2.9	2.8	2.8	2.7
	After	2.4	2.1	2.4	2.1	2.1	2.3	1.9	2.5	2.5	2.5	2.2
Developing one's own point of view	Before	2.3	2.3	2.3	2.1	2.0	2.3	2.0	2.3	2.3	2.6	2.2
	After	1.8	1.9	1.9	1.7	1.4	1.8	1.7	1.9	2.0	1.9	1.7

continued table S33

		Home country					Field of study					
		UK	F	D	S	US	Bus	Eng	NatSc	Law	Lang	Total**
Interactive learning												
Regular class attendance	Before	2.2	2.2	2.9	2.4	1.9	2.5	3.2	2.5	2.8	1.7	2.3
	After	1.8	2.4	2.8	2.5	1.9	2.7	2.6	2.7	2.7	1.5	2.3
Active participation in class discussions	Before	2.5	2.3	2.7	2.7	2.4	2.5	3.0	2.8	2.6	2.6	2.5
	After	1.8	1.9	2.3	2.2	1.7	2.1	2.1	2.2	2.3	1.9	2.0
Out of class communication between students and teaching staff	Before	2.8	3.2	3.2	2.6	2.6	3.1	3.1	2.8	3.3	2.7	2.9
	After	1.9	2.4	2.3	2.2	1.8	2.4	2.1	1.9	2.5	2.2	2.1
Obtaining regular feedback from teachers	Before	2.5	2.4	3.5	2.6	2.3	3.1	3.1	3.1	3.3	2.2	2.7
	After	1.9	2.2	3.1	2.1	1.9	2.8	2.2	2.6	3.0	2.0	2.3
Regarding the teachers as the main source of information	Before	3.0	3.0	2.8	3.0	2.5	2.7	3.5	2.6	3.1	2.9	2.8
	After	3.5	3.6	3.4	3.2	3.0	3.5	3.2	3.3	3.7	3.4	3.3
Work pressure												
Taking on a heavy workload	Before	2.7	2.5	2.7	2.3	2.4	2.6	2.5	2.5	2.7	2.4	2.4
	After	2.4	2.3	2.3	2.4	2.5	2.3	2.6	2.6	2.1	2.2	2.5
Selecting demanding courses	Before	3.1	2.7	2.6	2.5	2.2	2.6	2.7	2.8	2.7	2.8	2.5
	After	2.7	2.6	2.0	2.5	2.0	2.2	2.3	2.5	2.0	2.6	2.2
International/comparative perspectives												
Obtaining comparative (e.g. international/European/intercultural perspectives)	Before	2.9	2.9	2.9	3.0	2.7	2.7	3.1	3.4	3.1	2.7	2.9
	After	2.2	1.8	2.2	2.6	1.4	1.9	2.3	3.0	2.2	1.8	1.9

* Scale from 1 = "very important" to 5 = "not important at all" (question: "If you reflect over your ways of thinking and learning before your study abroad period and after you returned home, how important in your judgment are the following for your learning and intellectual development?")

** Also including other fields of study

*** The categories and sequence of items do not correspond to the questionnaire but rather to the results of a factor analysis conducted on the replies

Source: Post-Study Abroad Questionnaire SAEP F 47 (F 852-933)

Outside the domains produced by factor analysis was the finding that students' appreciation of utilising publications in foreign languages greatly increased as well.

The importance of "developing one's own point of view," which had been highly prized before study abroad, was even more valued afterwards. Conversely, the period abroad appeared to have aroused considerable scepticism about whether the teacher should be in a central position for the students' intellectual development. The change in view on this issue was pronounced for the German and French students; and, by field, for the Business and Natural Science students.

In the aftermath of study abroad, the overall range in students' views about the types of thinking and learning styles which should be important to their intellectual development (1.4 - 3.7) was greater than the overall range in students' post-sojourn perceptions about their actual abilities (1.8 - 3.1). Quite differently from what was observed for changes in abilities and accomplishments, then, students did not become more alike in their views after study abroad. Most notably, the range widened, across the entire sample, in degree of importance attached to the following aspects:
- becoming familiar with different schools of thought;
- examining relationships between observations, hypotheses, facts, and concepts;
- developing one's own point of view;
- cultivating comparative/international perspectives;
- active participation in class discussion; and
- regarding teachers as the main source of information.

Across all aspects, the British, German and American students had made the *greatest number* of significant changes of view (i.e. "significant" defined as a difference of .3 in the arithmetic means of the pre- vs. post-sojourn ratings). Among the Europeans, by field, the Business Studies and Natural Science students had made significant changes in the greatest number of their views, followed by the Law, Engineering, and last by the Foreign Language students.

If one looks instead for groups which showed the largest average *amount* of change, these were most frequently the German and American students. Among the fields, it was the Engineers, then the Law students, for whom the average amount of change was greatest.

The Germans had made the greatest change in views, relative to students from other countries, about the importance of:
- applying knowledge to practical areas;
- methodology (in research, computer programming etc.);
- assuming a heavy workload; and
- selecting demanding courses.

The Americans changed most in their views about the importance of:
- becoming familiar with different schools of thought;
- examining relationships between observations, hypotheses, facts, and concepts;
- obtaining knowledge from different disciplines;
- developing one's own point of view; and
- comparative/international perspectives.

The British changed most in their views about:
- regular class attendance; and
- regular feedback from teachers.

The French changed most in regard to systematic thinking.

Both German and British groups changed most, on average, in their views about the importance of out-of-class communication between teachers and students; German and French students changed most in views about teachers as the main source of information; and American and British students about the importance of active participation in class discussion.

For the European students by field, some patterns were evident. The Engineering students' views changed most, relative to students from other disciplines, concerning the importance of:
- becoming familiar with different schools of thought;
- obtaining knowledge from different disciplines;
- regular class attendance;
- active participation in class discussion;
- out-of-class communication between teachers and students; and
- obtaining regular feedback from teachers.

The Law students changed most regarding their views on:
- systematic thinking;
- assuming a heavy workload; and
- selecting demanding courses.

The Business Studies students' ideas changed most about:
- applying knowledge to practical areas; and
- viewing teachers as the main source of information.

The Foreign Language students' views changed most about the importance of developing a personal point of view while Law and Foreign Language students made the largest change toward recognising the importance of obtaining comparative/international perspectives. Business and Natural Science students more than others strengthened their views about the importance of:
- methodology (research, computer programming etc.); and
- examining relationships between observations, hypotheses, facts, and concepts.

Because the German students who went to the USA had shown the greatest amount of change in academic abilities as well as in views about what was important to their intellectual development, the research team searched the texts of their replies to several open-ended questions, looking for clues about what might have brought about such a remarkable effect. Descriptions of the "best" thing that happened to the Germans abroad highlighted a number of academically related experiences:
- "The ability to earn a Master of Science degree."

- "The accessibility of teaching staff and administrators in the international pro-
  grammes office who were willing to help foreign students."
- "Student-teacher interaction at American universities."
- "The pervasive feeling that study was *fun*."

Conversely, among the "most difficult" parts of the sojourn had been:
- "Coping successfully with the far greater workload in the USA compared with
  studying at home."
- "Working in group projects and having to deal with peer pressure to perform."
- "Having to take courses which were the second part of sequels, without any
  knowledge of the corresponding courses that had been offered the previous
  semester."

When asked about the "worst" experiences abroad, the Germans who had been in
the USA - in contrast to those who had studied in other countries - scarcely mentioned academic problems.

4.3.2   Re-assessing Education at the Home Institution

The immersion in a foreign environment during a period of study is a time when
participants are confronted with a plethora of stimuli and encounters which are
substantially different from the habitual ones of their home. Portions of the events
abroad have immediate conscious effects, other effects are more latent. All the
while, comparisons of home and host environments build on a growing reservoir
of encounters abroad. The comparisons are complex. It is not only the new elements encountered abroad, but also the absence of elements students had grown
accustomed to in the home environment which mould and refine their ideas and
viewpoints, no less about what they think is most important for their intellectual
development. What is more, students react differently, the one from the other.
This is illustrated in the following summaries of the British, French and German
data.

After study abroad, the British especially re-affirmed the importance of regular
class attendance and regular feedback from teachers. Based on their responses
about positive features of their home institutions, it appears they were moved by
the absence abroad of what they were accustomed to at home. The positive characteristics of their home institutions which British returnees highlighted were:
- small, informal tutorial groups (especially British participants from all subject
  areas who had gone to France);
- close contact with lecturers;
- "regular" coursework with fixed submission dates;
- very good lecturers (especially the British students in Social Sciences and Law
  who had been in France);
- form of examination and assessment (especially the Business and Law students
  who had been in France and Germany; they stressed that assessment mechanisms at their home institution were less arbitrary, and the returnees praised
  the style of written essays and examinations at home); and

- group project work (especially the Business and Engineering students who went to France and Germany).

The British students who had been in France were the most forthcoming with critical comments about their home institutions. Especially the Engineering students criticised the overcrowding and lack of sufficient tutorials at home. Several Law students were disappointed that there was little, if any, tuition in subjects unrelated to their degree at home. They were critical of the lack of interest in comparative law at home. Business students (those who had been in France *and* Germany) and Law students were critical of the over-emphasis at home in assessing students on the basis of their examination performance. Finally, the Engineering and Business students (among the former, mainly those who had gone to France; among the latter, those who had gone to France and Germany) felt studies at home lacked practical application, especially to industry.

The French returnees, who had re-affirmed the importance of "systematic thinking" to their own intellectual development, especially appreciated the seriousness and quality of the courses at home, the "cartesian spirit," the quality and relevance ("up-to-date") of the instruction, the organisation and planning of the courses, and the grading system. It was particularly the French students who had been in the UK - in all subject areas - who stressed the value of these characteristics in their home institutions. The Business and Foreign Language students were particularly complimentary about the grading system at home. One of the Business students insisted: "The French grading practice is clear and able to reflect the true level of a student's accomplishments." Also, Foreign Language students insisted: "We are obliged to learn to work on our own, so we are really the basis of our own success."

The French Business and Engineering students who had gone to the UK and to Germany appreciated the practical applications of their French education: "It provides a good opening to the world of enterprise." Also, these students especially appreciated the "flexibility" of the French system.

The greatest criticism the French held for their home institutions concerned all aspects of contact (i.e. the lack thereof) with instructors, and the formalism which did not at all encourage personal points of view.

Finally, the Germans had made the greatest change in their views about the importance of applying knowledge to practical areas, about methodology, assuming a heavy workload and selecting demanding courses. Interestingly, many of the returnees explicitly stated they appreciated that there was less pressure at home. Especially in the minds of German students in Natural Sciences and Engineering who returned from the USA, the fact that the times for courses and exams at home were not so "fixed" were positive features. Business students (who had been in the UK, USA and France) appreciated the greater degree of freedom and independence in choice of studies and in study habits at home. At the same time, many German students in Business and Natural Sciences who had been in the UK and USA criticised their home institutions for allowing students too much freedom and too little contact with instructors whom the students felt should monitor students' progress more closely. There was, however, an appreciation of the emphasis in Germany on assessing more what the students actually know, rather than how well they can compete with each other (part of this was a negative reaction to "grading on the curve" in the USA).

The German students were divided on the matter of theoretical vs. practical application of their studies. The Business students who had been in France and the UK were appreciative of the broader and more theoretical basis they had gained from earlier education in Germany. Business students who had gone to France and the USA, and Natural Science students who studied in the USA were critical of the lack of practical application of their German studies.

4.4   Academic Progress Abroad Compared With Home

Functioning in a foreign system set up linguistic and other challenges, requiring students to don a different academic mentality and in many cases to work far more independently than they had at home. There were also some mis-matches in levels of courses, with those abroad either much easier or far more difficult than courses the students were accustomed to at home. Despite all of this, students guessed that their academic progress abroad had been marginally higher than for a comparable period at home. This is the message of Table S34, which displays an arithmetic mean of 3.4 for the entire sample of students who had estimated their progress abroad on a five-point scale, where 1= "academic progress abroad much less than at home" and 5= "academic progress abroad much greater."

Table S34
Students' Self-Appraisal of Academic Progress Abroad Compared With Expected Level had They Stayed at Home, by Home Country and Field of Study (in arithmetic means)*

	Home country					Field of Study					
	UK	F	D	S	US	Bus	Eng	NatSc	Law	Lang	Total**
Academic Progress abroad compared with expected level for corresponding period at home	2.9	3.5	3.4	3.5	3.7	3.1	3.3	3.3	3.2	4.0	3.4

*   On a scale of 1 = "academic progress abroad much less" to 5 = "academic progress abroad much greater"
**   Also including other fields of study
Source: Post-Study Abroad Questionnaire SAEP F 13 (F 325)

From their comments, it was obvious that students had taken account of the effect of overcoming all the linguistic and other challenges. They had also taken account of the "broadening of horizons" due to study abroad: stepping outside more narrow academic specialisations begun at home to take courses from a wider field;

working more intensively in these new areas; becoming familiar with many new practical applications of their studies; using other learning sources and tools such as the library, computers and laboratories abroad.

The British students assessed their progress abroad most cautiously. This could be related to the results noted in Chapter 3 and in the previous section of this chapter, which indicate that the British students did not consider the education abroad was commensurate to that at home. At the same time, the British students mentioned some hindrances connected more explicitly with the study abroad programmes. The major points are summarised below:

-From Business students:
- "We did not have enough preparation beforehand." (study abroad in France)
- "Four months was not long enough really to settle into new methods of teaching and actually begin to learn something." (study abroad in France)
- "Although we took examinations while abroad, our success or failure was not important, so a lack of motivation and involvement occurred." (study abroad in France)
- "The lectures were one and a half hours; foreign students could not concentrate so long." (study in Germany)
- "We were studying in groups of about sixty with no seminars of smaller groups and no allowances being made for our nationality and possible problems." (study in Germany)
- "My language ability was too poor to understand and take part in technical lectures and assignments; the lectures were either too difficult due to a combination of content and language problems, or they had already been covered in the UK." (study in Germany)

From Law students who had been in France:
- "It took a long time to adjust to a different educational system and to the language, so grades suffered at first."
- "There was no incentive to do well; plus, the assessment was so arbitrary."
- "It is hard to shine next to French law students."

An Engineering student who had gone to France commented: "I had to make a huge effort to learn many new things."

A student in Social Sciences who had been in France felt "The study year abroad was not very relevant to our course,; most language was learnt outside college."

At the other end of the spectrum, American students assessed their academic progress abroad most positively. Thus, the question has to be raised as to whether the Americans tended to react more positively to the questions asked, or whether they were indeed better prepared to gain the most academically from their sojourns.

The righthand portion of Table S34 shows that by field (European students only), the Foreign Language students attributed the highest rate of success to study abroad. This is intriguing, given the finding reported in the previous volume, that directors of study abroad programmes in Foreign Languages recounted more problems than directors in other fields. Foreign language students assessed their achievement most moderately prior to study abroad and consequently had the most to gain in academic terms from the sojourn. The gain might also be attributable to the benefits of immersion in the language milieu, which obviously has a special meaning for just this field of study.

Chapter 5

Effects of Study Abroad upon Foreign Language Proficiency

5.1   Introduction

It is generally assumed that students make greater progress in acquiring a foreign language as a consequence of living in the language milieu. It is further known on the basis of the current evaluation that the expected increase in foreign language proficiency is one of the leading motivations for students to study abroad. It is necessary, therefore, to measure how much more skill and what kinds of skills are produced during such a study abroad experience.

The design and validation of instruments to assess foreign language capacity depends upon a great deal of trial testing and considerable statistical capacity. Because of the restriction in lead time and in resources for the current evaluation, it was not possible to develop a battery of entirely new instruments. Language tests were assembled from existing instruments; the major portion of the testing was incorporated within the questionnaires administered to students immediately prior to departure and, again, shortly after their return from the study period abroad. While many of the participants were proficient in more than one foreign language[1], they were requested to assess in greatest detail their level of proficiency in the language of the study abroad host country.

The lengthier of the two tests integrated in the questionnaires was adopted from an instrument devised by the Educational Testing Service (ETS) in the USA. This - commonly referred to as the "can do" test - had respondents appraise their speaking and listening comprehension skills, and their ability to read and write the specified foreign language. The aim in employing this instrument was not to measure the proportion of an absolute quantity of vocabulary or the percentage of a certain curriculum which students mastered, but rather to assess how well the respondents themselves felt they could function in the language in specifically defined contexts. The language items which characterised these contexts were largely descriptive and directive, in some cases alluding to situations which called for elaborate structures of messages, arguments or interpretations. In each speaking, listening comprehension etc. category, proficiencies were listed in a

---

[1]   Only the European students were asked (in the Pre-Study Abroad Questionnaire) about their knowledge of foreign language(s) other than of the study abroad host country. Half the Europeans indicated "good" or "very good" reading and listening comprehension proficiencies in a second foreign language. This was particularly prevalent among the German and Swedish students. Over a third of the Europeans were competent at a similarly high level in speaking and writing a second foreign language; especially the French and the Germans. A minor portion of the study abroad participants were proficient in a third foreign language as well. This was more the case for the French and British than for the Germans or Swedes.

progression from simpler (involving use or understanding of minimal word forms and syntactic fragments) to more complicated proficiencies which involved major structuring or comprehension of messages which had as their prime function to communicate topics or points of view to the listener or reader. Inherent in this was a progression from mere passive decoding of messages or delivering abbreviated bits of information, to conditions which required more preparation of a discourse or argument.

In each category, respondents were requested to check all items they could do well. The number of items to which they were to respond included:
- speaking proficiency: 14 general items; where relevant, an additional 6 which were academically related;
- listening comprehension: 12 general items; where relevant an additional 2 which were academically related; and
- reading proficiency: 8 general items; where relevant an additional 3 which were academically related.

A different procedure was followed for the writing proficiency, as students were asked which one among the six specified levels corresponded with their writing proficiency in the foreign language.

The order of items in the lists had been determined during the original development of the instrument (not part of the current evaluation), when repeated administration had shown which proficiencies could be mastered fairly easily and therefore could be expected to figure in most people's responses concerning what they could do, in contrast to those which were more difficult and therefore possessed by a minority of respondents. Most of the items pertained to general situations of daily life and not to types of scholarly settings likely to be encountered by persons studying abroad. For this reason, the research team for the current evaluation supplemented the original list with a number of items relating to language usage in uniquely academic contexts. This extended list was administered to the European students, both before and after their study abroad. The American students were asked to rate their academic linguistic competence only after the sojourn.

To obtain a differentiated perspective on language proficiency and some indication of whether students accurately assessed their abilities in the self-appraisal portion of the questionnaire, a limited sample of the American study abroad participants was tested through oral interviews. The interview format was originally developed by the American Council on Teaching Foreign Languages (ACTFL) and the ETS, based on the proficiency rating system of the Foreign Service Institute of the American Department of State. Interviews were conducted by trained interviewers with native speaker proficiency. The subjects tested conversed with the interviewer(s) between ten and forty minutes, depending upon the level of language proficiency. The speech sample for each subject was recorded, analysed and rated on a nine-point scale. The lowest level signified "no practical ability to function in the language", and the highest indicated "ability equivalent to that of a well-educated native speaker".

Furthermore, and following the same logic as the self-appraisal test of students' functional competence in the language of the study abroad host country, the research team devised its own items for the Post-Study Abroad Questionnaire so that returned students could indicate the extent to which they felt hampered in using the language of the host country at the beginning of their sojourn and at the end. Students were asked to judge the extent of their difficulties on a five-point scale, with respect to each of the following circumstances:
- entering into conversation with host country nationals;
- entering into academic conversations with instructors; and
- meeting the language requirements of daily life.

For the general speaking, academically related speaking, the listening comprehension, reading and writing proficiency categories of the "can do" instrument, as well as the three circumstances listed here, indices were compiled on the basis of magnitude of change between the aggregated pre- and post-study abroad assessments. Inter-correlations among these eight indices were relatively high, implying that it is not just certain skills (e.g. speaking more than reading) but rather a full range which are enhanced as a result of study abroad. The high inter-correlations also signify that the much more detailed self-appraisals of the ETS "can-do" test were tapping similar abilities as the students' more general assessments of degree of restraint in operating in the same language.

In further checking correlations between the "can-do" assessments and the oral interviews, it was found that these were as high as the inter-correlations solely among the self-appraisal indices. The correlations between the students' self-appraisals and those of the external examiners (the language interviewers) were certainly high enough not to be random, but they were not so high to provide unequivocal justification for using only one instrument to test foreign language acquisition.

The same Post-Study Abroad Questionnaire enquired about any significant problems students may have encountered abroad in taking courses and examinations in a foreign language or in communicating in a foreign language outside the classroom. They also rated the period in terms of how worthwhile it had been for their foreign language proficiency.

5.2   Self-Appraisal of Foreign Language Proficiency

5.2.1   General Abilities

In reviewing the students' pre-departure assessments, it was found at this stage that many of them already professed (whether their own assessments were accurate or not) solid proficiency in the prospective host country language. Essentially all students felt they could easily master the first six of the fourteen speaking proficiencies, which meant, for example, that they could say the days of the week, order a simple meal in a restaurant, and give simple biographical information about themselves (place of birth, composition of family). They could easily do the first four of the listening comprehension items. This meant that beyond understanding very simple statements or questions in the language ("Hello, how are you?", "What is your name?"), they could understand native speakers in face-to-face conversation or on the telephone, who spoke slowly and carefully, deliberately adapting their speech to suit the foreigner. Finally, the first three of the reading proficiencies could be handled with ease. Students could read newspaper headlines and signs on store fronts where the type of services (e.g. drycleaning, bookstore) was provided, and could read handwritten, personal letters addressed to them in which the writer had deliberately used simple words and constructions. Consequently, in presenting the results in Table S35 - 37 (as well as in the Tables on the academically-related proficiencies of the Europeans, which follow), only the ability levels for the more difficult items in each category are shown, as it is only in this region that perceptible differences emerged among the various groups of students.

In *general speaking ability* (Table S35) prior to departure for study abroad, a greater proportion of the British and Swedish students felt they could master the more difficult linguistic items such as talking about a favourite hobby at some length, using appropriate vocabulary, and describing their studies or other major life activities. This was least true of the Americans. Upon returning from their respective periods abroad, the Americans had attained a level of ability which was not appreciably inferior to the post-sojourn assessment of the other groups, except the Swedes, who were clearly more proficient than any of the others at this point. In some cases, other groups who had been "weaker" at the outset surpassed the formerly "stronger" ones. This was true, for example, in the case of the Germans' ability to state and support a position on a controversial topic, as compared with the ability of the British.

In viewing these results for the Europeans by field of study, the most striking finding is the comparatively weaker position of the Foreign Language students at the outset, which essentially remains so at the end of the study abroad period. In contrast, the Engineering students, who had reported approximately the same (i.e. a comparatively lower) level of competence in the pre-departure situation, acquired foreign language proficiency during the period abroad which put them near the highest of all groups. Could the Foreign Language students have been more objective in their assessments; or possibly, while realistic in their assessments at the outset, more ambitious about the level of accomplishment they expected by the end of their sojourn?

In *general listening comprehension* (Table S36), before entering their respective host countries, greater proportions of the Swedish and French students considered they would be capable of mastering the more difficult language situations. The Swedes assessed their competence to be relatively high. But one must also bear in mind that the Swedes in the current evaluation are primarily in programmes of study which send them to English-speaking countries, and English is regularly taught in Swedish schools from the early grades. Given this, the level of competence (even greater than the self-assessed level of the Swedes) perceived by the French students is even more meaningful. The Americans on average rated

Table S35
Study Abroad Participants' General Speaking Ability in Language of Host Country, Before and After the Study Abroad Period, by Home Country and Field of Study (in percentage of students)*

		Home country					Field of study					
		UK	F	D	S	US	Bus	Eng	NatSc	Law	Lang	Total**
Buy clothes in a department store	Before	94.1	89.1	90.1	97.3	86.4	90.1	92.6	88.1	94.0	87.0	90.2
	After	96.2	97.8	95.5	100.0	98.4	97.3	96.4	97.6	96.0	100.0	97.1
Introduce oneself in social situations using appropriate greetings and leave-taking expressions	Before	94.1	54.3	89.5	89.2	86.4	88.3	74.1	92.9	88.0	69.6	85.1
	After	98.1	91.3	96.1	100.0	100.0	98.2	96.4	100.0	96.0	87.0	97.3
Talk about a favorite hobby at some length, using appropriate vocabulary	Before	82.4	76.1	78.3	86.5	59.2	84.7	74.1	76.2	82.0	73.9	74.3
	After	92.3	93.5	94.2	97.4	96.7	95.5	100.0	92.9	96.0	91.3	94.9
Describe present studies or other major life activities	Before	88.2	82.6	68.4	75.7	55.3	82.0	70.4	73.8	72.0	82.6	69.9
	After	98.1	89.1	94.8	100.0	97.5	97.3	100.0	97.6	94.0	87.0	95.9
Tell what one plans to be doing in five years, using appropriate vocabulary	Before	66.7	63.0	63.8	78.4	48.5	72.1	59.3	69.0	64.0	56.5	61.4
	After	96.2	91.3	90.9	97.4	95.1	94.6	96.4	92.9	92.0	91.3	93.4
Describe home country's educational system in some detail	Before	70.6	50.0	60.5	78.4	46.6	64.9	63.0	71.4	54.0	47.8	58.6
	After	94.2	80.4	90.3	100.0	87.7	93.7	96.4	95.2	86.0	78.3	89.8
State and support with examples and reasons a position on a controversial topic (e.g. birth control, nuclear safety)	Before	60.8	65.2	45.4	48.6	26.2	55.9	48.1	40.5	54.0	60.9	45.0
	After	80.8	84.8	87.0	86.8	75.4	91.9	78.6	85.7	78.0	78.3	82.5
Describe system of government in one's country	Before	51.0	54.3	52.6	56.8	28.2	56.8	37.0	45.2	58.0	39.1	46.5
	After	75.0	82.6	84.4	92.1	77.0	84.7	78.6	76.2	88.0	73.9	81.6
(N)		(51)	(46)	(152)	(37)	(103)	(111)	(28)	(42)	(50)	(23)	(389)

* Multiple reply was possible
** Also including other fields of study
Source: Pre-Study Abroad Questionnaire SAEP D 36 (D 411 - 424); Post-Study Abroad Questionnaire SAEP F 19 (F 513-526)

Impacts of Study Abroad Programmes

Table S36
Study Abroad Participants' Listening Comprehension in Language of Host Country, Before and After the Study Abroad Period, by Home Country and Field of Study (in percentage of students)*

		Home country					Field of study					
		UK	F	D	S	US	Bus	Eng	NatSc	Law	Lang	Total**
Understand movies without subtitles	Before	70.6	65.2	65.4	84.2	24.8	70.9	70.4	57.1	68.0	73.9	55.7
	After	88.5	84.8	89.6	97.4	85.2	95.5	85.7	83.3	92.0	78.3	88.3
In face to face conversation, understand a native speaker who is speaking as quickly and as colloquially as he or she would to another native speaker	Before	62.7	84.8	45.8	68.4	33.9	62.7	63.0	33.3	66.0	65.2	50.9
	After	84.6	93.5	90.3	94.7	82.0	96.4	92.9	83.3	88.0	78.3	87.9
Understand news broadcasts on the radio	Before	56.9	65.2	70.6	89.5	20.7	76.4	66.7	66.7	60.0	52.2	55.3
	After	88.5	93.5	93.5	100.0	86.1	96.4	96.4	90.5	90.0	91.3	91.3
Understand other non-natives of the SAP country, speaking the language of that country	Before	78.4	76.1	64.1	73.7	0.0	75.5	74.1	61.9	60.0	73.9	49.1
	After	96.2	89.1	91.6	97.4	88.5	93.7	100.0	92.9	92.0	91.3	91.5
Understand two native speakers when they are talking rapidly with one another	Before	49.0	52.2	22.2	42.1	19.0	33.6	37.0	16.7	40.0	52.2	29.8
	After	76.9	73.9	77.3	78.9	74.6	85.6	78.6	57.1	72.0	69.6	76.2
Understand play-by-play descriptions of sports events (example a soccer match) on the radio	Before	31.4	30.4	23.5	63.2	9.1	31.8	63.0	26.2	22.0	21.7	24.7
	After	48.1	60.9	61.7	68.4	42.6	67.6	75.0	52.4	46.0	47.8	54.9
From the radio, understand the words of a popular song not heard before	Before	21.6	21.7	27.5	55.3	13.2	28.2	33.3	33.3	22.0	21.7	24.4
	After	44.2	45.7	58.4	84.2	39.3	61.3	71.4	50.0	52.0	30.4	51.9
On the telephone, understand a native speaker who is talking as quickly and as colloquially as he or she would to another native speaker	Before	37.3	54.3	24.2	44.7	0.0	35.5	37.0	16.7	42.0	39.1	24.0
	After	71.2	84.8	70.8	84.2	66.4	79.3	78.6	54.8	78.0	78.3	72.3
(N)		(52)	(46)	(154)	(38)	(122)	(111)	(28)	(42)	(50)	(23)	(412)

* Multiple reply was possible.
** Also including other fields of study
Source: Pre-Study Abroad Questionnaire SAEP D 36 (D 431-441, 444); Post-Study Abroad Questionnaire SAEP F 19 (F 533-543, 546)

Table S37
Study Abroad Participants' Reading Proficiency in Language of Host Country, Before and After the Study Abroad Period, by Home Country and Field of Study (in percentage of students)*

| | | Home country | | | | | Field of study | | | | | |
		UK	F	D	S	US	Bus	Eng	NatSc	Law	Lang	Total**
Read handwritten personal letters and notes written as they would be to a native user of the language	Before	86.5	73.9	62.7	84.2	65.8	77.5	70.4	66.7	64.0	82.6	69.9
	After	100.0	95.7	90.9	100.0	95.0	97.3	92.9	100.0	88.0	95.7	94.6
Read and understand magazine articles at a level similar to those found in Time without using a dictionary	Before	61.5	65.2	51.0	60.5	37.5	62.2	55.6	42.9	56.0	56.5	50.9
	After	78.4	89.1	81.8	92.1	73.6	84.7	89.3	75.6	86.0	78.3	80.7
Read popular novels without using a dictionary	Before	65.4	65.2	37.3	65.8	24.2	51.4	55.6	40.5	48.0	73.9	42.8
	After	86.3	78.3	74.7	100.0	66.9	84.7	89.3	68.3	74.0	82.6	76.6
Read technical material in a particular academic or professional field with no use or only very infrequent use of a dictionary	Before	26.9	23.9	35.9	50.0	7.5	30.6	51.9	57.1	30.0	4.3	26.4
	After	56.9	67.4	82.5	78.9	39.7	75.7	96.4	85.4	80.0	34.8	64.6
Read newspaper "want ads" with comprehension, even when many abbreviations are used	Before	25.0	34.8	29.4	15.8	14.2	34.2	22.2	23.8	30.0	30.4	23.7
	After	58.8	60.9	66.9	55.3	49.6	71.2	75.0	51.2	60.0	47.8	59.0
(N)		(52)	(46)	(153)	(38)	(120)	(111)	(27)	(42)	(50)	(23)	(409)

* Multiple reply was possible
** Also including other fields of study
Source: Pre-Study Abroad Questionnaire SAEP D 36 (D 445, 447, 448, 450, 452-455); Post-Study Abroad Questionnaire SAEP F 19 (F 547, 549, 550, 552, 554-557)

themselves least competent - in this case very significantly so - prior to departure for study abroad. By the end of their sojourn, the Americans had caught up with the others except in the proficiencies related to the three most difficult items. Two of these - understanding play-by-play descriptions of sports events and the words of popular songs heard for the first time on the radio - also remained difficult for the British students and to a certain extent also for the French. Overall, after the study abroad period, the Swedes, Germans and the French assessed their foreign language competence higher than the other two groups.

By field of study (European students only), the proportion of Business Studies and even more so of Engineering students who perceived they were competent in listening comprehension was consistently above average before going abroad, as well as afterwards. At the other extreme, study abroad participants in the Natural Sciences were markedly weak at the pre-departure point. During the period in the host country, the proficiency of the Natural Science students progressed to the extent that in half the situations described in the list, the proportion of this group who easily managed the items was greater than the corresponding proportion of students in Foreign Language programmes.

In *general reading ability* (Table S37), the Swedes, French and British students felt they were capable of mastering the more difficult items even before they went abroad. The Americans lagged considerably behind and in fact continued to do so in the post study abroad situation. Their comparatively weak proficiency is dramatically apparent for the one item which relates most directly to the academic context at the level of higher education: reading technical material in a particular academic or professional field with infrequent, or no, use of a dictionary. For students from the remaining four countries, language acquisition in terms of reading put them at very similar levels of ability as for listening comprehension, noted above.

By field of study, the range in general reading proficiency levels of the various groups at the pre-departure stage is the smallest of all situations mentioned so far, either by field or by country of origin of the participants, before or after the sojourn. One of the most remarkable findings is that, after the period abroad, the proportion of students in Foreign Languages who rate themselves as proficient in the specified items is equalled or in many cases surpassed by the participants in programmes in other fields. In this respect, the facility of the Business Studies and Engineering students is markedly high across the board. The Engineering and Natural Science students are strong in their ability to read technical material, presumably in their areas of specialisation, without having to consult a dictionary very often.

The post-study abroad oral interview results, based on a restricted sample of the previously specified subgroup of Americans who studied in Germany, offer supportive evidence for conclusions drawn from the self-appraisal instruments, that very substantial gains in foreign language proficiency were a result of the sojourn abroad. The interviewers judged that the majority of students had moved from the "intermediate" level (i.e. "able to satisfy most survival needs and limited social demands") to the "advanced" (i.e. "able to satisfy most work requirements and show some ability to communicate on concrete topics relating to particular interests and special fields of competence"), or "superior" categories. Half of the students interviewed after the sojourn were judged to be at the superior level, the highest in the scale.

In writing ability, slightly under ten percent of all study abroad participants felt prior to their study abroad period that their proficiency corresponded to that described at the fifth or the sixth level. They felt that they would be able to write complex personal and business letters and many other kinds of documents, using in each case the particular vocabulary and style of expression appropriate to the situation in question. There would: only be an occasional hint that they were not native writers of the language (= level 5); or their writing in all situations would not be distinguishable from that of educated native speakers in the host country (= Level 6). By the end of the period abroad, well over a quarter of the students appraised their ability at one of these two levels, as Table S38 shows.

In addition, approximately two-thirds of all students rated their proficiency to be on the fourth level. This meant they could write fairly long personal letters and uncomplicated business letters which conveyed meaning accurately and contained relatively few errors, although these would not be completely idiomatic in expression. The results also show that, for some students, writing ability in the host country language increased considerably during the sojourn.

The French students, who had assessed their ability to write in the study abroad host country language as comparatively strong even prior to departure were also strong in the post-sojourn period. Over half the French (52.2%) rated their proficiencies at one of the two highest levels at the end of the study abroad. The proportion of Americans and British students was lowest in this regard - less than a third and less than half that of the French, respectively. And despite the earlier suggested advantage for the Swedes in going to English-speaking countries, this group did not stand out as being above average in writing ability in the host country language either before or after the study period abroad.

By field of study for the Europeans, students in Business Studies and in Foreign Language programmes on the whole were more proficient in their writing abilities in the pre-departure situation, and the Business students continued to show large gains while abroad. Students in Law rated themselves weakest at the beginning of study abroad. By the end, the various groups were much closer in their assessed ability levels. The Law and Natural Science students showed the highest increases.

In sum, it appears that these tests elicited meaningful appraisals of language proficiency even with the inclusion of Europeans in an instrument originally designed to assess the foreign language proficiency of Americans, who at home obviously are enmeshed in a comparatively more mono-lingual climate. A fuller assessment of the Europeans' ability would probably have been gained from lengthening the categories of general speaking, listening comprehension and reading proficiencies, to include several more difficult items. Otherwise, with respect to the items which did figure in the test, the averages across all students sampled,

Table S38
Study Abroad Participants' Writing Ability in Language of Host Country, Before and After the Study Abroad Period, by Home Country and Field of Study (in percentage of students)*

		Home country					Field of study					
		UK	F	D	S	US	Bus	Eng	NatSc	Law	Lang	Total**
I cannot really communicate in the language of the SAP host country, through writing	Before	-	-	-	-	1.6	-	-	-	2.0	-	.7
	After	2.0	-	.7	-	-	-	-	2.4	-	-	.2
I can write a few sentences using very basic vocabulary and structures	Before	.5	-	-	-	-	-	-	-	2.0	-	.5
	After	-	-	-	-	-	-	-	2.4	-	-	-
I can write relatively simple items that communicate basic messages but usually contain a number of errors	Before	17.3	13.0	27.2	23.7	30.9	15.5	25.9	23.8	32.0	17.4	25.1
	After	2.0	2.2	4.5	5.4	5.8	1.8	7.1	-	10.0	4.3	4.4
I can write fairly long personal letters as well as uncomplicated business letters, which contain relatively few errors, although they are not completely idiomatic in expression	Before	65.4	69.6	62.3	63.2	64.2	70.0	59.3	66.7	52.0	73.9	64.1
	After	74.5	45.7	61.7	70.3	78.3	55.0	75.0	75.6	56.0	73.9	67.2
I can write complex personal and business letters, as well as many other kinds of documents (e.g. a "letter to the editor" of the local newspaper). There is only an occasional hint that I am not a native writer of the language	Before	7.7	17.4	9.3	13.2	3.3	13.6	14.8	7.1	8.0	8.7	8.5
	After	19.6	45.7	31.2	21.6	13.3	38.7	14.3	22.0	32.0	17.4	25.2
My writing, in all situations, cannot be distinguished from that of an educated native speaker of the language of the SAP host country	Before	5.8	-	.7	-	-	.9	-	-	4.0	-	1.0
	After	2.0	6.5	2.6	2.7	2.5	4.5	3.6	-	2.0	4.3	2.9
(N)		(51)	(46)	(154)	(37)	(120)	(111)	(28)	(41)	(50)	(23)	(408)

* Question: "Please assess the level of your current writing ability in the language of the SAP host country. Check only the one paragraph which best describes your writing ability."

** Also including other fields of study

Source: Pre-Study Abroad Questionnaire SAEP D 37 (D 456); Post-Study Abroad Questionnaire SAEP F 20 (F 558)

with only a few exceptions, did follow the originally established progression in order of difficulty.[2]

Contrary to what might have been expected, the Tables covering the general proficiencies show that a greater proportion of the respondents on average felt confident of their general speaking ability, even though this presumably demanded more active structuring and expression of messages on the part of the language user, and harboured the potential for more spontaneous, possibly unpredictable linguistic challenges where the speaker would not have recourse to a dictionary, than would be the case for reading, and the more passive proficiency of listening comprehension. It is also apparent that there are other than simply linguistic factors at play in the students' perceptions of their competence in the more difficult linguistic situations.

What has not been recorded in the Tables is that in each group of students, by home country, the self-assessed levels of proficiency prior to departure differed noticeably according to the host country for which students were headed. To illustrate, a greater proportion of the group of British bound for France felt competent in their speaking, reading and listening comprehension of the language of the host country, than did the British students bound for Germany. Greater numbers of Swedes going to the UK or the USA - in contrast to Germany - and a greater proportion of the Germans going to the UK or USA, in contrast to France, felt competent in all proficiencies in the host country language.

As far as the French and Americans were concerned, the patterns were more variable. For students of both countries, the self-appraisal of general speaking proficiency was rated approximately the same regardless of host country. In general listening comprehension, greater proportions of the French going to Germany (in comparison with French going to the UK) and a greater number of the Americans bound for Germany (in comparison with Americans going to France) felt competent in the language of the host country. But in reading, the French and Americans going to Germany felt **less** competent than their respective counterparts bound for the other countries. The length and regularity of these results suggest that the sense of proficiency in the host country language may rest upon factors which are not exclusively connected with the individual design of the study abroad programmes, particularly as would concern any pre-departure preparation they would provide. The pervasiveness of familiarity with the specified foreign language quite generally in the study abroad participants' native society, the extent to which the language is studied as a foreign language during earlier years of schooling, or the extent to which that language appears internationally could all be influencing the outcomes here.

---

[2]   The order of the items in Tables S35 - S37 is arranged according to the results of the current evaluation, rather than the original order, which was also the one used in the questionnaire.

5.2.2   *Academically Related Abilities of the Europeans*

For the academically related linguistic proficiencies, it was only the competence of the European study abroad participants which was recorded before *and* after study abroad. Consequently, it is only the European findings which are presented in Tables S39, S40 and S41. Here, in contrast to the pattern noted for the general abilities, greater portions of the student groups, on average, felt they could manage the academic reading and listening items, than the proportion who felt competent in the academic speaking situations described. Nevertheless, at the beginning of study abroad, the Europeans could easily do the first of the six academically related speaking proficiencies (asking for assistance in the library).

In this realm of academic abilities, it is also quite obvious that some of the more difficult linguistic conditions present challenges in terms of self-projection, mastering and organising content areas etc. which are unlikely to be demanded of the easier activities. Thus again, there are other than simply linguistic factors which play some role in the students' perceptions of their competence in these situations. To take an example, even if students were fluent in all respects in the host country language, the most difficult items in the academic speaking category - "presenting a paper in front of a large group of students and teacher(s)" and "leading a small group seminar" - would presumably be more difficult than "understanding class discussions" (the most difficult item in the academic listening category) or "reading handwritten notes on the blackboard" (the most difficult in the academic reading category). It is nevertheless quite outstanding that nearly half the (European) students could accomplish the most difficult task of leading a small group seminar by the time they had completed their period of study abroad.

In the pre-departure situation, across all three categories of academically related linguistic proficiency, the Swedish and French groups most frequently contained the largest proportion of students who felt they could do the language items listed. The lowest proportions are found in the German group. The British students stand out in one respect, for the highest proportion who can easily do the most difficult academic speaking items.

After the study period abroad, the Swedish students have done particularly well in their academically related reading and listening comprehension skills. They are the only group in which all students felt they could do all items listed in each of the two categories.

The proportion of German students who can easily manage the academically related linguistic situations of all three categories (speaking, reading, and listening) is in line with or even in some cases slightly better than the average for the majority of items listed. The Germans could present well in large classes; the British could lead seminars.

Viewing the students' assessments by subject area, in the pre-departure ratings, the Business Studies group shows that for the majority of items, the proportion of competent students is highest. The proportion of students who presume they can manage the various linguistic situations is most frequently low for students going abroad in Law programmes.

Table S39
European Study Abroad Participants' Speaking Ability in Academically Related Language of Host Country, Before and After the Study Abroad Period, by Home Country and Field of Study (in percentage of students)*

		Home country				Field of study					
		UK	F	D	S	Bus	Eng	NatSc	Law	Lang	Total**
Discuss coursework, ask for guidance etc. in conversation with teachers	Before	80.8	93.5	51.6	84.2	72.1	74.1	64.3	48.0	87.0	77.5
	After	96.2	95.7	90.3	97.4	96.4	92.9	97.6	82.0	91.3	92.0
Participate actively in small group discussion, project or laboratory work, with other students who are native speakers of the SAP host country language	Before	48.1	76.1	46.4	71.1	66.7	55.6	47.6	38.0	60.9	60.4
	After	82.7	89.1	87.0	86.8	93.7	75.0	85.7	82.0	78.3	85.9
Ask questions or participate in discussion in a large class setting	Before	46.2	63.0	47.1	47.4	56.8	51.9	38.1	42.0	52.2	50.9
	After	63.5	89.1	83.8	73.7	85.6	78.6	69.0	80.0	69.6	76.7
Present a paper, results of laboratory experiments etc. in front of a large group of students and teacher(s)	Before	42.3	32.6	26.1	31.6	42.3	25.9	19.0	32.0	21.7	33.2
	After	65.4	78.3	68.2	76.3	82.0	75.0	54.8	58.0	47.8	64.1
Lead a small group seminar	Before	34.6	26.1	11.8	21.1	26.1	25.9	11.9	18.0	17.4	23.4
	After	55.8	60.9	44.2	55.3	63.1	53.6	38.1	36.0	43.5	44.7
(N)		(52)	(46)	(153)	(38)	(111)	(27)	(42)	(50)	(23)	(289)

*   Multiple reply was possible
**   Also including other fields of study
Source: Pre-Study Abroad Questionnaire SAEP D 36 (D 425 - 430); Post-Study Abroad Questionnaire SAEP F 19 (F 527-532)

Table S40
European Study Abroad Participants' Listening Comprehension in Academically Related Language of Host Country, Before and After the Study Abroad Period, by Home Country and Field of Study (in percentage of students)*

| | | Home country | | | | Field of study | | | | | |
		UK	F	D	S	Bus	Eng	NatSc	Law	Lang	Total**
Understand a lecture in your field(s)	Before	70.6	76.1	62.1	78.9	73.6	59.3	71.4	56.0	91.3	71.9
	After	90.4	95.7	96.8	100.0	97.3	100.0	92.9	92.0	95.7	95.7
Understand students and teachers in a discussion, seminar situation, etc., concerning topics in your field(s)	Before	60.8	73.9	51.6	63.2	68.2	55.6	54.8	44.0	78.3	62.4
	After	84.6	87.0	94.8	100.0	95.5	89.3	88.1	90.0	82.6	91.6
(N)		(51)	(46)	(153)	(38)	(110)	(27)	(42)	(50)	(23)	(288)

*   Multiple reply was possible

**   Also including other fields of study

Source: Pre-Study Abroad Questionnaire SAEP D 36 (D 442 - 443); Post-Study Abroad Questionnaire SAEP F 19 (F 544-545)

Table S41
European Study Abroad Participants' Academically Related Reading Proficiency in Language of Host Country, Before and After the Study Abroad Period, by Home Country and Field of Study (in percentage of students)*

		Home country				Field of study					
		UK	F	D	S	Bus	Eng	NatSc	Law	Lang	Total**
Read handwritten notes on blackboard, view-graphs, etc. where writer has deliberately used simple words and constructions	Before	94.2	84.8	96.7	94.7	94.6	96.3	97.6	94.0	87.0	92.6
	After	98.0	95.7	96.8	100.0	98.2	96.4	100.0	96.0	100.0	97.6
Read signboards at the university which explain e.g. procedures for registering in course	Before	80.8	63.0	89.5	89.5	89.2	85.2	83.3	84.0	56.5	80.7
	After	98.0	95.7	96.8	100.0	98.2	96.4	100.0	96.0	95.7	97.6
Read handwritten notes on blackboard, view-graphs, etc., written as they would be to a native user of the language	Before	69.2	80.4	62.1	86.8	75.7	70.4	69.0	56.0	73.9	74.6
	After	98.0	100.0	94.8	100.0	95.5	96.4	100.0	96.0	95.7	98.2
(N)		(52)	(46)	(153)	(38)	(111)	(27)	(42)	(50)	(23)	(289)

*   Multiple reply was possible

** Also including other fields of study

Source: Pre-Study Abroad Questionnaire SAEP D 36 (D 446, 449, 451); Post-Study Abroad Questionnaire SAEP F 19 (F 548, 551, 553)

After the sojourn, the ability level of students in all subject areas has risen to such an extent that the Business students hold a leading position essentially only in terms of academic speaking ability. Further, the proficiency of Law students increased considerably, to the extent that the proportion of this group who can do the more difficult items slightly surpasses the corresponding proportion of Foreign Language students.

5.2.3   Summary of Proficiencies

To summarise across all of these proficiencies, the Swedes, French and British students stand out in the pre-departure ratings for comparatively higher assessments of their foreign language proficiencies than the Germans and the Americans. Prior to study abroad, the German students rate higher in most cases than the Americans. At the end of study abroad, the Americans continue to rate lower in most respects, but the differences are clearly smaller than before. The nature and amount of language acquisition during the sojourn enables the Swedish and French students to maintain comparatively higher levels of competence, although, in several instances, the Germans and the British (the latter capable of doing the most difficult tasks of all in the academically-related speaking category) reckon they have attained similarly high levels of proficiency.

For the Europeans by field of study, Business and Engineering students professed comparatively high levels of proficiency in their respective host country languages before they went abroad. Their language acquisition abroad enabled them, on average, to remain comparatively more competent. In many instances, the Natural Science students, who assessed their proficiencies at lower levels at the time of the pre-departure rating, made considerable gains in language acquisition in conjunction with their study abroad. This was not as characteristic of the Foreign Language students who, low or average in competence at the outset with the exception of their writing skills, felt themselves frequently surpassed in language proficiency by study abroad participants in the other fields.

5.3   Overall Degree Of Restraint in Using the Host Country Language

Since students were not tested *in situ* after arriving in the host country, it cannot be shown explicitly whether their self-appraisals of foreign language facility immediately prior to departure had been realistic, inflated or deflated in comparison with their actual ability to cope at the outset of their study period abroad. As far as a comparison is possible between the oral interviews (conducted with thirty-three Americans who studied in Germany) and the students' self-appraisals, it appears that the students did tend to overrate their foreign language proficiencies prior to entering the host country.[3] If this is so, and if it is further assumed that, at the end of the sojourn, students more accurately appraised their proficiencies, this would mean that the findings regarding the linguistic impact of the study abroad programmes are, if anything, underestimates of the change which took place.

Another way to assess the change was to compare the degree of restraint students felt in using the host language at the outset of their study abroad, compared with at the end of the sojourn (see Table S42). Their responses did indicate they felt somewhat hampered in using the language of the host country at the beginning, more acutely in the academic setting and particularly in conversing with instructors. The marked restraint felt by the Americans (as high as a mean of 1.7 in conversation with host country teachers, where 1 = "very restrained" and 5 = "not at all restrained") contrasts with that of the Europeans. This provides further evidence for the testimony of programme directors that American students face comparatively greater problems in communicating in a foreign language abroad (starting from a much lower proficiency level) Because of the stronger foreign language background of the Europeans, this situation is true of the American students even though the American programmes emphasise foreign language study more than tends to be the case of the European programmes included in this evaluation. The amount of restraint recalled by the German and British students is also apparent, yet by the end of the sojourn there were no appreciable differences in the restraint felt, on average, by students from these two countries compared with the French and Swedes. Among the fields of study, participants in the Law and Natural Science programmes felt most restrained in using the language of their host countries at the beginning of their sojourn, but this is not the pattern in the assessments concerning the end of the sojourn.

To sum up, by the end of the period abroad, students felt only minimally restrained in using the language of their study abroad host country in academic settings as well as in social occasions and daily rituals. Conversations with instructors remained the weakest area of proficiency, but it was primarily a situation encountered by a few of the British and Americans who had studied abroad in France or Germany. By field of study, this affected some Law and a few Foreign Language students more than any of the others.

The detailed information which underlies the Table above, as well as the others of this chapter, reveal that there were several differences from one category of participants - by individual sending country or by field of study - to the next which should be considered in analysing the enhancement value for foreign language proficiency of an extended period of living in that linguistic milieu. Categories in which the proportion of linguistically capable students had been comparatively low at the outset did not always remain lower in comparison with the other categories by the end of the period abroad. Frequently, the less competent (or more

---

3   The results of the oral interviews showed that students who went to Germany had rather limited knowledge of the German language. The median level on the scale was "intermediate," defined as "Able to satisfy most survival needs and limited social demands."

Table S42
Study Abroad Participants' Restraint in Using Language of Host Country, at Beginning and at End of Study Abroad Period, by Home Country and Field of Study (in arithmetic means)*

		Home country					Field of study					
		UK	F	D	S	US	Bus	Eng	NatSc	Law	Lang	Total**
Entering into conversations with host country students	Beginning	2.7	3.3	2.6	3.1	1.9	2.9	2.9	2.5	2.6	2.9	2.5
	End	4.5	4.6	4.5	4.6	4.3	4.6	4.5	4.4	4.4	4.3	4.4
Entering into academic conversations with instructors	Beginning	2.1	3.3	2.3	2.5	1.7	2.5	2.5	2.4	2.2	2.6	2.2
	End	3.7	4.4	4.2	4.3	3.7	4.2	4.5	4.3	3.8	3.7	4.0
Meeting the language requirements of daily life	Beginning	3.0	3.4	3.0	3.4	2.2	3.1	3.4	2.7	3.2	3.2	2.8
	End	4.6	4.6	4.8	4.9	4.8	4.8	4.7	4.5	4.8	4.5	4.7

* Scale from 1 = "very restrained" to 5 = "not at all restrained"
** Also including other fields of study
Source: Post-Study Abroad Questionnaire SAEP F 21 (F 559 - 564)

modest or realistic) categories from the outset are shown by the end of the period abroad to have attained the same level of proficiency or even to have surpassed the formerly more competent groups.

It is also well in line with the above that, on average, the Swedes and French more than others reported that there had not been any problems in taking courses and examinations in a foreign language abroad, nor in communicating in the language outside of class. Generally, across all students by sending country, 68 percent indicated they had no problem communicating in academic settings, and 80 percent indicated no problem in the extracurricular domain. Where there had been problems, this had occurred more frequently among the British, French and American students who had spent their study abroad programme in Germany. The problems had been least for students who went to the UK or to the United States.

By field of study, comparatively greater percentages of the study abroad participants in Engineering, Natural Sciences and Foreign Languages reported little or no problems either in participating in courses or in taking their exams in a foreign language, or in communicating in extra-curricular settings. With respect to this finding for the Foreign Language students, this puts into context the occasional suggestion in the previous narrative, which compared the self-assessments of proficiency, that there may have been a problem particularly for the Foreign Language participants.

In considering these results, it should also be recalled that students rated foreign language acquisition as one of the two most worthwhile aspects of their experiences in the study abroad programmes. It probably comes as no surprise that the Americans did so more than participants in programmes from any other sending country. The Swedes were least inclined to have this view, although a substantial majority nevertheless did subscribe to it. In fact, across all sending countries, over three-quarters of the students felt the gains in foreign language proficiency had made the study abroad period not only worthwhile, but *extremely* worthwhile.[4]

5.4   Determinants of Language Acquisition Abroad

The variations in patterns of language acquisition - most particularly the situations in which comparatively weaker groups at the outset catch up or even surpass the formerly strong groups in language competence by the end of the period abroad - argue for a closer look at how programme design and the opportunity afforded to practice certain linguistic skills in the host culture may influence language acqui-

---

[4]   "Extremely worthwhile" represents a "1" on a scale from 1 - 5, where the "5" signifies "not at all worthwhile." If responses to points 1 and 2 on this scale are taken together, the result is that 96 percent of the participants overall felt their study abroad had been extremely or at least very worthwhile. Obviously, the British students going to the USA and the Americans studying in the UK are not included in any results reported concerning this type of question, since the two nationalities speak the same language.

sition. This was tested systematically through multivariate analysis, also taking into account certain factors, for example, in the students' backgrounds.[5]

This analysis shows that language proficiency is hardly linked to any of the aggregate indicators[6] on the extent to which the study abroad participants were integrated into the host institution of higher education. The indicators were the extent to which the students: utilised host country newspapers and novels, professional books and journals, lectures and discussion groups for information about the host country; communicated actively with host country nationals; took courses involving content or teaching methods not available at their home institution, to broaden their academic or cultural backgrounds; took language courses (in the host country language); and visited museums, concerts, cinema and travelled.

The only element which correlated across the board with the indicators of foreign language acquisition (although with varying intensity) was taking courses in the host country language. These were not courses which were arranged by the study abroad programme to provide intensive language training. Three more aspects appeared to be linked with language acquisition only in some cases, and in this respect the links were more appreciable by field, rather than sending country. The students' having availed themselves of host country newspapers, books etc. correlated most consistently with foreign language acquisition among Natural Science, Engineering and Foreign Language students. Coursework which provided content or methods not available at home, or enabled students to broaden their background, correlated with the language acquisition of participants in Natural Science and Law programmes. Museum visits were significantly linked with language acquisition for participants in the Natural Science, Engineering, Law and Business programmes.

As the more in-depth analysis in chapter 8 shows, the degree of improvement in foreign language proficiency during the study abroad period may indeed be influenced by some of the arrangements of the study abroad programmes, or, by decisions taken by students on how to make use of their study abroad. According to the analysis, these factors certainly play a more important role regarding improvement in foreign language proficiency than they do regarding improvements in academic learning or regarding the cultural values and attitudes of students analysed in this study.

---

[5]   The results of the full analysis are reported in chapter 8.

[6]   The indicators which were compiled to represent fundamental aspects of the experience abroad are the same ones employed in the multivariate analysis of Chapter 8: Determinants of Change in Students' Competencies, Attitudes and Views.

Chapter 6

Cultural Impacts

6.1 Underlying Concepts and Questions

It is often assumed that studying in another country for a period of time provides an excellent opportunity for cultural enrichment. Furthermore, as higher education is considered not only to develop a thorough understanding of theories, methods, and facts within a given disciplinary structure but also to contribute to responsible citizenship, understanding of cultural heritage, and reflection about values, concepts, and lifestyles, a study abroad period is widely considered to make an especially important contribution. Academic learning in a foreign environment is likely to make students aware of their attitudes and *mindset, the limits of their knowledge about other parts of the world and the degree to which their academic learning in their home country is bound by that country's cultural and national interests.

The broad consensus that it is incumbent upon higher education to contribute to individual growth and to transmit and promote wider cultural knowledge and values does not provide explicit signals for the weight which institutions should actually place upon the personal, cultural, and political development of students. Thus, the general debate about the cultural function of higher education does not point to any generally accepted criteria for the cultural impacts of study abroad which should be aimed at. Literature and research on student exchange and study abroad programmes are more forthcoming in calling attention to four major dimensions which have to be taken into consideration:

- Study abroad provides a direct opportunity for cultural learning through the broadening of knowledge and views internationally. As a consequence, one of the most obvious impacts is expected to be better understanding of the conditions in certain other countries. However, the value of study abroad is not confined to this. It is widely assumed that an understanding of other cultures stimulates, in turn, some *reflection about one's own culture*, and even a reconsideration of values in general, apart from application to any specific country. Examples of this type of impact include improved understanding of political rationales, and tolerance for different views.
- Study abroad most directly provides the opportunity to acquire *knowledge about the culture and other aspects of the host country*. At the same time the impact of such knowledge acquisition is considered to extend beyond the cognitive domain into the area of motivation, views, and opinions. It is expected that interest in getting to know and understand foreign cultures will be quickened, and that views based on both cognitive and effective bases will be touched. This may or may not affect deeply rooted values.

- The *direction of expected change* cannot be predicted. Students could shed very distinct views in the process of being exposed to a different environment. Or, students could develop new views as a consequence of further reflection stimulated by the period abroad. A student might lose self-confidence due to the broadening of experience; or, on the contrary, could become more self-confident in coping with new challenges. Students might become cosmopolitan by crossing the bounds of a more national experience or might become more nationally oriented by coming to the conclusion that life is superior or at least more desirable at home.

- Cultural knowledge and understanding *play a different role for students from one country to the next, as well as from one field of study* to the next. For example, fields of study differ both in the extent to which the core knowledge of the field is related to what is generally conceived to be a cultural experience - a visit to a museum plays a different role for an engineer than for an art historian - as well as in the extent to which certain areas of cultural learning are encouraged or discouraged.

This study has assessed a broad range of cultural impacts concerning the previously outlined dimensions. Students were polled regarding their knowledge about the host country culture, interest in getting to know other cultures, opinions on various aspects of the home and host countries, their (the students') international orientations and values. More or less identical questions were posed before and after the study period abroad, with the aim to measure the impact of the sojourn.

To keep the questionnaire at a realistic length, only a limited number of all possible dimensions of cultural learning could be addressed. In several cases, a list of broad areas (political system, cultural life, social structure etc.) was provided, rather than a more detailed set of items. In other cases, more in-depth information was solicited on a limited selection of topics within a broader area, at the expense of tracing in-depth information on other topics within the same area.

The questions asked and the categories presented were in most cases based on prior surveys. Adjustments were made in light of the specific concepts which formed the underlying rationale for the evaluation, the international composition of the intended respondents, and also because of limitations of space in the questionnaire.

6.2   Knowledge and Interest Regarding Other Countries

Changes in the range and depth of students' knowledge about the culture and society of the country in which they spend their study abroad is important to analyse because the changes in extent and nature of knowledge must be viewed as prerequisites for potential changes in opinions, basic values, and beliefs. Certainly it is expected that knowledge about the host country would increase as a matter of course while students are abroad. It is crucial, though, to examine whether knowledge on all aspects of culture and society increases across a broad range of these aspects or whether certain areas stand out and others lag behind.

Students were requested, before and after the study abroad period, to rate their level of knowledge on several dimensions of the political and social milieu of the host country. The research team assumed that this self-rating would assure greater co-operation from the students than would have been possible with any knowledge test embedded in the questionnaires. As Table S43 shows, prior to the study abroad period, students did not consider their knowledge about the host country to be very extensive. Arithmetic means ranged from 2.6 (on geography) to 3.4 (treatment of recently arrived immigrant groups), on a scale from 1 = "extensive knowledge" to 5 = "very minimal knowledge".

Table S43
Knowledge about Various Aspects of Host Country Before and After the Study Abroad Period, by Home Country (in arithmetic means*)

Problem		UK	F	D	S	US	Total
				Home Country			
System of post-secondary or	Before	2.6	3.0	2.9	3.1	2.7	2.8
higher education	After	2.1	2.1	1.9	2.1	1.8	1.9
Political system and	Before	3.1	2.5	2.7	2.8	3.2	2.9
institutions	After	2.6	2.3	2.1	2.6	2.4	2.3
Governmental foreign policy	Before	3.6	3.0	2.6	2.8	3.4	3.1
in general	After	3.2	2.7	2.2	2.6	2.8	2.6
Governmental policy toward	Before	3.4	2.4	2.4	3.0	3.0	2.8
your own country	After	2.9	2.3	2.2	2.8	2.3	2.4
Dominant political	Before	**	**	**	**	**	**
issues	After	2.7	2.2	2.0	2.3	2.3	2.3
Treatment of recently	Before	3.3	3.4	3.5	3.6	3.4	3.4
arrived immigrant groups	After	2.6	2.6	2.6	2.7	2.4	2.5
Economic system	Before	3.4	2.5	2.7	2.7	3.2	3.0
	After	3.2	2.3	2.3	2.3	2.7	2.6
The country's geography	Before	2.8	2.6	2.5	2.6	2.7	2.6
	After	2.6	2.7	2.1	2.2	1.9	2.2
Social structure (e.g. family,	Before	2.8	2.9	3.0	2.9	2.7	2.8
class system etc.)	After	2.4	2.4	2.2	2.0	1.9	2.2
Dominant social issues	Before	**	**	**	**	**	**
	After	2.6	1.9	2.3	2.4	2.1	2.2
Customs, traditions	Before	3.3	2.9	3.2	2.9	2.8	3.0
(including religious)	After	2.5	2.5	2.3	2.3	2.1	2.3
Cultural life (e.g. art, music,	Before	3.0	2.9	3.1	2.6	2.5	2.8
theater, cinema, literature)	After	2.2	2.6	2.4	2.4	2.0	2.3
Sports, leisure/recreational	Before	3.1	2.9	2.9	2.9	2.9	2.9
activities	After	2.7	2.3	2.4	2.5	2.3	2.4

* Scale from 1 = "extensive knowledge" to 5 = "very minimal knowledge"
** Item was not included in Pre-Study Abroad Questionnaire.
Source: Pre-Study Abroad Questionnaire SAEP D 39 (D 465-475); Post-Study Abroad Questionnaire SAEP F 25 (F 713-725).

Following the sojourn, their knowledge about all aspects had increased substantially: by 0.6 on average, with a range from 0.4 to 0.9. On a five-point scale, this obviously represents considerable improvement. To illustrate this in another way, prior to the period abroad, 37.2 percent of the students thought they were well informed (scale points 1 and 2) about politics in the host country. This percentage had nearly doubled (63.3%) after the period abroad.

Not surprisingly, the greatest increase in knowledge was reported in regard to higher education in the host country. The proportion of well-informed students increased from 41.0 to 77.9 percent. On the other hand, a relatively low increase in knowledge was reported with respect to the economic system and the geography of the host country.

British students rated their level of knowledge lower than students from other countries, both before and after the study abroad period, and the magnitude of the increase during that period was slightly below the five-country average. Before the stay abroad, French and German students reported the highest level of knowledge; and after, the highest levels were recorded for the German and American students. These dimensions of knowledge vary, as French students are well informed on social issues, Germans on foreign policies, and Swedes on the economic system of their respective host countries.

Among Europeans, students in Business Studies and Law consider themselves to be better informed about their respective host countries than students of Foreign Languages, Engineering and, especially, Natural Sciences. The latter rate their knowledge relatively low in all aspects except geography, the higher education system, and leisure activities.

It is intriguing to note that the level of knowledge in these respects differs more strongly between the student groups when categorised by home country than by the country in which students spent their study abroad. This implies that differences in knowledge acquisition have to be attributed more strongly to dispositions in the respective sending countries than solely to factors connected with the host countries.

It is frequently assumed that increased knowledge will reduce scepticism or even prejudice about another country, and possibly also foster empathy for other cultures. This hypothesis is not clearly supported by the findings of the current evaluation. It is true (see Table S44) that in the pre-departure stage, the greater the European students' knowledge about various aspects of their host country, the more positive were their opinions. But the post-sojourn assessments did not show links between increase in knowledge and increasingly positive opinions. The relationship between knowledge and opinion had obviously become less pronounced. On the basis of the European findings, it might be argued that the degree of knowledge and corresponding opinions are closely linked almost in a stereotype fashion as long as knowledge is generally low, and that information acquired during the period abroad counteracts such stereotyped thinking in differing ways. In the case of the American students, however, the opposite could be observed. Their knowledge and opinions about the host country were not related prior to study abroad, but afterwards, there were moderately positive correlations between an increase in knowledge and the students' reportedly more positive opinions about the host country.

Table S44
Relationship Between Knowledge Level and Favourable Opinion of Various Aspects of Host Countries Before and After the Study Abroad Period, by Home Country (Pearson correlation coefficient)

Aspects of host country		Home country					
		UK	F	D	S	US	Total
Post-secondary or	Before	.24	.43	.63	.40	.10	.42
higher education	After	-.11	.19	.38	-.06	.14	.16
	Change	.12	.12	.31	-.45	-.00	-.02
Governmental foreign	Before	.70	.28	.37	.40	.20	.37
policies in general	After	.42	.20	.13	.43	.41	.33
	Change	.06	.09	-.03	.15	-.20	.06
Treatment of recently	Before	.40	.49	.51	.47	-.04	.43
arrived immigrant groups	After	.34	.46	.13	.47	.33	.29
	Change	.17	.05	-.05	-.12	-.02	.01
Cultural life	Before	.48	.56	.52	.28	.29	.49
	After	.22	.47	.60	.29	.12	.44
	Change	.32	.10	.09	.03	-.00	.09
Social structure	Before	.47	.47	.44	.31	.04	.39
(e.g. family, class, system)	After	.42	.40	.11	.21	.20	.27
	Change	.10	.49	-.06	.07	.14	.09
Customs, traditions	Before	.58	.58	.59	.36	.12	.49
	After	.32	.66	.20	.17	.23	.31
	Change	.16	.53	.13	.19	.17	.18

Source: Pre-Study Abroad Questionnaire SAEP D 39-41 (D 465-475, 511-517) and Post-Study Abroad Questionnaire SAEP F 25-26 (F 713-732 CP 6A-J, CP 8A-G)

Increase in knowledge might not be spurred simply by the opportunity to get to know another country, but by the particular motivation to do so. Most students already reported a strong interest in other countries and international issues prior to their study abroad. The average score on a scale from 1 = "extremely interested" to 5 = "not at all interested" changed from 1.9 to 1.6 after the sojourn. It thus surpassed the interest in current events of the home country, which remained constant. As Table S45 shows, French and German students reported higher interest than the Swedish and British concerning home and host country issues, before as well as after the study abroad period.

For this particular issue of current events, American students were questioned only after the study abroad period. At that point, slightly over a third reported no interest at all in issues related to the host country, or in international issues. This extreme attitude was not observed among any of the Europeans.

Table S45
Student's Being Interested in Current Events of their Own Country and in Other Countries and International Affairs Before and After the Study Abroad Period (in arithmetic means*)

					Home country			
		UK	F	D	S	Total EUR	US	Total
Current events relating	Before	2.2	1.6	1.7	2.2	1.8	·	·
to your own country	After	2.1	1.8	1.7	2.1	1.8	2.0	1.9
Other countries, European	Before	2.4	1.7	1.7	2.3	1.9	·	·
and/or international affairs	After	2.1	1.4	1.4	1.9	3.1	1.6	2.1

*   Scale from 1 = "extremly interested" to 5 = "not at all interested"
Source: Pre-Study Abroad Questionnaire SAEP D 27 and 28 (D 274-275); Post-Study Abroad
         Questionnaire SAEP F 3 and 4 (F 132-133)

6.3   Opinions on Culture and Society of the Host and Home Countries

In general, people's attitudes and interpretations of other countries, their people, culture, politics and living conditions may range from xenophilia to xenophobia, even in situations where people are quite familiar with other countries. Consequently, the process of acquiring knowledge and experiences might lead to changes of opinion, but one cannot exclude the possibility that these experiences will have quite diverse effects. A person's feelings of empathy might grow in accordance with experience, or attitudes might become more negative, as a result of discovering problems about which a foreigner is usually oblivious upon first encountering the country in question. It is also possible that opinions might become more diverse as the knowledge base becomes more solid.

In this study, students were first asked to state their opinions about various aspects of the country in which they spent their study period abroad, and then about their home countries. This provides some point of departure for comparing their opinions about the home and host countries. For example, one comparison was whether students viewed higher education more favourably in their host country than in their home country. Second, students' opinions were examined to see whether their attitudes about other countries could in some way be reactions to opinions they have about their own country, and vice versa. Would students be more likely to express positive opinions about the host country if their opinions about the home country were negative? Or are these two realms independent of each other? Third, are changes of opinion on various aspects of the host country associated with any reconsideration or change of attitude about the home country?

Table S46 indicates that there are neither exceptionally positive nor very negative opinions about the host and home countries. Changes during the study abroad period are also marginal on average. The attitude toward home country became

Table S46
Opinions about Culture and Society of Study Abroad Host Country and of Home Country Before and After the Study Abroad Period, by Home Country (in arithmetic means)*

		Home country											
		UK		F		D		S		US		Total	
		Host	Home	Host	Home	Host	Home	Host	Home	Host	Home	Host	Home
Post secondary or higher education	Before	2.8	2.3	2.5	2.6	2.8	2.8	2.5	2.0	2.1	2.1	2.5	2.4
	After	2.8	2.2	2.3	2.7	2.9	2.4	2.9	2.0	2.8	2.0	2.8	2.3
Governmental foreign policies in general	Before	3.3	3.1	2.7	2.7	3.3	2.7	3.6	2.2	2.7	3.4	3.1	3.0
	After	3.2	3.3	3.3	2.3	3.3	2.8	3.6	2.1	2.9	3.7	3.2	3.0
Treatment of recently arrived immigrant groups	Before	3.7	3.3	3.0	3.6	3.7	3.7	3.8	2.5	3.3	3.2	3.5	3.4
	After	3.8	3.5	3.2	3.9	3.8	3.5	3.6	2.9	3.8	3.1	3.7	3.4
Cultural live (e.g. art, music, theater, literature)	Before	2.4	2.2	1.9	2.2	2.2	2.4	1.9	3.1	1.7	2.3	2.0	2.4
	After	2.0	2.2	2.2	1.8	2.1	2.4	1.7	2.8	1.5	2.4	1.9	2.4
Television, radio, newspapers, magazines	Before	3.2	2.2	2.2	2.8	2.5	2.5	2.6	3.0	2.5	2.5	2.6	2.5
	After	3.2	1.8	2.3	2.4	2.5	2.5	2.2	3.0	2.4	2.3	2.5	2.4
Customs, traditions	Before	2.5	2.7	2.2	2.8	2.5	2.8	2.6	2.4	2.1	2.7	2.4	2.7
	After	2.4	2.6	2.2	2.8	2.7	2.7	2.5	2.5	1.9	2.6	2.3	2.6
Social structure (e.g. family, class system)	Before	3.1	3.3	2.7	2.9	3.3	2.7	3.4	2.5	2.8	2.8	3.1	2.8
	After	2.9	3.4	3.3	3.0	3.6	2.5	3.3	2.4	2.9	2.8	3.2	2.7

*   Scale from 1 = "highly positive opinion" to 5 = "highly negative opinion"
Source: Pre-Study Abroad Questionnaire SAEP D 41 and 42 (D 511-524) and Post-Study Abroad Questionnaire SAEP F 27 and 28
    (F 726-743)

slightly more positive after study abroad than it had been before, but the difference was not statistically significant.

There are several noteworthy differences among the individual aspects, however. Cultural life (art, music, theatre, etc.) as well as customs and traditions abroad tend to be viewed more favourably - both before and after the study abroad period - than those at home, though attitudes toward the home country are also positive in these respects. On the other hand, the social structure of the home country is viewed - on average across these five countries - more positively than that of the host both before and after the study abroad period. Even though it would be misleading to say that study abroad fosters feelings after the sojourn that all is best at home, there are nevertheless three aspects about the host country which students tended to view more negatively than the corresponding aspects at home. One that is especially pronounced concerns higher education. A considerable number of students apparently became disappointed with higher education in the country of their study abroad experience. This slightly more negative view was also evident for the host country's foreign relations and its policies on the treatment of recently arrived immigrant groups.

Altogether the students' opinions do differ from one aspect of politics, society and culture to another, and very few students tend to express decidedly positive or negative attitudes about the home or host countries in a global way, as a block. This was additionally confirmed by two separate factor analyses conducted on the students' responses prior to and after the study abroad period. These analyses yielded **three** factors based on the numerous items about politics, customs and tradition, higher education, etc., rather than a **single** factor.

In many cases, the obvious pre-departure differences in opinion about the host country fade away. For example, prior to their sojourn, American and French students assessed their prospective host countries more positively than their home countries. The difference in opinion about home and host almost disappeared after the stay abroad. On the other hand, Swedish and British students viewed their host countries more negatively than their home countries before they went abroad. After their sojourn, the assessments of their host countries became slightly more positive, although the change was not statistically significant. The German participants, whose views were rather mixed about their prospective host countries before the sojourn, assessed the host more negatively in comparison with the home country after the study abroad.

Students' opinions about the various aspects of politics, society and culture presented in Table S46 show the British students have a surprisingly negative opinion about the media in their country. On the other hand , they show high appreciation for cultural life at home both before the study abroad and even more so thereafter. French students viewed foreign policy, cultural life and media in their home country more positively after the sojourn than before it. They assessed these aspects of their respective host countries less favourably after the study abroad.

German students on average hardly changed opinion about their home country or their respective host countries, with the exception of greater appreciation of German higher education upon return. Both before and after the sojourn, they viewed the foreign policy and social structure of their respective host countries much more negatively than these elements at home.

Swedish students display the sharpest contrast in their opinions about the home country in comparison with the host. On the one hand, they assessed Swedish foreign policies, immigrant policies and social structure much more favourably than those abroad; on the other hand, they preferred cultural life abroad to that at home. Whereas these opinions remained more or less constant, their view on higher education in their host country was more negative after the study abroad period, thereby assessing it considerably less favourable than their opinion on higher education at home.

American students viewed cultural life, customs, traditions and foreign policies of their host countries more favourably than those at home. This was true both before and after their study abroad period. Not so for higher education in their respective host countries: many American students were quite disappointed about it.

Table S47
U.S. Study Abroad Participants' Opinion about Culture and Society of Study Abroad Host Country and Home Country Before and After the Study Abroad Period in Comparison to U.S. Non-participating Students (in arithmetic means)*

		On foreign country		On home country	
		SAP-partici-pants	Non-partici-pants	SAP-partici-pants	Non-partici-pants
Post secondary or higher	Before	2.2	2.2	2.1	1.8
education	After**	2.8	2.5	2.1	1.9
Governmental foreign	Before	2.7	3.0	3.4	3.0
policies in general	After	3.0	3.1	3.7	3.1
Treatment of recently	Before	3.3	3.0	3.3	3.2
arrived immigrant groups	After	3.8	3.1	3.2	3.2
Cultural life (e.g. art,	Before	1.7	2.0	2.3	2.0
music, theater, literature)	After	1.6	1.8	2.5	2.4
Television, radio	Before	2.5	2.7	2.6	2.3
newspapers, magazines	After	2.3	2.8	2.5	2.1
Customs, traditions	Before	2.0	2.0	2.6	2.6
	After	2.0	1.8	2.6	2.6
Social structure (e.g.	Before	2.7	2.6	2.7	2.7
family, class system)	After	3.0	2.6	2.8	2.8

* On a scale from 1 = "highly positive opinion" to 5 = "highly negative opinion"
** In the case of the U.S. non-participants: replies to the follow-up survey about one year later.
Source: Pre-Study Abroad Questionnaire SAEP US D 30 and Post-Study Abroad Questionnaire SAEP US F 36

Table S47 provides an overview of the extent to which the Americans participating in the study abroad programmes under evaluation here differ from students who did not participate in these programmes. In the case of the comparison group, they were asked to state their opinion about the foreign country they knew best.[1] On average, views on foreign countries hardly differed between the American study abroad participants and the students of the American comparison group, before as well as after the one group's study period abroad. The participants had a more positive view on cultural life in the host country before they went abroad, which was also evident afterwards. In regard to foreign policy, they had a more positive view before the stay abroad than after. Concerning higher education and social structure abroad, the appreciation of the host country declined on the part of the study abroad participants to the extent that it was less favourable than that of the comparison group.

Up to this point, the analysis has been simplified in the sense that students' opinions from each country were recorded in the aggregate with respect to all host countries. It is presumably more realistic to expect students' views to differ depending upon the specific country they have visited. This more complex analysis was constructed with the help of Diagrams S7 - S13.

The first question to pursue is whether certain countries tend to be seen positively or negatively by students from certain other countries across all areas analyzed. This should provide a clue as to whether some "emotional loading" could overshadow perceptions. Only one example of this was found. Germany was viewed in four of seven aspects most negatively by British students prior to the study abroad period. This pattern disappears, however, after the study abroad.

A second avenue to explore is whether a certain country - again, across all areas analyzed - is viewed more positively or more negatively by students from other countries after the study abroad period than it had been assessed before. Does a country gain a more positive or a more negative image? Only one case stood out. The USA in all aspects except media was viewed more positively by the study abroad participants it hosted - after their stay there - as compared with their relatively negative opinion prior to arrival.

The third question is whether students from certain countries view all others very positively or very negatively, either before or after the study abroad period, and whether any change takes place in this respect. Again, there is only one category of students who show a decided change in attitude. Swedish students, who actually viewed their own country most positively prior to their study abroad period, assessed their respective host countries more positively in the majority of aspects after the sojourn than they did before.

---

[1]   Unlike Table S46, the arithmetic means in Table S47 also include replies from students responding to the Pre-Study Abroad Questionnaire only.

Diagram S 7
Students' Opinion about Host Country Governmental Foreign Policies, by Home Country (in arithmetic means)*

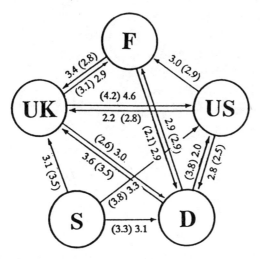

* Scale from 1 = "strongly emphasized" to 5 = "not at all emphasized"

Assessment of home country is presented in circles, those of the host country to the arrows, whereby the direction of the arrows represents the home ---> host relationship.

Source: Post-Study Abroad Questionnaire SAEP F 8, 9, 10 (F213-324)

Diagram S 8
Students' Opinion about Host Country Policies Concerning Recently Arrived Immigrant Groups (in arithmetic means)*

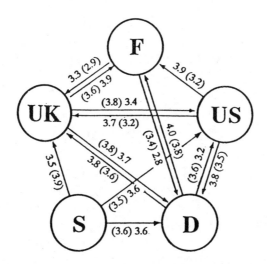

Diagram S 9
Students' Opinion about Host Country Cultural Life (in arithmetic means)*

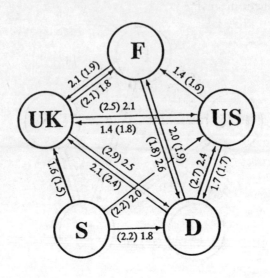

Diagram S 10
Students' Opinion about Host Country Media (Television, Radio, Newspapers, Magazines) (in arithmetic means)*

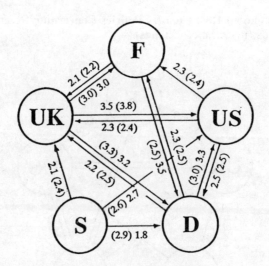

Diagram S 11
Students' Opinion about Host Country Post-secondary or Higher Education (in arithmetic means)*

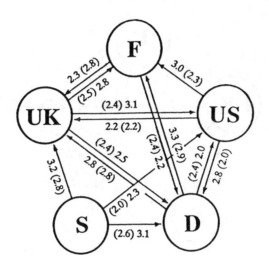

Diagram S 12
Students' Opinion about Host Country Customs and Traditions
(in arithmetic means)*

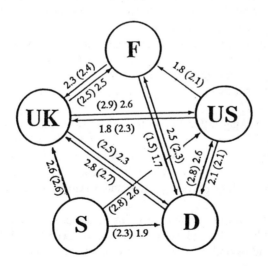

Diagram S 13
Students' Opinion about Host Country Social Structure
(in arithmetic means)*

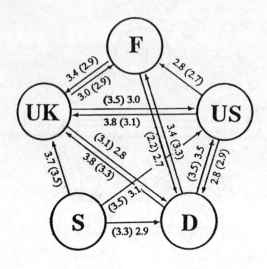

For the fourth, and most central, portion of this analysis, the underlying question is whether students' opinions indicate a more or less consistent hierarchy among the countries with respect to students' opinions on each of the aspects in question. (Sweden can only be included in an indirect way, since the number of students going to that country is so small.) The patterns which emerge are different for each of the seven aspects investigated:

- Concerning media, the opinions remained stable in regard to the extremes. British media were viewed most positively both before and after the study abroad period. On the other hand, American media continued to be viewed most negatively. A moderate change can be observed in opinions related to the other three countries.
- There was no striking difference in the pre-sojourn stage concerning students' opinions on policies governing newly arrived immigrants, and afterwards only a moderate change was noted. Sweden might be put in first place both before and after the study abroad period. The most negative views were directed at the USA before the study abroad period and toward France in the post study abroad phase.
- The pattern of change is similar for opinions about social structure in the host countries: Sweden in first place, with Germany second, both before and after the study abroad period. Britain is viewed much more negatively in this respect after the study abroad period than before.
- In the case of customs and traditions, a rank order is somewhat more consistent after the study abroad period than before. Germany is more clearly in

first place in this respect according to students' opinions after their period abroad. There is one exception, however, in that the American students view German customs and traditions relatively negatively.

- Views on the foreign policies of the individual study abroad host countries showed a consistent hierarchy before the students departed for the period abroad. Again, Sweden might be put in first place, followed by Germany, France, Britain and finally the USA. After the study abroad period, this pattern dissolved completely.
- Concerning views on cultural life, the situation was the reverse. Before study abroad, there was no clear pattern in the opinions about the various countries. After study abroad, cultural life in France was most highly appreciated, followed by that in the UK. Cultural life in Sweden was ranked least favourably.
- The pattern in views on the system of higher education in the study abroad host countries is especially complex. The majority allow the conclusion that British higher education was viewed most negatively whereas American and German higher education were seen most positively prior to the study abroad period. Both French and German higher education were rated lower after the study abroad period, whereas the British was rated higher. After the study abroad period, American higher education is more positively viewed than the German, and British higher education viewed less negatively than the French. Americans are somewhat of an exception in that both before and after their study abroad, they view British higher education most positively. It is not known to what extent this exception may be attributed to the lack of a language barrier.

Altogether, there is little evidence of sweeping stereotypes which determine positive or negative views about the respective host countries for the study abroad. Rather, opinions relate to individual aspects in these countries, and in many cases are shown to have changed as a result of the period abroad. The opinions finally emerging, however, do not necessarily contradict conventional wisdom in pointing to appreciation of French cultural life, British media, German customs and traditions, Swedish social structures and American universities.

6.4   International Orientations

It has been shown that experiences in other countries contribute to increasing knowledge about those countries and in some cases to changing opinions about those and the home country. The heightened international knowledge can lead as well to greater appreciation of common needs, interests and prospects in international relations and co-operation. Consequently, three instruments were employed to tap students' international attitudes. In the first, they were asked to describe their own values about other countries and global political issues. In the second, they were to assess international policies and types of co-operation. In the third, their attitudes were polled specifically about European co-operation.

Table S48
European Students' Global Awareness Before and After the Study Abroad Period, by Home Country (in arithmetic means)*

		Home country				
		UK	F	D	S	Total
Desire to travel to foreign nations**	Before	1.3	1.2	1.4	1.2	1.3
	After	1.2	1.2	1.2	1.2	1.2
Belief that there is a need for	Before	1.4	1.6	1.2	1.4	1.3
closer cooperation among nations	After	1.4	1.3	1.2	1.4	1.3
Desire for international peace	Before	1.6	2.0	1.2	1.4	1.5
	After	1.5	1.5	1.2	1.4	1.3
Desire to meet and interact with	Before	1.7	1.5	1.5	1.7	1.5
persons not from your own country	After	1.4	1.4	1.6	1.4	1.5
Negative feelings about foreigners	Before	4.2	4.3	4.6	4.5	4.5
	After	4.2	4.4	4.4	4.3	4.3
View that values of your own society are not universal and that values of	Before	2.0	1.4	1.5	1.7	1.6
other societies are also valid	After	1.5	1.4	1.5	1.7	1.5
Respect for achievements of nations	Before	1.8	2.0	1.9	1.6	1.9
other than your own	After	1.8	1.8	1.8	1.8	1.8
Concern with problems of	Before	2.5	2.2	2.1	2.3	2.2
Third World countries	After	2.1	2.2	2.0	2.3	2.1
Critical views of your own country	Before	2.4	2.6	2.1	2.7	2.4
	After	2.4	2.6	1.9	2.4	2.2
Average	Before	1.8	1.8	1.6	1.7	1.7
	After	1.7	1.7	1.6	1.7	1.6

* Scale from 1 = "considerable" to 5 = "non-existent" (question: "How would you describe your position on the following?")
** The sequence of categories does not correspond the questionnaire, but rather is a rank order according to replies prior to the study abroad period
Source: Pre-Study Abroad Questionnaire SAEP D 43 (D 525-533) and Post-Study Abroad Questionnaire SAEP F 29 (F 744-752)

The first instrument was derived from a scale developed by the American Educational Testing Service in 1981, entitled "International Awareness and Orientation I." This was part of a survey on "College Students' Knowledge and Beliefs: A Survey of Global Understanding". All seventeen items of the survey were incorporated within the questionnaires distributed in the American portion of the present study (study abroad participants as well as the comparison group), and students were asked to reply on a seven-point scale. In the European questionnaires, the list of items was reduced to nine, and a five-point scale was utilised for the students' responses. The following analysis is based only on the nine items which appeared in both questionnaires. Since identical items were presented in the Pre- and Post Study Abroad Questionnaires, it was possible to measure whatever change occurred in global awareness during the sojourn. In addition to measuring changes in responses to each item singly, comparisons were made of the various student groups with respect to their scores on a "global understanding" index constructed through factor analysis.

Considering first the single items, there was an especially pronounced desire to travel to foreign nations (1.3) and a belief in the need for closer international co-operation (1.3 in the case of the European students on the five-point scale, and 1.6 for the Americans, on the seven-point scale) already prior to the sojourn. Nearly as strong overall was the students' desire to meet and interact with people from other countries. They had few if any negative feelings about foreigners. They felt that the values of their own society were not universal, and that the values of other societies were also valid. Most sought international peace. Only with respect to three issues were the views less than unanimous: respect for achievement of other nations, concern with problems of Third World countries, and critical views on one's own country.

As Table S48 shows, global awareness was only marginally higher after the period abroad. If it had increased at all, there was only a slight increase across countries and fields of study where the scores had been lowest prior to departure (France and the UK, and Foreign Languages, respectively).

In this context, it is interesting to look at the replies of the American comparison group. The global awareness of the Americans who participated in the study abroad programmes was considerably higher than that of students who did not participate (see Table S49). Since the increase in the case of the comparison group within a year was equivalent to students participating in a study abroad programme, it appears that the increase noted for the students who went abroad might have been due to general socialisation in higher education rather than to specific experiences abroad during that interval of time.

All these findings lead us to conclude that students participating in study abroad programmes are a select group in demonstrating a high global awareness already prior to their period abroad. It is not surprising that, under these conditions, they do not move any further in that direction than what might generally be expected during the continued socialisation in higher education anyway. Nor is it surprising that significant changes could be observed only among those subgroups which were shown to be somewhat less globally oriented before departing for studies abroad.

As already mentioned, a second instrument on "international understanding" addressed the students' views on policies regarding international mobility, economic co-operation, and defence policy. This was based largely on the "International Awareness and Orientation II" scale of the previously mentioned ETS survey. Since this was heavily influenced by the American political environment, it had to be adapted in Europe to conform to the target group of the current evaluation. A set of fourteen items was administered to the European students, and a list of thirteen to the USA. Of these, ten were similar or identical in both versions. Again, the American questionnaire used a seven-point scale, whereas a five-point scale was employed for the European. The statements in the questionnaire describe opinions in a stereotyped manner, but it was nevertheless expected that students would recognise these as fairly common views even if some of the statements - as students pointed out later - were rather extreme. The extent to which this polarised the answers could not be determined.

Table S49
U.S. Study Abroad Participants' Global Awareness* in Comparison with U.S. Non-participating Students (in arithmetic means)**

		US SAP students***	US comparison group***
Actual or desired travel	Before	1.4	1.9
to foreign nations	After****	1.3	2.3
Need for closer cooperation	Before	1.6	2.0
among nations	After	1.5	2.0
Desire for international peace	Before	1.7	2.0
	After	1.5	1.9
Desire to meet and interact with	Before	1.4	2.3
persons not from your home country	After	1.5	2.5
Negative feelings about	Before	5.6	3.5
foreigners	After	5.9	5.5
View that values of your own society are not universal and that values of	Before	1.9	2.4
other societies are just as valid	After	1.7	2.3
Respect for historical, cultural etc. traditions and achievement of nations	Before	1.7	2.2
other than your own	After	1.6	2.2
Concern with problems of	Before	3.1	3.4
Third World countries	After	3.1	3.6
Critical views of your own	Before	3.2	3.6
country	After	2.9	3.6
Average	Before	2.0	2.7
	After	1.9	2.5

*	Presented here are the replies to only the 9 (out of 17) items which are identical or similar to items in the European students' questionnaire
**	Scale from 1 = "extensive" to 7 = "non-existent" (Question: "How would you describe your position on the following?")
***	Pre-Study Abroad data also include replies from students who subsequently did not reply to the Post-Study Abroad Questionnaire
****	In the case of the U.S. non-participating students: replies to the follow-up survey about one year later
Source:	Pre-Study Abroad Questionnaire SAEP US D 33 (US D 336-349) and Post-Study Abroad Questionnaire US F (US F 815-831)

In their response, students endorsed internationally oriented policies less strongly than items in the "global awareness" scale. Almost all students were emphatic in believing in political freedom as well as the right to leave one's country and also return to it unhindered. The results are set out in Table S50.

Table S50
European Students' International Understanding Before and After the Study Abroad Period, by Home Country (in arithmetic means)*

		Home	country			
		UK	F	D	S	Total
Freedom and right to be mobile						
Everyone should have the right to	Before	1.5	1.2	1.1	1.1	1.2
leave his country and return to it	After	1.6	1.1	1.2	1.1	1.2
Political freedom is a basic						
human right and no government	Before	1.6	1.2	1.3	1.2	1.3
should be permitted to abridge it	After	1.7	1.3	1.4	1.3	1.4
Any individual should be allowed	Before	2.3	1.6	1.4	1.6	1.6
to live whatever country he choses	After	2.3	1.5	1.5	2.0	1.7
It is none of your country's business						
if other governments restrict the	Before	4.0	4.2	4.3	4.6	4.3
personal freedom of their citizens**	After	4.1	4.3	4.1	4.5	4.2
The immigration of foreigners to your						
country should be kept down so that it	Before	3.3	3.5	3.7	3.6	3.6
can provide for its own people first**	After	3.4	3.6	3.4	3.7	3.5
Cosmopolitan						
You prefer to be a citizen of the	Before	3.0	2.9	2.8	3.0	2.9
world rather than of any other country	After	2.8	2.6	2.7	2.7	2.7
There should be a world government						
with the power to make laws that would	Before	3.9	3.9	3.0	3.3	3.4
be binding to all its member nations	After	3.2	3.8	2.9	3.2	3.2
Aid						
Your country should send food and						
materials to any other country that	Before	2.6	2.7	2.3	2.3	2.4
needs them	After	2.3	2.7	2.3	2.4	2.4
People in developed nations should						
voluntarily cut back on their food						
consumption and contribute food to						
the inadequately fed in underdeveloped	Before	2.4	3.1	2.8	2.3	2.7
nations	After	2.2	3.1	3.0	2.5	2.8
Favouring armament						
People should refuse to engage in any						
war, no matter how serious the con-	Before	3.2	3.2	2.4	3.3	2.8
sequences to their country may be**	After	3.3	3.0	2.6	3.3	2.9

continued Table S 50

		Home country				
		UK	F	D	S	Total
The best way to keep your own country out of war is to keep it so well-armed that no other nations would dare to	Before	3.7	3.7	4.0	3.7	3.9
attack it	After	3.8	4.1	3.9	3.7	3.9
Others						
Environmental protection should be	Before	2.1	1.9	1.5	2.0	1.7
regulated by an international authority	After	2.0	2.1	1.6	1.8	1.8
No duties are more impotant than	Before	3.8	3.9	4.2	4.0	4.0
duties towards one's own country	After	3.9	3.9	4.3	4.0	4.1
Foreign enterprises should not be allowed to have substantial	Before	3.6	4.3	4.0	3.6	3.9
holdings in your country	After	3.8	4.5	4.0	3.6	4.0

*   Scale from 1 = "strongly agree" to 5 = "strongly disagree" (question: "Please indicate the extent to which you agree or disagree with the following statements")
**   Negative factor loading
Source: Pre-Study Abroad Questionnaire SAEP D 44 (D 534-547) and Post Study Abroad Questionnaire SAEP F 30 (F 553-566)

Again, attitudes towards internationally-oriented politics, as measured by the "international understanding" scale, hardly changed during the study abroad period. Among European as well as American students, the increase on average was about 0.1, which is not significant (at the 99% level). As Table S51 indicates, the "international understanding" of the Americans participating in study abroad programmes initially was on average 0.4 higher than that of the comparison group, but the increase on the part of the comparison group was not less than on the part of the study abroad participants. European students emphasised world citizenship and a world government slightly more after the study abroad period, whereas the Americans indicated they would be more in favour of aid to developing countries.

Factor analyses of the European data of the Pre- and Post-Study Abroad Questionnaires produced similar factor structures. They were similar in suggesting four indices: (1) Emphasis on freedom and mobility; (2) Cosmopolitan orientation; (3) Emphasis on aid to developing countries; and (4) Attitude towards disarmament.(The higher the score, the greater the emphasis).

In comparing the indices by country (see Table S52), it was found that
- German students emphasised disarmament and cosmopolitan attitudes most strongly. "Freedom and mobility" was as strongly emphasized as in the case of Swedish students. On average, German students did not change their attitudes much during the sojourn. At most, there was slightly less emphasis on freedom and mobility at the end of the period abroad.
- The Swedish students' emphasis on freedom and mobility declined slightly during the stay abroad, as did their support for foreign aid, which was relatively high prior to the sojourn. On the other hand, their reluctance to endorse cosmopolitan views decreased slightly.

- French and British students scored very low on almost all indices: the only exception was the British students' favourable view on aid to developing countries, which was even more pronounced after their period abroad. Both British and French became less reserved in their cosmopolitan views.

Table S51

U.S. Study Abroad Participants' International Understanding Before and After the Study Abroad Period in Comparison to U.S. Non-participating Students (in arithmetic means)*

		SAP students**	Comparison group**
Freedom and right to be mobile			
It is none of our business if other governments restrict the personal freedom of their citizens	Before After***	2.6 2.5	2.7 2.5
The immigration of foreigners to my country should be kept down so that we can provide for our own people first	Before After	3.8 3.6	4.1 4.0
Cosmopolitan			
I prefer to be a citizen of the world rather than of any country	Before After	4.4 4.7	3.8 3.7
We should have a World Government with the power to make laws that would be binding to all its member nations	Before After	3.5 3.4	3.5 3.4
Aid			
I believe that my country should send food and materials to any country that needs them	Before After	4.4 4.8	4.2 4.2
It is our responsibility to do everything possible to prevent people from starving anywhere in the world	Before After	5.1 5.5	4.8 5.0
Others			
Since the world's supplies of essential minerals are limited, the mining and distribution of mineral resources should be controlled by an international authority	Before After	4.1 4.0	3.8 3.6
No duties are more important than duties towards one's country	Before After	2.6 2.2	3.2 3.0
We should not allow foreign business enterprises to have substantial holdings in our country	Before After	3.4 4.1	3.9 3.5
Categories presented to U.S. students only			
Pacific demonstrations - picketing missile bases, peace walks, etc. are harmful to the best interests of my home country	Before After	2.2 1.9	2.8 2.8
Patriotism and loyalty are the first and most important requirements of a good citizen	Before After	3.1 2.6	3.7 3.3
Immigrants should not be permitted to come into our country if they compete with our own workers	Before After	3.0 2.8	3.3 2.9
An international authority should be established and given direct control over the production of nuclear energy in all countries	Before After	4.1 4.0	3.9 3.7

*	Scale from 1 "strongly disagree" to 7 = "strongly agree"
**	Pre-Study Abroad data also include replies by students who subsequently did not reply to the Post-Study Abroad Questionnaire
***	In the case of the U.S. non-participating students: replies to the follow-up survey about one year later

Source: Pre-Study Abroad Questionnaire SAEP US 34 D and Post-Study Abroad Questionnaire
SAEP US 39 F

Analysing the replies of the American study abroad participants in a similar way brought out a substantial increase in their support for foreign aid as well as a moderate increase in their endorsement of freedom and mobility. In various respects, American study abroad participants after the sojourn considered patriotism to a lesser extent the first responsibility of a citizen and they were less concerned about the possible harmful repercussions of peaceful demonstrations. On the other hand, more of the American students after the study abroad (than before) tended to favour restrictions on foreign business operations in the USA.

Table S52
Changes of European Student's Global Awareness and Global Understanding - Indices, by Home Country (in percentage of students)

Index	Measures	Home country				
		UK	F	D	S	Total
	High before (1.0 - 1.75)*	50.0	46.5	65.8	54.3	58.1
	High after (1.0-1.75)	56.7	62.8	74.7	54.0	70.0
Global awareness	Considerable increase**	15.5	7.3	10.7	11.4	11.3
	Considerable decrease	5.2	2.4	7.1	2.9	5.5
	High before (1.0 - 1.75)	36.9	65.7	70.2	70.2	62.6
Favoring freedom	High after (1.0-1.75)	39.0	60.4	56.9	54.0	55.4
and right to be	Considerable increase	17.9	14.3	5.8	8.1	5.8
mobile	Considerable decrease	11.7	18.9	16.8	8.3	14.8
	High before (1.0 - 2.25)	10.0	18.0	32.4	16.6	23.6
Cosmopolitan	High after (1.0-2.25)	25.0	26.2	38.8	29.7	32.9
view	Considerable increase	33.3	29.7	24.8	30.6	28.1
	Considerable decrease	11.7	18.9	16.8	8.3	14.8
	High before (1.0 - 2.25)	48.3	43.3	42.6	54.0	44.2
	High after (1.0-2.25)	53.3	31.7	38.8	37.8	40.7
Favoring aid	Considerable increase	21.7	28.9	19.1	16.2	20.7
	Considerable decrease	11.7	21.1	16.9	24.3	17.3
	High before (1.0 - 2.25)	53.4	48.6	28.0	48.6	38.7
Favoring	High after (1.0-2.25)	48.4	36.6	31.4	52.7	37.9
armament	Considerable increase	8.6	9.1	7.1	-	6.7
	Considerable decrease	8.6	18.2	6.4	-	7.5

*   Arithmetic mean of replies to all corresponding items
**   Average difference of score for all corresponding items of .50 and more

Source: Pre-Study Abroad Questionnaire SAEP D 43-44 and Post-Study Abroad
          Questionnaire SAEP 29-30 (VGLOBD, VGLOBF, VGLOBX, VIUFRED,
          VIUFREF, VIUFREX, VIUCOSD, VIUCOSF, VIUCOSX, VIUAIDD, VIUAIDF,
          VIUAIDX, VIUARMD, VIUARMF, VIUARMX)

As regards the relationship between home and host country, there was only one consistent finding: students going to Germany emphasised freedom and mobility aspects more strongly upon their return, whereas students going to the USA emphasised freedom and mobility less strongly afterwards.

The few noteworthy findings for the European students when categorised by field of study include the finding that, prior to study abroad, Natural Science students were most strongly cosmopolitan, in favour of aid·to developing countries and in favour of disarmament. They hardly changed their views during the stay abroad except for a decrease in favourable opinion about aid to developing countries. Foreign language students changed their views substantially during their stay abroad. Before, they had been least in favour of freedom and mobility, least cosmopolitan and second most in favour of armament. After the sojourn, they emerged as one of the fields which endorsed all three aspects most strongly.

In efforts to reduce the complexity of the analysis, what has been said above in relation to Table S52 has taken account of average differences for all students or averages by each home country or field of study. It has to be admitted that in some cases, these averages disguised considerable variations in both directions. To illustrate, if 0.5 is taken as a threshold for noteworthy change, then 28.1 percent of the European students had a stronger cosmopolitan orientation after the study abroad period than they had before. The reverse was true for 14.8 percent of all European students. It can therefore be concluded that study abroad had a noteworthy impact on many students' attitudes toward international relations. This impact could be in either direction and cannot be characterised as overwhelmingly more "international" or more "national-centred."

Attitudes towards European co-operation were addressed in a somewhat similar fashion as for the previous questions. Students were asked to indicate their views in reaction to pre-supplied statements such as "The E.E.C. should be strengthened." In part, these statements combined political opinion with some reasoning about European co-operation, for example "Closer European co-operation is an essential prerequisite to economic progress." The most obvious result as Table S53 shows, is the clear difference in attitudes according to the country from which students come. French students emphasised Europe most strongly for all six items. On a five point-scale(1 = "strong support" to 5 = "strong opposition"), their support was on average 1.7 both prior to the study abroad and after. German students emphasised Europe second most strongly before the stay abroad (1.9). Afterwards they emphasised Europe almost as strongly as the French students (1.8). British students were much more reserved about Europe. This difference by country was much more pronounced than any differences in cultural impact measures discussed above. Their support for Europe somewhat increased from 2.3 prior to the study abroad period to 2.2 thereafter. Again, the average change of attitude is very small and remains below the level of statistical significance. Furthermore, the marginal increase was not found in cases where the attitudes had been positive prior to the study abroad period.

Not surprisingly, Swedish students favoured European integration least (2.6 prior to study abroad and 2.8 after) since the questions did not, in the main, refer to Europe in general, but rather explicitly to the EC or its policies, and Sweden is not a member of the EC. On the more general question on European co-operation in culture and education, Swedish students were even slightly more positively inclined than the British. Finally, the American students were asked about European co-operation after their study period abroad. Their average score was 2.4, i.e. only slightly less supportive than British students prior to their sojourn.

Table S53
European Students' Opinion on European Cooperation Before and After the Study Abroad Period, by Home Country (in arithmetic means)*

				Home country			
		UK	F	D	EC	S	Total EUR
The E.E.C. should	Before	2.2	1.4	1.4	1.6	3.1	1.8
be strengthened	After	2.0	1.3	1.3	1.5	3.0	1.7
Closer European cooperation is an essential prerequisite	Before	1.9	1.3	1.6	1.6	2.4	1.7
to economic progress	After	1.8	1.4	1.6	1.6	2.6	1.8
Only European cooperation can help Europe catch up with the technological advance of the	Before	2.4	1.5	2.0	2.0	2.9	2.1
US and Japan	After	2.2	1.6	1.7	1.8	2.7	1.9
The goal of European political	Before	3.7	4.1	4.1	4.0	3.4	3.9
union is not important	After	3.7	3.9	4.5	4.2	3.3	4.1
European cooperation is less important than worldwide	Before	3.0	3.6	3.5	3.5	2.5	3.3
international cooperation	After	3.1	3.7	3.3	3.3	2.5	3.2
More emphasis should be placed on European cooperation in the	Before	2.2	1.6	1.9	1.9	2.0	1.9
fields of education and culture	After	2.2	1.7	1.8	1.9	2.2	1.9

*　Scale from 1 = "strongly agree" to 5 = "strongly disagree"
Source:　Pre-Study Abroad Questionnaire SAEP D 45 (D 548-553) and Post-Study Abroad
　　　　　Questionnaire SAEP F 31 (F 767-772)

Students from countries which were members of the EC emphasised most strongly that the EC should be strengthened and that the EC was essential to economic progress. These students were slightly less in agreement that political union was important and that the EC was needed in order to stand up to technological competition. In both cases, these aspects were slightly more strongly emphasised upon the students' return to their home countries. Co-operation on educational and cultural matters was stressed both before and after the study period abroad, and there was no difference, on average, between the ratings given at these two periods of time. Finally, students from EC countries were, both before and after the study abroad period, much less inclined to view European co-operation as being more important than, or equally important to, worldwide co-operation.

Altogether, the international orientation of study abroad participants is already high in most cases before they actually go abroad. The subsequent sojourn does not contribute to significantly stronger international interests and opinions if the *average* of replies given by the students is taken as the yardstick. On average, increases are marginal, and as far as comparison is possible, the increases occur similarly for students who do not participate in these programmes. Moderate change towards international orientation is visible among students of those countries and fields who somewhat lagged behind in international orientation prior to departure for study abroad.

6.5 Self-Efficacy

The experience of being exposed to another culture and of communicating frequently with people from another country, might both give a new perspective to the way a person thinks about societies and about him/herself. It could affect students' feelings of self-efficacy, defined as feelings of self worth. It could be assumed that students would lose a bit of self-confidence if their prior perceptions are shaken by experiences in other countries which lead them to rethink what they had known before. Or it could be argued that coping with different cultures and persons helps to improve self-confidence.

In the Pre- and Post-Study Abroad Questionnaires, students were presented with fourteen items on which they were asked to assess themselves in the general areas of social and personal competence. These had been taken from a "Perceived Competence Scale" constructed by the American psychologist Susan Harter. The scale was administered to the students prior to and after the study period abroad.

Factor analysis of the pre-departure and post-study abroad replies revealed three factors (which were more or less identical as regards items loading at least 0.40):
- One factor can be labelled "social confidence", for five items of sociability such as "some students are really easy to like."
- A second factor can be labelled "personal confidence" (it includes such items as "Some students are pretty sure of themselves"). However, only three of the seven supposedly relevant items load highly.
- A third factor can be called "negative self-efficacy," because it was based on negatively phrased items about sociability (i.e. "some students don't think they are very important members of their group") and personal efficacy ("some students feel there are a lot of things about themselves they would change if they could").

Prior to the study abroad period, students tended to be fairly confident. Arithmetic means of replies from all students on items related to social confidence ranged from 2.1 to 2.5 on the scale from 1 = "very true for me" to 4 = "not at all true for me." Those related to personal confidence ranged from 2.2 to 2.4. Con-

Table S54
Changes of Students' Self-Efficiency - Indices, by Home Country
(in percentage of students)

| Index | Measures | Home country | | | | | |
		UK	F	D	S	US	Total
Social	High before (1.0-2.25)*	29.3	24.4	52.1	35.3	38.8	40.1
confidence	High after (1.0-2.25)	27.8	30.7	56.9	28.6	45.9	44.5
+	Considerable increase**	17.3	17.2	9.8	12.9	10.9	11.8
	Considerable decrease	5.8	10.3	7.6	9.7	7.8	7.9
Personal	High before (1.0-2.25)	43.9	4.6	41.3	56.7	71.4	49.1
confidence	High after (1.0-2.25)	45.0	18.6	53.3	48.5	71.2	53.8
+ +	Considerable increase	15.8	9.5	20.5	8.8	20.6	17.8
	Considerable decrease	15.8	14.3	7.5	26.5	19.1	14.6
Negative	High before (2.75-4.0)	6.9	2.3	.7	2.7	5.1	3.3
self-efficacy	High after (2.75-4.0)	-	2.3	4.6	5.3	8.2	5.0
+ + +	Considerable increase	12.5	7.5	5.6	13.5	12.2	9.5
	Considerable decrease	5.4	9.5	6.3	8.1	10.7	8.1

+ Based on "Some students find it hard to make friends" (neg.), "Some students have a lot of friends", "Some students are popular with their classmates", "Some people are really easy to like"

+ + Based on "Some students are pretty sure of themselves", "Some students feel good about the way they act", "Some people are usually sure that what they are doing is the right thing"

+ + + Based on "Some students find it hard to make friends", "Some students feel there are a lot of things about themselves they would change if they could", "Some students don't think they are a very important member of their group", "Some students think maybe they are not a very good person", "Some people wish more people liked them", "Some people aren't very happy with the way they do a lot of things". The question was introduced as follows: "From your experience, rate the following statements by indicating how true each statement is for you, als compared with the hypothetical "some".

* Arithmetic mean of replies to all corresponding items

** Average difference of score for all corresponding items of .50 and more

Source: Pre-Study Abroad Questionnaire SAEP D 25 and Post-Study Abroad Questionnaire SAEP F 24 (VHSSOCD; VHSSOCF; VHSSOCX, VHSCOND, VHSCONF, VHSCONX, VHSSED, VHSSEF, VHSSEX)

versely, means related to negative self-efficacy were in the range between 2.9 and 3.2. There were no significant positive changes in any of the fourteen items. Neither social confidence nor personal confidence was higher, on average, after the study abroad period as compared with before. There were essentially no changes in "negative self-efficacy." This does not mean, however, that there was virtually no change on a more detailed level. Indices based on the three factors revealed (see Table S54) that social confidence increased by 0.5 and more (on the scale from 1 to 4) in 11.8 percent of the cases; whereas 7.9 percent of the students reported a substantial decline in social confidence. There were stronger changes in personal confidence: 17.8 percent of the students became visibly more self-confident, whereas 14.6 percent revealed the opposite.[2]

The French students were least confident socially and personally both before and after the study abroad period. Their score on negative self-efficacy was around average before the study period abroad, but was the most negative upon return. The French differed from students of the other countries most strongly in negative terms as regards "some people are usually sure that what they are doing is the right thing." On the other hand, American students were on average the most personally confident and also rated relatively high in most items of social confidence. They were correspondingly low in most items of negative self-efficacy and differed most strongly from students in other countries as regards "some students feel good about the way they act."

British, German, and Swedish students tend to place between the French and the Americans except in their responses to one item where their responses are markedly extreme: British and Swedish students reacted in the negative when asked about whether the statement "some students are always doing things with a lot of kids" (3.3/3.2 and 3.1/2.9) applied to them. The German students' replies were strongly affirmative (2.1/2.1 as compared to 2.5/2.4 and 2.6/2.7 for the French and American students). These differences might be attributed to the phrasing of the item since "kids" seems to be an appropriate expression for the Americans for relationships with their peers, but British and Swedish students most likely have different associations for that word. On the other hand, the German translations "manche Studenten machen viel mit anderen Leuten zusammen" relates to any kind of persons.

Altogether, the differences are not extreme by country. On average per item, American students' self-confidence after the study abroad period is 0.2 higher than that of French students.

These self-assessments of personality show similar results to those observed for students' international orientations. Such basic views and beliefs do not seem to be substantially changed by the study abroad experience when the average responses of the students are considered. Where there is change, this tends to be for students who were comparatively less internationally oriented and less confident about their competence than the majority of students surveyed prior to the study abroad experience. It could nevertheless be argued that average change should not be the only criterion. One could assume that both an increase and a decrease in international orientation and self-efficacy could be signalling reconsideration and change of values and perceptions due to the experience acquired abroad. However, such ups and downs could best be conceived as likely indicators of reflection and re-orientation only if it could be established that there were systematic links between certain experiences or problems abroad and changes in values

---

[2] The stronger change in the case of personal confidence might be explained by the fact that this index is based on three items only, as compared with five and six items, respectively. Thus any change in nature of the reply is more likely to be calculated as a substantial change for stochastical reasons.

and self-perception. As the corresponding analysis shows (in chapter 8), no systematic relationships of this kind were noted.

6.6 Summary

Students obviously augmented their knowledge about the culture, politics and society of their respective host countries to a considerable extent during their study abroad period. The change in knowledge was not reflected, however, in changes in their values regarding international issues. Most of the participants were already internationally oriented before they went abroad and they had hardly moved further in this direction after their experience abroad. Nor did students change significantly on average, in their personal and social self-confidence. Whatever changes in values and self-confidence were observed to be significant at all were noted for students who had lagged slightly behind others before the study abroad period. Speaking about averages, however, obscures the fact that changes of values and attitudes did take place, for individual students, in both directions to about the same extent (many of the changes therefore cancelled each other out).

Differences according to home country and field of study were relatively small. The ones concerning European co-operation were the most obvious, with British students less enthusiastic about European co-operation than the German and, notably, the French students.

Asked about their opinion on various aspects of the culture, politics, and society of their home and host countries, study abroad participants failed to express any generally negative or positive attitudes in either direction. Instead, their opinions very specifically addressed certain aspects. Changes of opinion did not all head in the same direction, but did seem to dissolve some stereotyped views held prior to the study abroad period. The opinions which finally emerged - about culture, society, and politics in each of the five countries surveyed - did not necessarily contradict conventional wisdom.

Chapter 7

The Importance of Study Abroad for the Career

7.1 The Questions Raised

Study abroad programmes commonly aim to advance participants' academic qualifications, improve their foreign language proficiency and encourage the students' personal development by challenging them with unfamiliar cultural experiences. In many cases, this is connected with the expectation that qualifications and competences acquired in the study abroad will later prove useful in the graduates' careers[1]. The degree to which this expectation is explicitly placed in the foreground as an objective varies from one programme to the next and from one student to the next. However, in almost every case, there is some expectation that study abroad will positively affect participants' careers.

The current study addressed three major questions in the relationship between study abroad and a subsequent career:

- To what extent would employment prospects be more favourable if part of the higher education was undertaken abroad? Are there advantages in terms of access to interesting and professionally suitable jobs or high income?
- Do participants in study abroad programmes later take assignments abroad in international organisations, or in areas where knowledge is required of foreign languages, the behaviours of other cultures, and scientific and other developments in other countries? In this same respect, what dimensions does study abroad offer, over and above an internationally oriented degree pursued in a single country?
- Is study abroad profitable for a career even when it does not require participants to use a foreign language or systematically study the conditions of another country?

The directors, as explained in the first volume, assessed the possible career benefits of study abroad, partly on the feedback they had received from the graduates in their programmes. In addition, the 1984/85 participants speculated about the professional advantages that might accrue from their sojourns. However, to gain a more specific picture of the type of career situation that can be expected of former study abroad participants and the use that can be made of academic qualifications developed abroad, the study had to be expanded to include a cohort of students who had studied abroad and already graduated, in the four European countries surveyed. The analysis of the graduates begins in Section 7.3, below.

---

[1]   The terms "career," "employment," "occupation," "profession," and "job" are used interchangeably in this chapter.

7.2   Anticipated Occupational Advantages of Study Abroad

The 1984/85 study abroad participants returning from their sojourns were largely optimistic about the future occupational utility of those experiences. As shown in Table S55, three-quarters of this group felt their study abroad had been worthwhile - or extremely worthwhile - with regard to career prospects. French study abroad students were by far the most positive about the effects of study abroad, with nearly three-quarters (70.7%) answering that it was "extremely worthwhile." English (48.3%) and German (46.6%) students rated study abroad as extremely worthwhile also, in contrast to much lower percentages of American (30.1%) and Swedish (24.3%) students.

Table S55
Expected Occupational Utility of Study Abroad as Seen by Returning Study Abroad Students, by Home Country (in percentage of students)

| | Home country | | | | | |
	UK	F	D	S	US	Total
Extremely worthwhile with regard to career prospects	48.3	70.7	46.6	24.3	30.1	41.9
Worthwhile with regard to career prospects	34.5	22.0	34.0	37.8	36.1	33.9
Hardly worthwhile with regard to career prospects*	17.2	7.3	19.5	37.9	33.9	24.2
Very useful for achieving professional/ work-related goals	46.6	60.9	46.1	42.9	.	48.1
Useful for achieving professional/ work-related goals	34.5	26.1	38.8	42.9	.	36.4
Hardly useful for achieving professional/work-related goals*	19.0	13.0	15.2	14.3	.	15.4
Anticipate that career or work-related roles will involve:						
- Utilizing the particular expertise with regard to the SAP host country	59.6	62.2	63.9	41.2	50.4	57.1
- Utilizing the general international experience obtained through SAP	78.8	86.7	79.6	73.5	89.6	82.9
- Considerable contact/cooperation with SAP host country	48.1	51.1	44.2	47.1	44.8	45.9
- Considerable international contact/cooperation	61.5	73.3	59.9	55.9	63.2	62.3
- Living and working in SAP host country	46.2	28.9	44.9	29.4	48.8	43.2
- Living and working in other foreign country	51.9	44.4	57.1	64.7	60.0	56.6

*   Value of 3 - 5 on a scale from 1 = "extremely worthwhile" or "most probably" to 5 = "not at all worthwhile" or "not likely at all"
Source: Post-Study Abroad Questionnaire SAEP F 52, 57, 58 (F 939, 949 - 955)

The data when viewed by field of study (European students only) showed that the Foreign Language students estimated that study abroad would be extremely worthwhile for their careers, whereas less than half the Law students and a third of those in Natural Sciences felt this way.

A more distinctly expressed question directed only at European students, asking whether they thought the period of study abroad would help them attain their professional aims, yielded similarly positive assessments. However, the different nuance of this question evokes consideration of external market conditions more than the less precisely delineated question above. This may be one reason why the response to the second question shows fewer differences from one country to the next, and why the responses by field of study reveal a trend in the opposite direction of that noted above. In response to the second question, only a third of the Foreign Language students answered that they thought it was very probable that their study abroad would help in attaining their professional aims, whereas a larger percentage - 40-59 percent - of the students in other fields thought their study abroad would have this effect.

There are three plausible explanations for these various findings. First, of the goals pursued by many study abroad programmes, the promotion of career prospects is not centrally involved. For example, it appears that the American programmes as a whole put less emphasis on professional qualification through study abroad, and more on cultural enrichment from experiences abroad. Second, the occupational utility of study abroad is rated particularly highly in cases in which there is also a phase of work placement abroad; of the programmes surveyed, only those from Britain, France and Germany included a work placement component abroad. Third, the labour market in certain countries may reinforce the assumption that experiences abroad are not adequately rewarded. Furthermore, the difficult employment situation for humanities graduates in many countries may dampen the hopes of Foreign Language students that they will be able to obtain jobs directly in line with the specialisation of their higher education degree.

The details of how highly students estimate the probability of using the skills acquired abroad in future activity are also shown in Table S55.

- 82.9 percent of the study abroad students thought they would generally be able to use the international experiences acquired abroad. This was stressed most frequently by the American students who otherwise had been very hesitant about the direct labour market utility of study abroad.
- 57.1 percent expected they would be able to utilise the particular expertise acquired from study abroad in their subsequent occupation.
- Almost half the study abroad students expected that, in their future occupation, they would have close contacts with the study abroad country or that they would live and work there. Somewhat higher was the percentage of students who expected to have such occupational contacts and to work in other countries than the study abroad host.

The Table does not show the results by field of study, which were somewhat surprising on two counts. For one, students of the Natural Sciences, although the least optimistic about the possibility of using knowledge acquired abroad in their occupation, expected to live and work in the study abroad country in proportions equal to students in other fields of study. For the other, the Foreign Language students considered that returning to live and work in the study abroad country was most improbable. Some of the testimony later quoted from the graduate survey sheds light on why students may plan to live and work in the host country even though not impelled primarily by professional reasons to do so.

How firm are students' career plans? Almost half (48.6%) the students felt they were largely decided about their choice of future career before they studied abroad. Apparent differences in the degree of their determination could be attributed to the labour market situation or the occupational bent of their degree courses, and fields of study. For example, two-thirds of the students in Engineering were decided on their future careers, but this was true of less than a third of the Foreign Language students. There were hardly any differences according to country.

After the study abroad, the percentage of students who felt their future careers were largely decided was somewhat higher (61.5%). The establishment of career options usually evolves as students advance in higher education, so one should not assume on the basis of the current findings that the study abroad experience itself accelerates or substantially facilitates the establishment of students' career options. It may only influence their decisions about strategies to pursue to use the skills acquired during the study abroad.

At any rate, after the sojourn, many students were convinced that study abroad would be important to their future occupations. This was often the case even for students who had no prior expectation that they would be in occupations which required foreign language proficiency and/or knowledge of and contacts in the study abroad host country. It is striking that many students did expect to be involved in work which would in some way relate to the host country of their study abroad.

Do the gains from study abroad in fact turn out to be of such importance? We examine this question in considering the results of the graduate survey.

7.3   Survey of European Graduates

7.3.1   Survey Method

In the case of the four European countries, a questionnaire was sent in 1986 to former participants (in the study abroad programmes analysed here) who had graduated between 1980 and 1984. Altogether, 485 graduates were surveyed in this manner:
- 194 former participants in British programmes;
- 115 in the German programmes;
- 83 in French programmes; and
- 66 former participants in Swedish programmes.

In the case of the USA, telephone interviews were conducted with 77 individuals who graduated from the four American institutions between 1960 and 1981 and who in their third year of university study, had spent a year abroad in one of the four European countries. The analysis in the remainder of this chapter is based only on the results of the questionnaire sent to European graduates. The results of the American interviews are presented in a separate publication.[2]

7.3.2 Description of the Sample

The average age of the graduates who responded to the survey was twenty-seven. Such a young age was to be expected, since the investigation included European graduates who had concluded their studies on average about a year and a quarter prior to responding to the questionnaire. Only 6.8 percent of the graduates interviewed were over 30. This substantiates the findings based on the programme survey in 1984/85 that most students participate in the study abroad programmes when they are in their early twenties.

Table S56 shows that the majority of German and Swedish graduates were 26-30 years old at the time of the questionnaire; the English and French graduates were two years younger on average. The differences can be attributed to the age on beginning studies, the duration of the study, and the period of time that had elapsed since graduation. Time taken from studies for military service or professional training also accounts for age variations.

Table S56
Age of European Graduates at Beginning and Completion of Studies and when Surveyed, by Home Country (in arithmetic means of years)

	Home country				
	UK	F	D	S	Total
Age at enrollment	18.8	18.4	20.2	20.3	19.3
Length of study in higher education	4.1	4.5	5.5	4.4	4.5
Age at graduation	22.9	22.9	25.7	24.7	23.8
Length of time since graduation	3.3	3.3	2.8	3.7	3.3
Age when surveyed	26.2	26.2	28.2	28.4	27.1

* Estimated based on information supplied concerning year of birth, year first enrolled in higher education and year of graduation

Source: Questionnaire for Graduates SAEP G 1, 13 and 14 (G 113-114, G 135-138)

Not much over a third (39.3%) of the graduates sampled were female. This again is consistent with the gender profile of the European 1984/85 study abroad par-

---

[2] Carlson, J. et al. *Study Abroad: The Experience of American Undergraduates in Western Europe and in the United States* (forthcoming).

ticipants (41.9% of whom were female). It should be remembered that, in the study abroad programmes examined here, there is a preponderance of fields of study which customarily attract few female students. Thus, for the individual fields of study, there is not any under-representation of women participating in study abroad. The differing proportion of women among the British (53.1%), French (44.6%), German (27.8%) and Swedish (12.1%) respondents is to be attributed mainly to the distribution of fields of study.

As was the case for the 1984/85 group, the graduates were predominantly citizens of the country of their sending institutions in the study abroad. 3.3 percent of the graduates did not have citizenship from the country of the sending institution of higher education.

Among the graduates, there is a greater portion of former university students (in contrast to students in higher education institutions outside the university sector) than among the 1984/85 group. As far as their parents were concerned, slightly more than a third of the graduates' fathers were themselves university graduates, as were a fifth of the mothers. The respective figures by country were:
- UK: 35.9 percent of fathers and 21.9 percent of mothers were university graduates;
- France: 39.8 percent of fathers and 26.8 percent of mothers were university graduates;
- Germany: 44.3 percent of fathers and 17.5 percent of mothers were university graduates; and
- Sweden: 27.3 percent of fathers and 15.2 percent of mothers were university graduates.

These findings are in line with generally accepted statistics that, in European countries, students from academic families are substantially represented, although not to such an extent that the majority of students in higher education come from families with academic backgrounds. Comparing the graduate data with that from the study abroad participants of 1984/85, there are two noteworthy differences. Among the Swedish graduates, the percentage whose mothers completed higher education is smaller than among the 1984/85 students. Among the German graduates, the percentage whose fathers or mothers have university degrees is higher.

The graduates' assessments of their academic achievement were more positive than those the 1984/85 European participants in study abroad expressed before their sojourn. Among the latter, 53.1 percent thought their study achievements were above average, in contrast to 68.4 percent of the graduates who felt this way about themselves. It is conceivable that the study abroad programmes were more selective before 1984/85. It is also likely that, as a consequence of the study abroad, there was an increase in achievement that naturally could not be detected in questionnaire responses given before the sojourn. Finally, we cannot exclude the possibility that graduates overestimated their academic achievement level a few years after the fact.

In financing their studies, as Table S57 shows, the French graduates stated that their parents had paid the greater part of study costs both at home and abroad. For the Germans, study at the home institution was financed 58.6 percent by the

Table S57
European Graduates' Sources of Financing Their Studies at Home Institution and While Abroad
(in percentage of costs)*

| | Home country | | | | | | | | | |
| Source | UK | | F | | D | | S | | Total | |
	At home	SAP	At home	SAP	At home	SAP	At home	SAP	At home	SAP
Parents**	28.8	26.0	81.3	75.7	58.6	45.0	4.4	5.0	41.7	35.9
Own work	2.6	8.3	11.4	10.5	17.2	10.6	13.6	10.4	9.5	9.6
Grant, loan	67.1	60.1	5.9	8.8	22.5	21.8	77.8	71.3	46.9	43.4
Special SAP grant or loan	.	4.1	.	4.6	.	21.7	.	7.8	.	9.3
Other sources***	1.5	1.6	1.5	0.4	1.7	0.9	4.2	5.4	2.0	1.8
Total	100.0	100.0	100.0	100.0	100.0	100.0	100.0	100.0	100.0	100.0
(N)	(191)	(185)	(75)	(72)	(115)	(114)	(66)	(66)	(447)	(437)

* Arithmetic mean of percentages in respondents' replies
** Students were requested to consider living with their parents rent-free as a contribution of 30 % toward overall study costs.
*** Including "income from working spouse/partner"
Source: Questionnaire for Graduates SAEP G 18 (G 145-177)

parents. The corresponding share for the study period abroad - 45 percent - was lower, since the grants and loans during the period abroad covered, on average, twice as large a share of the study costs of the German graduates as during their study at home. In absolute terms, the burden for the parents of the German graduates during the period of study abroad would have been greater than during the study at home. The Swedish and British graduates reported that four-fifths and two-thirds, respectively, of their study both at home and during the study abroad was paid for by grants or loans.

As can be gathered from other sources (see Table P46 in volume one), student grants for study abroad participation improved in France and Sweden over the course of the 1980's. The 1983/84 French students received a somewhat higher proportion of grants or loans at home, and especially so during the period of study abroad, than the graduates under consideration (28.4% compared to 13.4%). Likewise, the Swedish participants in study abroad during 1983/84 were able to cover a somewhat higher portion of the costs during the sojourn with the help of their student allowance than the Swedish graduates had been able to do (89.3% compared to 79.1%).

For a large share of the graduates, the study abroad was in no way their only lengthy experience of the host country prior to or during their higher education years. Over a third had spent at some other time more than one month in the same country. The corresponding percentage is far higher for the French (77.1%) than for the Germans (33.9%) and the British (31.5%) although the lowest percentage of all was found for the Swedes (22.7%).

The research team assumed that the international dimensions of the graduates' professional activities could be influenced by whether they were living with a partner, and if so, how internationally versed and interested these partners were. Thus, through several items in the questionnaire, the graduates provided some information on their partners.

At the time of the questionnaire, half the graduates were married or living with a partner. For most, this was new since graduation. 6.8 percent of the graduates with citizenship of the country of their sending institution for study abroad had a partner from the country in which they studied abroad. This percentage, as Table S58 shows, is lower for the German graduates (6.1%) than for the French (10.8%) and the British (8.7%). For the Swedish graduates on the other hand, there was no case of such a partnership. More of the women (10%) than the men (5%) reported having a partner from the host country of their former study abroad programme.

A further 7.6 percent of the indigenous graduates reported that their partners had a different nationality. The extent of international partner relations is still more strongly evidenced if we exclude from consideration graduates without partners. Of all the indigenous respondents who had a partner at the time of the questionnaire, in 14.1 percent of the cases the partner came from the study abroad host country, and in 15.4 percent of the cases from other countries.

Another interesting point is the distribution of partner relations according to countries: in 19 of 37 cases there were English-French bonds. Nearly ten percent of the graduates who had studied abroad in the UK, France and Sweden reported that they had partners from the host country. Among those who had studied in the USA, this share was 6 percent; while, for those who studied in Germany, it was only 2 percent.

Table S58
Nationality of European Graduates' Spouse/Partner, by Home Country
(in absolute number of graduates)

Respondent	Spouse/partner	Home country				
		UK	F	D	S	Total
Native*	No Spouse/partner	94	32	57	33	216
Foreign national	No Spouse/partner	6	2	0	2	10
Native	Native*	60	35	41	24	160
Native	SAP country native	16	9	7	0	32
Native	Native of other country	14	5	9	7	35
Foreign national	Native*	2	0	1	0	3
Foreign national	SAP country native	1	0	0	0	1
Foreign national	Native of other country	1	0	0	0	1
Total		194	83	115	66	458

* Citizen of home country, i.e. sending country of SAP
Source: Questionnaire for Graduates SAEP G 3 and 8 (G VINTPART)

Slightly over half (58%) the respondents who were married or who lived with a partner reported that their partners were active in highly skilled professions (as a rule, in professions requiring a university degree). This applied to 61.8 percent of the French, 61.4 percent of the German, 51.6 percent of the Swedish and 41.2 percent of the British graduates. In only 7.9 percent of the cases, the partners were not employed.

The majority of the graduates' partners had lived abroad for some period. Over half (57.8%) had reportedly lived abroad for at least three consecutive months. The percentage among the partners of the German graduates was the lowest, at 42.1 percent.

The foreign language qualifications of the graduates' partners were notably high: 74-84 percent had mastered one foreign language and 47-52 percent a second foreign language with at least a moderate degree of proficiency in writing, speaking, reading and oral comprehension. As Table S59 shows, almost all the partners of the Swedish and German graduates had mastered one foreign language. A second foreign language was cited most frequently by the Germans, which is intriguing, given the finding in the paragraph above.

For both the first and second foreign languages, the British partners of the British graduates possessed these skills to a much lesser degree. Here, without doubt, the fact that foreign language teaching in British secondary schools is less extensive than in Swedish, German and French schools, and is not mandatory in upper secondary, plays a role. In addition, the employment situation of the partners, noted above, implies there is a larger percentage of British than of the other graduates whose partners did not complete a university education and consequently could not have profited from additional foreign language training in some manner at that level.

Table S59
Foreign Language Proficiency of European Graduates' Spouse or Partner, by Home Country of Respondents (percentage of partners whose proficiency is at least fair* according to the respondents' assessments)

Foreign language proficiency	Home country				
	UK	F	D	S	Gesamt
First foreign language					
Reading	68.1	83.7	96.6	100.0	82.8
Speaking	60.6	85.7	93.1	96.8	78.9
Listening comprehension	70.2	85.7	93.1	100.0	83.2
Writing	53.2	75.5	89.7	96.8	72.8
Second foreign language					
Reading	35.1	61.2	70.7	64.5	53.4
Speaking	31.9	55.1	62.1	54.8	47.4
Listening comprehension	35.1	59.2	65.5	61.3	51.3
Writing	25.5	51.0	60.3	48.4	47.7
(N)	(94)	(49)	(58)	(31)	(232)

* On a scale of 1 = "very good", 2 = "good", 3 = "fair", 4 = "poor"
Source: Questionnaire for Graduates SAEP G 12 (G 127-134)

7.4   Graduates' Study Abroad

The European graduates responding had on average a 13.6 month sojourn through the study abroad programme. The average duration by sending country is as follows:
- 15.2 months in the French programmes;
- 14.2 months in the British programmes;

- 13.7 months in the German programmes; but only
- 9.9 months in the Swedish programmes.

The graduates had made good use of studies offered at the host university which were not available at their home institution. Thus:
- 75 percent took courses involving topics not available at home;
- 52.6 percent participated in courses using teaching methods not usually practised at their home institutions;
- 48.8 percent participated in non-compulsory courses to broaden their academic and cultural horizons;
- 24.8 percent used language laboratories or other facilities abroad which were not available at their home institutions or, if available, of more inferior quality at home;
- 21.7 percent took up new specialisations abroad; a further 5.4 percent said they had changed their specialisations during the study abroad;
- 14.2 percent participated in language courses in the language of the host country, which were not part of the intensive language courses arranged by the study abroad programme as such.

These results are fairly similar to the data for the participants in study abroad during 1984/85, even when broken down according to countries and academic specialisations.

While studying abroad, eleven percent of the graduates enrolled in a faculty different from theirs at the home institution. This percentage was highest (14.2%) among former participants in the German programmes. A relatively high percentage (43%) of the graduates who commented on the purpose of the period abroad had not only studied but also participated in a work placement connected with the study in the host country.

Like the 1984/85 participants, the graduates recalled that contacts with students in the host country had been the most important in shaping their overall experience during study abroad. On a scale of 1 = "very important" to 5 = "not at all important," they rated such contacts an average of 1.8. Contacts with host country teachers, other persons in the host country and with other foreign students in that country were all given ratings in the 2.2 - 2.5 range.

Contact with the host country remained relatively stable since graduation. As Table S60 shows, this was achieved most frequently via information through the media, communication with people in the host country, and travel in the host country.

If we compare the graduates' statements with the corresponding statements of students returning from their sojourn in 1984/85 (see the last two columns of Table S60), it appears that two aspects may have diminished over the years since graduation: participation in conferences (etc.) dealing with the host country, and communication with persons in the home country who are knowledgeable about the host country. There is also a slight reduction in reading popular literature from the study abroad host country, whereas visits to exhibitions or membership of organisations dealing with the host country probably remained more or less constant.

Table S60
Maintaining Contacts and Interest in the Host Country of the Study Abroad Period by European Graduates, by Home Country and by Field of Study (in arithmetic means)*

	Home country				Field of study						
	UK	F	D	S	Bus	Eng	Nat	Law	Lang	Tot**	(***)
By reading or watching media on that country	2.4	2.3	2.2	2.4	2.3	2.4	2.6	2.4	2.6	2.3	(2.2)
By communicating with persons in your own country knowledgeable about the SAP host country society	3.3	2.5	2.9	3.4	3.0	3.5	3.4	2.9	3.4	3.1	(2.7)
By communicating with persons living in the SAP host country	2.3	2.4	2.3	2.9	2.3	2.4	2.7	2.2	2.6	2.4	(2.2)
By reading popular journals/literature from the SAP host country	3.1	3.1	3.1	3.0	3.1	3.0	3.1	3.0	3.1	3.1	(2.9)
By reading professional journals/literature about the SAP host country	3.8	3.0	3.5	3.6	3.5	3.4	4.1	3.5	3.8	3.6	(3.6)
By further studies in an academic institution	4.3	4.4	4.3	4.4	4.6	4.6	4.3	4.0	3.9	4.3	(.)
By attending conferences seminars, lectures etc., dealing with the SAP host country	4.7	4.7	3.9	4.5	4.5	4.5	4.6	4.3	4.3	4.4	(3.9)
By being a member of organization(s) involved with the SAP host country	4.4	4.4	4.5	4.8	4.3	4.6	4.7	4.1	4.8	4.5	(4.5)
By attending art exhibitions, concerts, cinema, and other cultural activities	3.5	3.6	2.9	3.8	4.3	3.6	3.9	2.9	3.5	3.4	(3.4)
By receiving visitors from the SAP host country	3.1	2.5	2.4	3.5	2.6	2.9	3.4	3.1	3.3	2.9	(.)
By travelling to the SAP host country	2.5	2.2	2.5	3.2	2.2	2.6	3.2	1.9	2.2	2.6	(.)

*   Scale from 1 = "very much" to 5 = "not at all"
**   Including also other fields of study
(***)   All students 1984/85
Source: Questionnaire for Graduates SAEP G 23 (G 313-323) and Post-Study Abroad
           Questionnaire SAEP F 44 (F 823-836)

7.5   Graduates' Employment Profile

7.5.1   *Employment Status*

In 1986 when the graduates responded to the questionnaire, 93.2 percent were employed (see Table S61). This share was particularly high among the Swedes (96.2%). By former field of study, clear contrasts are discernible. Only a few business students (1.1%) and engineers (2.2%) were unemployed, whereas for the other fields, the share was more than 8 percent. Unemployment was reported most by Foreign Language graduates (10.5%). It is also noticeable that the differences in the unemployment ratios for the graduates by country are relatively small, and they do not follow the prevailing pattern of unemployment generally in the respective countries.

When surveyed, three-quarters of the European graduates were employed full-time, and a further five percent were self-employed. The share of graduates in part-time employment was nine percent. Of these, more than half were also studying. In comparing the countries, one thing stands out: that the Germans and the Swedes in the first years after graduation frequently combined further study with part-time employment. In the UK, further study tended to be connected with full-time employment. Hardly any of the French graduates decided on further study. Further studies were frequently chosen by Natural Science graduates (57.1%). This is in no way a peculiarity of former participants in study abroad programmes. Hence the relatively small percentage of natural scientists in full-time employment (46.4%) cannot, apart from one or two cases, be interpreted as a sign of employment problems.

The graduates' job classifications and locus of employment are delineated in Tables S62 and S63.

Also, when holding the distribution constant according to field of study and country, clear differences emerge when the sample is categorised by sex. At the time of the questionnaire, women were much more frequently in full-time employment than men; and, among the total group who chose part-time employment combined with further studies, the women were also represented in larger percentages than the men.

From the short narrative descriptions the graduates supplied about their jobs, it is possible only to estimate that 70-90 percent were employed in jobs for which a higher education degree is normally a precondition. Very few of the respondents had positions in public administration. In fact, many of the graduates complained that their specific international qualifications only met disinterest from the public service. A comparatively larger number of German law and foreign language graduates emphasised that when applying for jobs in government agencies, they could not as a rule count on their foreign qualifications being appreciated:

"My study and teaching periods abroad certainly give me better chances in the private employment market. For public jobs, this experience, according to what I have so far found, is irrelevant or even a handicap." (German Law graduate)

Table S61
Employment Status of European Graduates, by Home Country and Field of Study (in percentage)

Employment status	Home country				Field of study					
	UK	F	D	S	Bus	Eng	Nat	Law	Lang	Tot*
Full-time employed	68.5	80.5	60.2	54.0	82.3	71.7	32.1	57.5	52.6	66.6
Self-employed	4.5	-	5.1	1.6	2.8	-	3.6	7.5	5.3	3.4
Part-time employed	4.5	5.2	8.2	1.6	4.4	-	5.4	5.0	13.2	5.0
Unemployed	3.4	3.9	3.1	1.6	2.2	-	1.8	-	10.5	3.1
Military service/alternative service	-	3.9	1.0	-	1.1	2.2	-	2.5	-	1.0
Studies and other full-time activities**	10.1	5.2	7.1	15.9	6.1	17.4	14.3	15.0	10.5	9.4
Studies and part-time employment	1.1	-	9.2	11.1	0.6	2.2	17.9	2.5	-	4.3
Studies (only)***	7.9	1.3	6.1	14.3	0.6	6.5	25.0	10.0	7.9	7.2
Total	100.0	100.0	100.0	100.0	100.0	100.0	100.0	100.0	100.0	100.0
(N)	(178)	(77)	(98)	(63)	(181)	(46)	(56)	(40)	(38)	(416)

*   Including other fields of study
**   Employment, self-employment and military/alternative service.
*** Including 4 graduates, who stated studies and unemployment at the same time.

Source: Questionnaire for Graduates SAEP G26 (G Status).

Table S62
Current Occupation of European Graduates, by Home Country
(in percentage of employed graduates)

	Home country				
Occupation	UK	F	D	S	Total
Manager, top administrator and senior administrative civil servant	32.0	55.7	35.3	30.5	36.8
Engineer, natural scientist	4.1	-	7.8	10.2	5.2
Professions in higher education	3.5	2.7	23.5	32.2	12.6
Health and other liberal professions	0.6	1.4	-	-	0.5
School teachers	5.8	1.4	4.9	-	4.0
Writer, artist etc.	1.7	-	-	1.7	1.0
Other professions	6.4	-	6.9	11.9	6.2
Middle level personel	35.5	38.6	4.9	10.2	24.6
Other occupations	2.3	-	-	-	1.0
Trainees, preparatory status	8.1	-	16.7	3.4	8.0
Total	100.0	100.0	100.0	100.0	100.0
(N)	(172)	(70)	(102)	(59)	(403)

Source: Questionnaire for Graduates SAEP G 27-28

Table S63
Type of Employing Agencies of European Graduates, by Field of Study
(in percentage of employed graduates)*

	Field of study					
Employing agency	Business-studies	Engi-neering	Natural sciences	Law	Foreign languages	Total*
Industrial or commercial firm	70.1	79.5	40.8	42.5	50.0	57.8
Private service organization	17.8	2.3	6.1	15.0	8.3	12.6
Public administration	2.9	2.3	6.0	17.5	8.3	6.8
International/intergovern-mental organization	1.1	-	-	-	2.8	0.8
University, school etc.	7.5	13.6	44.9	25.0	27.8	19.7
Other	0.6	2.3	6.1	-	2.8	2.3
Total	100.0	100.0	100.0	100.0	100.0	100.0
(N)	(174)	(44)	(49)	(40)	(36)	(396)

* Also including other fields of study
Source: Questionnaire for Graduates SAEP G 27

More of this type of testimony follows.

It is noticeable that the majority of Foreign Language graduates had jobs in industry, commerce and private service companies. This lends credence to the assumption that study abroad opens only some job opportunities outside the area of education and science for foreign language students. In fact, overall when graduates were asked about how well their first job and/or their job at the time of the questionnaire corresponded to the expectations they had at the point of graduation, their judgements were more reserved than the research team had expected. Concerning the first job, the average rating was 2.7, based on a 5-point scale where 1 = "fully corresponded to expectations" and 5 = "did not correspond at all." The average rating was higher for the job held at the time of the questionnaire: 2.3. Slightly over half (56%) indicated that the current job corresponded to their earlier expectations (points 1 and 2 on the scale), 13.6 percent said they were disappointed (points 4 and 5), while 12.3 percent said they had not had any expectations. Here the British graduates considered the job corresponded less to expectations than the graduates of the other three countries (U.K.: 2.5; other countries: 2.2). In these terms, the Foreign Language graduates seemed less satisfied with their jobs (2.5) than the graduates from Business Studies, Law, Engineering and Natural Sciences (all in the 2.1 - 2.2 range).

7.5.2   International Contacts and Job Tasks

It is not the purpose of the study abroad programmes exclusively to prepare students for international careers, but by imparting a habit of looking at issues comparatively, it can give participants new insights into their own culture and society. By imparting specialist knowledge not available at the students' home institutions, it can make an important contribution to their future occupational activities which may not even have explicit international dimensions. The research team believed it would certainly be a criterion of success nonetheless for a study abroad programme if many of its graduates took on international responsibilities as they moved into their careers.

Many graduates who studied abroad were subsequently employed by organisations with marked international relations. As Table S64 shows, over half the graduates were even employed in firms or organisations which had contacts in the country for their former study abroad. Two-thirds of the respondents worked in organisations with significant international relations with other countries. In both cases, French graduates were far less represented.

Table S65 presents the same according to field of study. Graduates in Engineering and Natural Sciences were particularly active in organisations with significant international relations not restricted to the study abroad host country. For graduates in Law, Foreign Languages and Business Studies, this had happened less often. However, the percentages of graduates in organisations for which contacts with the host country of their study abroad played some role were roughly the same for all fields.

Table S64
Employment in Organizations with International Contacts and Internationally Oriented Work of European Graduates, by Home Country
(in percentage of employed graduates replying)*

	Home country				
	UK	F	D	S	Total
Organization does business/has contact with SAP host country	53.8	35.1	63.4	58.0	53.3
Organization does business/has contact with other countries	65.5	59.6	70.0	74.4	67.5
Using the language of your SAP host country in work-related telephone conversations, face-to-face discussions with people from that country etc.	44.1	57.9	59.0	62.9	54.0
Using the language of your SAP host country in writing/reading business related memoranda, reports etc.	40.3	51.4	61.0	69.3	53.0
Using firsthand professionel knowledge related predominantly to the SAP host country	24.0	33.6	40.4	17.8	28.7
Using firsthand knowledge of the country and people of your SAP host country	24.9	28.9	52.0	14.3	30.7
Professional travel to the SAP host country	18.6	21.2	26.8	11.3	19.9
Professional travel to foreign countries other than the host country of your SAP	19.1	31.1	28.0	24.2	24.2
Using knowledge of your field of study acquired during your SAP	30.1	48.0	48.0	38.7	39.1

* Percent of respondents replying 1 or 2 on a scale from 1 = "continually" to 5 = "not at all"
Source: Questionnaire for Graduates SAEP G 38 - 40 (G 466, 468, 513-519)

Insofar as they had been mobile in the first years of their profession, graduates had indeed often switched to organisations in which relations with the host country of their study abroad, or other international relations, figured more prominently. The foreign language graduates were the ones who had most frequently changed to organisations which dealt internationally. Tables S64 and S65 point out that a substantial proportion of the graduates called up specific study abroad skills though the share of those not utilizing their international competences in such an obvious way is equally noticeable.
- More than half the graduates reported they frequently used the language of the study abroad host country in the job;

- 39.1 percent reported that in their present job, they frequently used the specialist knowledge acquired in their study abroad programme;
- Firsthand knowledge acquired about the country and the people during study abroad could be applied frequently in their professional activity by 30.7 percent of the respondents; 28.7 percent made frequent use in their present activity of the professional knowledge related predominantly to the study abroad host country; and
- 19.9 percent of the graduates travelled frequently on business to the host country of their study abroad.

Table S65
Employment in Organizations with International Contacts and Internationally Oriented Work of European Graduates, by Field of Study (percentage of employed graduates replying)*

	Field of study					
	Business studies	Engi-neering	Natural sciences	Law	Foreign languages	Total**
Organization does business/has contact with SAP host country	56.0	56.5	58.2	50.0	57.6	53.3
Organization does business/has contact with other countries	69.9	76.1	80.0	55.2	68.8	67.5
Using the language of your SAP host country in work-related telephone conversations, face-to-face discussions with people from that country etc.	59.1	58.7	59.2	40.0	41.2	54.0
Using the language of your SAP host country in writing/reading business related memoranda, re-ports etc.	56.2	65.2	63.2	37.5	29.5	53.0
Using firsthand professional knowledge related predominantly to the SAP host country	37.6	30.4	14.8	27.5	11.7	28.7
Using firsthand knowledge of the country and people of your SAP host country	37.0	23.9	17.0	32.5	26.4	30.7
Professional travel to the SAP host country	26.5	22.2	11.2	21.3	14.7	19.9
Professional travel to foreign countries other than the host country of your SAP	34.2	26.7	22.3	10.2	9.1	24.2
Using knowledge of your field of study acquired during your SAP	45.1	44.4	33.3	30.0	15.6	39.1

*   Percent of respondents replying 1 or 2 on a scale from 1 = "continually" to 5 = "not at all"
**   Also including other fields of study
Source: Questionnaire for Graduates SAEP G 38 and 40 (G 466, 468, 513 - 519)

Surprisingly, the French graduates most often reported using the qualifications they had acquired in connection with their study abroad, although they reported less frequently that they worked in organisations with close relations with foreign countries. The British graduates were relatively active in organisations which dealt with the host country of their study abroad, but they reported making less use of the qualifications in their job than the graduates from other countries.

By their own admission, Foreign Language graduates made the least use in their profession of any knowledge acquired during their study abroad. They and the Law students reported least frequently using the language of their host country.

A content analysis of the graduates' summaries of their job activities described elsewhere in the questionnaire reveals many different manifestations of "internationality" and, as well, that the threshold for what was considered "international" was not always the same across the group of respondents. The following comment, compared with the numerous quotations which follow, is illustrative:

> "I am unsure as to what your question means. I work abroad in an international organisation with a multinational staff. However, I have no international business dealings on a day-to-day basis." (British Business Studies graduate)

Some of the Business Studies graduates referred only to the fact that their firm had pronounced international connections, without going into detail about their own jobs: "Exports account for some thirty percent of the firm's total sales." (German Business graduate) Nevertheless, on the whole, graduates from this field of study tended to characterise their jobs as international if this meant they spoke by telephone to foreign customers, participated in negotiations with foreign visitors, conducted market analyses related to other countries, or made occasional trips abroad:

> "My work involves assessment of foreign acquisitions both because of my language capabilities and marketing/industry knowledge." (British Business Studies graduate)

> "I am responsible for legal and logistical concerns for exports and imports." (French Law graduate)

> "I conduct international market surveys, prepare for international trade fairs, participate in international congresses." (German Business Studies graduate)

> "Half my job is directed at the export of our products, so it requires considerable travel." (French Business graduate)

> "All my work involves international contacts. Study abroad was vital to build international experience for this job." (British Business Studies graduate)

Some of the Business Studies graduates were employed in foreign firms or international concerns, and conducted negotiations, wrote business reports, and carried out other assignments in the language of the firm's headquarters:

"I am a German citizen working in a branch of an American firm, so the business language is English. I am in contact with foreign affiliates and colleagues, half of whom are not German." (German Business Studies graduate)

"I joined an international manufacturing company based in my study abroad host country (France). I remain in touch with people I met in factories and marketing departments while I was studying abroad." (British Business Studies graduate)

While the engineers described the international dimensions of their jobs very similarly to the Business Studies graduates, the former Law students less often mentioned any international characteristics of their work.

The Natural Science and other graduates employed in higher education or in comparable research positions pointed to their place in international networks:

"I am part of a European research project team." (German Natural Science graduate)

"My field, Astronomy, is by its very nature international; nor could it be otherwise." (Swedish Natural Science graduate)

"70 percent of our scientific activities relate to questions of international law." (German Law graduate)

Two of the university-based respondents were themselves, at the time of the questionnaire, co-ordinators of study abroad programmes.

There is no doubt that an international core lies in the work of foreign language teachers. A Swedish teacher of English who, among other things, teaches a day course in a large firm said:

"My employing organisation is not directly internationally involved, but as what the organisation mainly teaches is languages, an international outlook is naturally important." (Foreign Language graduate)

In contrast, there were several other foreign language teachers who felt that a job with international aspects should surely be understood as something more than just foreign language teaching, and that the job of a foreign language teacher could not be classified as "international" per se. One of the graduates who had a job in media wrote:

"My work as an editorial secretary in the regional office of a German press group naturally means we have a fundamental relationship with colleagues in at least one other country, Germany." (French Foreign Language graduate)

Another, a psychologist, wrote:

"In my job, I am regarded as an expert for English-speaking clients and everything to do with the USA and with American psychology." (German Psychology graduate)

Finally, in jobs in which the graduates did not appear to regard a higher education degree as a precondition (e.g. the auxiliary worker in a printing firm, the gardener), international relations were mentioned only in exceptional cases. One of these was a British Foreign Language graduate employed as hotel receptionist based in France who dealt with group bookings, telexes, and the like for people from other countries.

7.5.3   Using a Foreign Language in the Job

If we assume that of the three foreign languages the European graduates used during their study abroad, English has greatest international significance, French the second greatest, and German the third, it could be expected that the later use of these languages would vary correspondingly. But this is not the situation in all cases, as Table S66 shows:

The proportion of British graduates who spent their study abroad period in Germany and used German in their jobs is essentially equivalent to the proportion of British graduates who studied in France and used their French. French graduates who studied in Germany used their knowledge of that language as much as French graduates who studied in the UK. However, the German graduates who spent their study abroad period in the UK or the USA used English more in the job than German graduates who studied for some time in France.

7.5.4   Income Levels

Graduates were asked about their first annual gross income and their income in the year surveyed. In view of the small numbers and the necessary disaggregation of data according to country, field of study and year of graduation, there are certainly some cases in which the findings are of a random nature. One result, however, can be unequivocally read from Table S67. If we assume that in 1986 a British pound was about DM3, FF10 and SEK10, then the incomes of the British graduates in question were about thirty percent lower than those of their colleagues in France, Sweden and Germany. If we go further and look at the differences according to fields of study, the incomes of Foreign Language graduates are on average thirty percent below those of graduates from Business Studies, Law, Natural Sciences and Engineering.

The data as a whole do not permit any estimate of the income of former participants in study abroad compared to other graduates who did not study abroad. Consequently, whether there is a certain income advantage from study abroad cannot be ascertained.

Table S66
Internationally Oriented Work Responsibilities of European Graduates, by Home and Host Country (percentage of employed graduates)*

Home country Host country	UK F	UK D	UK S	UK US	F UK	F D	D UK	D F	D US	S UK	S US
Using the language of your SAP host country in work-related telephone conversations, face-to-face discussions with people from that country etc.	45.9	50.0	-	**	58.1	57.1	73.3	50.9	63.4	79.2	54.0
Using the language of your SAP host country in writing/reading business related memoranda, reports etc.	42.8	43.4	-	**	51.6	50.0	73.7	51.0	70.0	83.3	62.1
Using firsthand professional knowledge related predominantly to the SAP host country	29.6	20.0	10.0	17.1	32.8	35.7	31.6	41.2	44.8	8.4	24.3
Using firsthand knowledge of the country and people of your SAP host country	24.7	36.7	10.0	17.5	27.4	35.7	42.1	45.1	69.0	4.2	21.6
Professional travel to the SAP host country	25.4	14.3	-	12.9	18.9	30.8	31.6	33.3	13.3	-	18.9
Professional travel to foreign countries other than the host country of your SAP	20.6	20.7	20.0	14.4	35.0	14.2	26.3	33.4	20.0	25.0	24.3
Using knowledge of your field of study acquired during your SAP	31.0	27.6	20.0	31.7	47.5	50.0	52.6	41.2	56.7	41.6	37.8

*   Percent of respondents replying 1 or 2 on a scale from 1 = "continually" to 5 = "not at all"
**   Not applicable
Source: Questionnaire for Graduates SAEP G 40 (G 513-519)

Table S67
European Graduates' Starting and Current Annual Salary, by Home Country
(arithmetic mean in respective currencies)

Year of graduation	Home country			
	UK (£)	F (ffr)	D (DM)	S (skr)
Starting salary				
1980	5,219	85,000	(37,333)*	62,730
1981	6,183	93,625	(26,000)	69,944
1982	6,266	89,000	34,200	93,662
1983	6,327	98,476	39,236	97,875
1984	7,537	103,750	36,816	91,460
Current (last) salary				
1980	13,942	163,750	(48,750)	134,312
1981	11,602	206,571	(57,500)	123,022
1982	10,396	156,764	53,185	151,720
1983	10,435	138,727	46,075	139,294
1984	8,636	119,150	42,500	131,700

* Numbers in brackets ( ) denote information based on small number of respondents
Source: Questionnaire for Graduates SAEP G 31 - 37 (G 439-444)

7.6 Measuring the Effects of Study Abroad on Graduates' Occupations

7.6.1 Basis for Measuring the Effects

The graduates were invited to assess directly the contribution they felt their study sojourns had made to their development in the workforce in terms of specific skills and work habits, as well as promotions and income level. The research team also took account of the extent, described earlier, to which the graduates' job tasks involved international communication and knowledge of other countries and cultures. Finally, the design of the study allowed exploration of the correlations between particular characteristics of the study abroad programmes and certain occupational outcomes. To illustrate, with the aid of various statistical processes, one could examine whether the duration of the period of study abroad or the country in which it was spent were factors which correlated with graduates' higher incomes, with careers which were clearly international, or with other relevant international aspects in the graduates' working lives.

7.6.2   Graduates' Assessments of Occupational Utility of Study Abroad

"I am working at the present time as an economist in the French affiliate of a British multinational. In this work, the two years of study in Great Britain, including six months of practical experience in a firm, have been very helpful to me in mastering the language and understanding the psychology of my business partners." (French Business Studies graduate)

"I would like to point out that I am not in a job that has any strong connection to what I studied at university. I teach foreign language to Japanese businessmen. It is only in this connection that I use my knowledge of economics. It is the linguistic knowledge I acquired in my study in the UK which has proven extraordinarily useful." (French Business Studies graduate)

"Knowledge of languages certainly did play a role in my getting the job, although, according to my experience so far, lawyers in this organisation are used only to a limited extent in the international sector. But the study abroad certainly allowed conclusions to be drawn about my readiness to be mobile and transfer, and these qualities are demanded to a greater extent in this organisation." (German Law graduate)

Graduates in their first four years of professional activity gave high ratings to the experiences gained from study abroad. The boundaries are blurred between specific "scientific" knowledge and the more general impressions and practical experiences and proficiencies refined in the foreign setting. The graduates acknowledged how study abroad had enabled them to communicate adequately in a foreign language, to build up a network of foreign contacts and to become familiar with ways of life in other countries. When graduates were explicitly requested to rate these, all were rated 1.5 on average, on a scale from 1 = "very strongly" to 5 = "not at all" (see Table S68). This compares with the average rating of 1.3 given to these effects by the 1984/85 group shortly after their return from study abroad.

The graduates also emphasised that study abroad had given them a fuller perspective on their home countries: rated on average 1.9. This is slightly more positive than the 2.1 rating given by the 1984/85 sojourners soon after their return. The graduates stressed that the effects went beyond international and comparative acquisitions in the narrow sense. The capacity for working independently was significantly promoted by study abroad (2.2), and it had provided the opportunity to get a new perspective on themselves (2.3), although it had less often led to change in personal values (2.8).

Study abroad as preparation for internationally oriented job tasks in the home country rated sixth in a list of fourteen benefits (average rating of 2.4 on the 1-5 scale). Less frequently mentioned in the graduates' retrospective views were that study abroad had proven useful for further academic development or for more detailed knowledge of the employment situation in various countries. The same applied to the benefit of study abroad in assisting them in their choice of occupation.

Table S68
European Graduates' Retrospective Assessment of Study Abroad Experience, by Field of Study (in arithmetic means)*

	Field of study					
	Business-studies	Engi-neering	Natural sciences	Law	Foreign languages	Total**
It increased your ability to work independently	2.0	2.2	2.1	2.3	2.7	2.2
It gave you an opportunity to learn and use a foreign language in non-academic contexts	1.3	1.6	2.2	1.7	1.6	1.5
It gave you a chance to get to know people and their way of life in another country	1.4	1.7	1.5	1.7	1.7	1.5
It gave you a perspective on your home country	2.0	1.7	2.0	2.0	2.1	1.9
It gave you an opportunity to get a new perspective on yourself	2.3	2.2	2.5	2.7	2.4	2.3
It influenced you to change some of your personal values	2.6	2.5	3.3	3.2	3.1	2.8
It acquainted you with subspecializations/specific topics related to your field of study but not offered at your home institution	3.6	3.2	2.7	2.5	3.5	3.1
It helped you choose a specialization within your field of study	3.6	3.1	3.5	3.1	4.1	3.4
It broadened your your knowledge of scholarly approaches and teaching methods related to your field of study	2.4	2.7	2.9	2.5	3.2	2.6
It helped acquaint you with other cultures' business and/or industrial techniques	1.8	2.5	3.6	3.4	3.4	2.7
It gave you insight into working relations (e.g. employer-employee relations) in a country other than your own	2.0	2.7	3.7	3.4	3.7	2.8
It prepared you for internationally oriented job tasks in your home country	1.9	2.0	3.0	2.6	3.2	2.4
It influenced your goals/preferences for employment after graduation	2.2	2.3	3.1	2.2	3.1	2.5
It acquainted you with different orientations available within your career field	3.3	3.1	3.4	3.2	3.9	3.4

*   Scale from 1 = "very strongly" to 5 = "not at all"
**   Includes students surveyed from other fields of study
Source: Questionnaire for Graduates SAEP G 24 (G 340 - 353)

Here, as for other portions of the questionnaire, one cannot exclude the possibility that the graduates, if surveyed immediately after the study abroad, could have made different judgements. This likelihood is suggested by the visible difference between the graduates' and the 1984/85 students' responses about how the sojourn had broadened their knowledge of scholarly approaches and teaching methods related to their field of study (graduates: 2.6; 1984/85 students: 2.0) and had acquainted them with various alternatives in their career field (graduates: 3.4; 1984/85 students: 2.4).

Table S68 points out, however, that there are obvious differences in the graduates' responses according to the field in which they had studied. Graduates from Business Studies and Engineering rated many aspects of the study abroad more highly than graduates from the other fields: i.e. the direct preparation for an occupation, preparation for international job tasks, additional familiarity with occupational choices open to them (this point was also expressed by the former Law students), knowledge gained about business practices and industrial techniques, and insight into the relations between employers and employees abroad. Furthermore, a larger portion of the Business and Engineering graduates had the impression that study abroad had led to a change in their personal values. Doubtless, these differences cannot be attributed exclusively to the work placement which was provided to accompany the study abroad, since among the graduates in Engineering, only a minority had participated in such programmes.

Graduates in Natural Sciences and Law perceived a greater value (than did graduates in the three other fields) in the study abroad for getting to know specialisations not available at the home institution.

"In Law, a study abroad programme permits one to increase one's technical vocabulary and to have a very basic understanding of a foreign legal system." (British Law graduate)

Otherwise, the Natural Science and Law respondents were quite close to the other fields in their views on the effects of study abroad outside the academic and professional realms.

In contrast to the other fields, graduates of Foreign Languages not only rated study abroad as less worthwhile in directly preparing them for a career, they also gave lower ratings to the academic effects of study abroad (e.g. getting to know different teaching methods and new specialisations), in its ability to give them direction in choosing a specialisation, or in training their capacity for independent work.

The differences according to home country turned out to be small, with only a couple findings requiring mention. One is that the French graduates welcomed to a far greater extent the fact that the study abroad had acquainted them with other teaching methods (mean of 1.6). Recall in this connection that the French participants from 1984/85, after their study abroad, frequently evaluated the higher education system of the host country more positively than did students from the other countries. Secondly, the German graduates were least convinced that the study abroad had paved the way for a better understanding of their own country (mean rating of 2.3).

Focussing now on the graduates by gender, in only one respect did females judge the qualification benefits from the foreign study more negatively than the males. The females were less adamant in stressing that the study abroad had helped them in getting to know specialist fields that were not represented at their home institutions.

But how much can be attributed to study abroad? Many competences possibly gained from the study abroad programmes with which we are dealing here could conceivably have been developed by other international experiences as well. Since many of the respondents, apart from the study abroad programmes, had a wide range of other foreign experiences before or during their study in higher education, it was expected that the qualifying effects of international experiences as a whole would be rated higher than solely that part of the international experience which is the particular subject of this analysis - the phenomenon of the study abroad programme. What actually emerged, however, was that the international experience as a whole was rated somewhat lower (by 0.3 on average) than the targeted study abroad programmes. The only possible interpretation of this result is that the respondents, in answering this question, saw the study abroad as distinct from their other international experiences. This underscores the extent to which graduates rated the study abroad programmes as important and worthwhile. The following quotation makes some relevant distinctions:

"I would most certainly not have been accepted in my present job had I not taken my degree course. It made me confident and gave me the essential profile that the company needed. I love the challenge of my current position but am disappointed by the monetary rewards. The work placement in marketing that I completed in the study abroad country provided me with an insight into marketing, foreign marketing jargon, and particularly valuable references." (British Business Studies graduate)

The development of the graduates' international skills and facilities through study and subsequent learning on the job was shown in three additional self-assessments:

- 83.5 percent who used the language of the host country in their occupational activities (four-fifths of them said they did), estimated their conversational ability in professional telephone contacts or in speaking in person with people from the host country of their study abroad as high or very high (rated 1 or 2 on the scale from 1 = "very high" to 5 = "very low").

- 80.8 percent rated their ability to write and read the language of the host country for business purposes as high or very high. Here the French and Swedish graduates rated their skills somewhat higher than the Germans. The lowest self-assessment in this matter was given by the British. These differences are far less pronounced than the differences according to field of study. Law graduates assessed their reading and writing skills lower than graduates from Business Studies, Engineering and Natural Sciences. Surprisingly, the graduates from Foreign Languages were most reserved in the assessment of their ability to use the language of the host country in their occupation, in reading, writing, and speaking.

- 52 percent of the employed graduates reported some professional activity involving the former host country for their study abroad programme. Nearly all this group gave themselves high ratings for using the knowledge gained through study abroad on their present job.

7.6.3   Getting a Job - Job Mobility - Income Level

The reigning opinion was that study abroad had facilitated gaining employment after graduation (average rating of 2.7 on scale from 1 = "greatly facilitated" to 7 = "greatly impeded"). Responses from the four European countries are strikingly similar, as can be seen from Table S69. The similarity does not hold up when the results are viewed by field of study (see Table S70). Here, the graduates from Business Studies gave the highest rating to the study abroad for access to both the first employment and to the present job (average rating of 2.4 to 2.5), followed by the former Law students (2.7 in each case). Lower ratings were given by graduates from Natural Sciences (3.0 in each case) and from Foreign Languages (3.1 to 3.2). The assessment of the latter may have been influenced by their generally less favourable situation on the employment market. It is only for the engineers that we find a certain difference in their statements about the first employment after graduation as compared with the present activity. For access to the first employment, the importance of the study abroad was rated highly (2.5); but less so for access to the present professional activity (2.9).

Elsewhere in the questionnaire, quite a few of the graduates wrote that reference to a study abroad in their job applications had apparently increased their chances of an invitation to a job interview, and that the experience of study abroad gave them a decided advantage among the applicants. This was mentioned in several cases even when the jobs required no direct international qualifications.

> "It is evident that a period of study abroad and possibly even a foreign diploma are plus points in the curriculum vitae and attract the attention of those who have to select from among the candidates." (French Business Studies graduate)

> "I answered an advertisement for a job as interpreter and translator. Although my application was incomplete, I was surprised at being invited for a job interview. During the interview, it was revealed that their interest was in getting precisely the type of European Business student I had been, by virtue of the study abroad." (German Business Studies graduate)

> "Although my present activity has nothing to do with my study abroad, and I cannot use my knowledge of foreign languages, these were positive factors in my recruitment." (German graduate 3158)

> "The study abroad in France was regarded, in my recruitment, as a proof of initiative, persistence, capacity for adaptation and mobility. The question of which country was chosen for the study abroad was in this context a question of secondary importance." (German Business Studies graduate)

Table S69
Impact of International Experience on European Graduates' Employment and Career, by Home Country (in arithmetic means)*

	Home country				
Employment and career	UK	F	D	S	Total
a) Due to particular SAP experience					
1. Getting first job was facilitated	2.8	2.6	2.6	2.7	2.7
2. Getting current (last) job was facilitated	2.8	2.6	2.5	3.1	2.7
3. Getting job transfer(s)/ promotion(s) was influenced	3.2	2.7	2.5	3.1	2.9
4. Salary in first occupation was higher	3.8	3.9	3.6	3.8	3.8
5. Salary in current (last) occupation was higher	3.8	3.7	3.6	3.8	3.7
b) Due to degree programme incorporating SAP					
1. Getting first job was facilitated	2.1	2.5	2.5	1.9	2.2
2. Getting current (last) job was facilitated	2.2	2.3	2.4	2.2	2.2
3. Getting job transfer(s)/ promotion was influenced	2.6	2.7	2.5	2.6	2.6
4. Salary in first occupation was higher	3.7	4.0	3.7	3.7	3.8
5. Salary in current (last) occupation was higher	3.6	3.7	3.7	3.5	3.6
c) Due to all international experience					
1. Getting first job was facilitated	2.7	2.8	2.6	3.0	2.8
2. Getting current (last) job was facilitated	2.6	2.4	2.5	3.1	2.6
3. Getting job transfer(s)/ promotion was influenced	2.9	2.7	2.4	3.2	2.8
4. Salary in first occupation was higher	3.8	3.9	3.7	3.9	3.8
5. Salary in current (last) occupation was higher	3.6	3.6	3.6	3.7	3.6

*   Scale from 1 = "very positively influenced" or "substantially higher" to 7 = "very negatively influenced" or "substantially lower"
Source: Questionnaire for Graduates SAEP G 33 - 37 (G 451-465)

"The most valuable and most exploitable gain from study abroad generally - thus not only in France - is the gain in mobility, in the capacity for conversion and adaptation. This is easy to bring out in job interviews. Without these characteristics and without proven experience of living abroad, the search for employment in France would certainly not have been so easy for me." (German Business graduate)

Table S70
Impact of International Experience on European Graduates' Employment and Career, by Field of Study (in arithmetic means)*

	Field of study				
Employment and career	Business studies	Engi- neering	Natural sciences	Law	Foreign languages
a) Due to particular SAP experience					
1. Getting first job was facilitated	2.4	2.4	3.0	2.7	3.2
2. Getting current (last) job was facilitated	2.5	2.9	3.0	2.7	3.1
3. Getting job transfer(s)/ promotion(s) was influenced	2.8	3.1	2.9	2.6	3.5
4. Salary in first occupation was higher	3.6	3.7	4.1	3.7	3.9
5. Salary in current (last) occupation was higher	3.6	3.7	3.8	3.7	3.8
b) Due to degree programme incorporating SAP					
1. Getting first job was facilitated	2.1	1.8	1.9	2.4	2.6
2. Getting current (last) job was facilitated	2.1	2.1	2.0	2.3	2.6
3. Getting job transfer(s)/ promotion was influenced	2.5	2.6	2.3	2.4	3.1
4. Salary in first occupation was higher	3.7	3.5	4.1	3.5	3.7
5. Salary in current (last) occupation was higher	3.5	3.4	3.7	3.5	3.6
c) Due to all international experience					
1. Getting first job was facilitated	2.5	2.8	3.2	2.8	2.8
2. Getting current (last) job was facilitated	2.3	2.9	3.0	2.8	2.7
3. Getting job transfer(s)/ promotion was influenced	2.6	3.2	2.9	2.3	3.1
4. Salary in first occupation was higher	3.6	3.8	4.0	3.7	3.9
5. Salary in current (last) occupation was higher	3.4	3.6	3.7	3.7	3.7

* Scale from 1 = "very positively influenced" or "substantially higher" to 7 = "very negatively influenced" or "substantially lower"
Source: Questionnaire for Graduates SAEP G 33 - 37 (G 451-465)

"I am due to start work with a firm of solicitors in London. This firm has significant contact in the legal field with the country in which I did my study abroad (France). There is no doubt that one of the main reasons for my getting the job was the fact that I had studied for two years in France." (British Law graduate)

"In my opinion, the importance of study abroad will continue to increase in the selection of job applicants. The points regarded as important in this connection are flexibility, mobility, readiness and capacity for adaptation, the enjoyment of risk. Competition is getting tougher in the job market, and it is quite important to have a certain plus in one's education, languages for example, or to be able to demonstrate that one has already had to face up to new and complex situations. Without these experiences, my own entry into the job market would certainly have been more difficult." (German Business Studies graduate)

Some respondents pointed out that, during the job interview, the potential employer knew little about the study abroad programme or the quality of the foreign institution of higher education visited:

"Job opportunities improve if the candidate can succeed in communicating to the potential employer the value of the foreign university, which is largely an unknown factor for the potential employer." (German Business Studies graduate)

Finally, there were graduates who registered disappointment:

"The successful completion of a study abroad programme symbolises a great accomplishment for an engineer, on the human level as well as in more technical respects. Regrettably, all the employers I have met take no account of this. In their eyes, only the foreign language proficiency is of a certain interest. I think this hostile attitude toward study abroad would disappear if employers could be educated to think otherwise through more ambitious and positive reporting in the journals they read and set stock by." (French Engineering graduate)

"Employers I have been involved with do not regard my being able to speak a foreign language fluently as a particularly outstanding achievement. I have often been told to forget it as any kind of qualification and use it only if I find myself in a position to while on holiday. This is not the attitude I was led to expect from employers whilst actually doing my degree. We were always given the impression we could have something extra to offer when looking for jobs. I have not as yet found this to be helpful." (British Business Studies graduate)

"In other European countries, study abroad is highly esteemed. Not so in the Federal Republic: nobody cares! Here they look for people who are 25 years old, who have graduated with 'very good' marks, have studied very rapidly, and have at least three years of work experience." (German Business Studies graduate)

"The significance of the study abroad is minimal to my current and my first employment after graduation. Very little - if any - of what I learned whilst on the study abroad has been useful to me in my employment, although it has often been of great interest to prospective employers, often in a detrimental way. I mean, they think that someone who lived abroad for one year and speaks the language fluently must want to continue in employment which involves further contact with that country." (British Business Studies graduate)

"The employment situation for young teacher candidates should be sufficiently known by now. Since for me employment outside this sector - in the private sector, for example - is out of the question, the knowledge and experience I acquired abroad and which I prize are important only in a private sense." (German Foreign Language graduate)

"The study abroad programme helped considerably to increase my verbal fluency in the two languages concerned: French and German. It gave me greater confidence in using my languages and also in myself as a person. Unfortunately, however, this has since been shattered by my continuous period of unemployment. Despite my language ability which was greatly aided by my study abroad, there are very few employment opportunities in the UK for people with my qualifications who have little work experience. I believe a period of work placement abroad would be more valuable than study in view of the current employment situation." (British Foreign Language graduate)

"I should like to point out that my first employment after I graduated bore absolutely no relation to my studies and that is why, after a short time, I abandoned the job. I am now searching for a position in which I can make better use of the knowledge and experience from my study abroad programme." (German Business Studies graduate)

The type of employment in which the importance of study abroad was repeatedly emphasised was one with job activity abroad.

"I am in the fortunate position of having obtained a job in the host country directly after finishing the study period. I am still working in this job." (German Business Studies graduate)

"I have been employed by a multinational company under the same conditions as any French graduate since I left higher education." (British Business Studies graduate)

International jobs had not been abundantly available, and a considerable number of the graduates reported they had encountered great difficulty in finding jobs in which they could make proper use of their international qualifications. For reasons which should be obvious by now, the Foreign Language graduates had run into the most substantial difficulty finding jobs, although the Law graduates also complained about a lack of job offerings in the international line, and there were also problems among the Business students:

"My degree, including the study abroad programme, was a boost in getting my first job, but I couldn't find anything where I could fully utilise the knowledge and experience I had from abroad. There were very few jobs at graduate level in international or European marketing." (British Business Studies graduate)

There were also a number of cases where it was stressed that the study abroad had led to a job abroad, but there was no relationship between the qualifications acquired through the study abroad programme and the later job. One chose to work in the host country because that was where the graduate's partner lived; or the graduate wanted to live in the host country even though there was no work offered in line with the person's academic credentials:

"I should like to point out that my present occupation bears little relevance academically to my degree, which may be a little unusual considering that mine was a 'vocational' degree. However, I consider the study abroad experience instrumental in my decision to live abroad more permanently thus quite highly relevant to my present activities." (British Business Studies graduate)

"I took the study abroad course to see America for the first time. I now live in America. I have never really been able to use my degrees in American History to obtain a job over here." (British American History graduate)

Thus, the message that comes across most strongly when graduates are allowed to formulate it in their own words (rather than to rate fixed answers in a questionnaire) is that the desire to live and work in another country is strong, but - according to experiences of former students - there are not many clearly available jobs in line with the graduates' academic qualifications which enable them to fulfil their international career goals in the short term.

"Demanding careers for graduates of such programmes do not seem to be immediately available after graduation. In my experience, a rather mediocre interim of one to three years is unavoidable before the positions one had really wanted become available." (British Business Studies graduate)

"It is true that in my present (first) job I have almost no contact with my former host country. But I see the experiences I gained as very valuable for the career that still lies ahead. And of course, later study periods are not to be excluded." (German Business Studies graduate)

"The return on my investment in study abroad (in every sense of the word, since it did cost me a lot of money) will not be immediate. In the grand order of things, I first have to take my professional exams in France. After two to three years, I can use that opening I had to another country and try to live and work abroad." (French Business Studies graduate)

"The foreign language qualifications I acquired will show their effects only in the medium term, since the precondition for being seconded abroad is also a considerable portion of specialist knowledge. The decisive factors for the first job were not so much the foreign language qualifications but rather the proof of mobility and the capacity of adapting to a strange environment." (German Business Studies graduate)

This makes it more difficult to delineate the direct impact of study abroad upon the earlier portion of a graduate's career. In some cases, too, the graduates pointed out that their study abroad had not been as meaningful as it could have been:

"The study abroad programme should have concentrated more on teaching me the language, which I feel is still not very strong." (British Law graduate)

"In retrospect, I do not think I would choose to study abroad again. Except for students wishing to pursue a career in education, I believe that a work placement abroad would be of greater value." (British Foreign Language graduate)

"Having walked my way through this questionnaire, I now realise that because of the short period of time (6 weeks at most) the study abroad programme was virtually useless. We were at X University - all the students had departed other than the North African students - the courses provided were not really intensive and direct contact with French people was very limited." (British Foreign Language graduate)

"In principle, I consider a study period abroad as very instructive, since for many jobs it is almost a necessity, and within Europe it promotes the process of European integration in the long term. But looking back on my own experience, I decisively reject today an integrated course that has you studying at home and abroad. What I would prefer is first to complete a course of study in one country, and subsequently, as a student or trainee, spend at least a year abroad for language qualifications and possible further training. The integrated course of study offers the advantage of getting to know a little about everything. The decisive disadvantage: you don't really master anything.." (German Business Studies graduate)

"The study abroad programme had no significant effect, either positive or negative. It did however make me realise how fortunate British students are compared to French students in terms of education techniques, freedom, etc." (British Law graduate)

"Summing up, it may be said that my period of study abroad had little to do with my own field of study. Although I wanted to take legal courses, I stayed away from courses that were taught in the language of the country. My presence at the university was limited to the foreign language courses offered. Obviously this conditioned the effect on my professional career." (British Law graduate)

"I fell a bit behind in my studies when I had to change language. Although I had studied German for five years in school, it took me a long time to read the scientific texts. Also, as I was left to choose the courses myself (in my area), it was difficult to figure out what they were all about: level, expected knowledge, etc. But it is a totally personal experience, even considering the minor drawbacks and hard times." (Swedish Engineering graduate)

7.6.4   Medium-Term Effect on Career

For graduates who had come somewhat further in their career, then, how did they view the influence of study abroad upon getting promotions or even making job changes? Viewing Tables S69 and S70 again, it is evident that graduates perceived the influence was rather moderate. And as usual, there are differences among the four countries (see Table S69). The British (3.2) and Swedish (3.1) graduates believed that study abroad had been less important in opportunities to change careers or in promotions than did the German graduates (2.5). The most salient findings by field of study are that former Law students rated the study abroad most positively with respect to occupational mobility (2.6), whereas the former Foreign Language students gave this the lowest rating (3.5).

Some graduates also linked study abroad to attaining a higher income, although this effect was felt to be far weaker than the influence on obtaining employment or upon occupational mobility.

The analysis in conjunction with Tables S69 and S70 should be handled with caution. The graduates obviously have only limited insight into how such decisions were reached in the employing organisations. Nor is it possible for the graduates unequivocally to attribute each of their skills and qualifications to discrete learning experiences. They may attribute successes to themselves and failures to their universities, or vice versa. And skills which are most difficult to pinpoint as having been honed by the study abroad experience may not be attributed properly at all: the ability to project oneself favourably to other people, for example.

Even when dealing with such concrete matters as speaking a foreign language or developing an academic specialisation abroad, it is not easy to judge whether these qualifications were furthered by the study abroad phase, or, as implied earlier, by the whole of the course of studies of which study abroad was part, or in the wider context of all experiences acquired abroad. The graduates were nevertheless asked outright to give this a try, to make comparative assessments about the impact of the period of study abroad, the course of studies which included this period, and their international experiences as a whole. These comparisons are also found in Tables S69 and S70.

In getting the first and present job after graduation, the graduates gave a significantly higher rating to the course of study as a whole, with its study abroad component (2.2) than to the study abroad period per se (2.7) or their international experiences generally (2.6 - 2.8). Among the notable differences by country and field of study, the Swedish graduates gave relatively high ratings to the influence of the overall degree programme with its study abroad component in accessing their first employment and in landing their present occupation (1.9 and 2.2), while they rated the influence of the study abroad period and international experience as a whole much lower (2.7 - 3.1). In contrast, the Germans detected no appreciable difference in the influence of these three factors in accessing their first or their present employment (all values 2.4 - 2.6).

Similarly, Natural Science graduates and some of the Engineering graduates rated the study abroad phase and the international experiences significantly lower in facilitating their employment than they rated the course of study as a whole.

Graduates from the other fields did not make as sharp distinctions between these three aspects.

Comments elsewhere in the questionnaire pointed again to the symbiotic relationship between the study abroad programme and the larger degree programme of which it was part:

> "Although having participated in a study abroad programme might be important in the immediate post-university situation, it soon becomes just 'another feather in your cap' or another experience on a list once other more recent and more career-oriented experiences have been gained. Having said that, doing a study abroad programme undoubtedly increases one's chances of getting a good degree grade (over those who do not do a study abroad programme; in my course, the third year abroad was optional) which does remain an important factor in later job prospects, despite the fact that I have since gained higher academic qualifications." (British Business Studies graduate)

> "The study abroad programme enabled me to obtain a better degree than would have been likely otherwise, and some valuable and rewarding contacts." (British Natural Science graduate)

> "I think the fact that my study abroad was at a prestigious university will possibly reinforce my potential, so to speak, if my published work is accepted. The study abroad will certainly not have a negative influence." (Swedish Engineering graduate)

7.6.5   Correlations between Personal Background - Study Abroad - Job Tasks

Male and female graduates rated the professional utility of the study abroad (as defined by the items in Table S68) at about the same level. The more significant differences appeared to be in how they felt about their employment as such. Males who studied Foreign Languages indicated with more frequency that their job at the time of the survey corresponded with expectations they had when they left higher education (arithmetic mean values of 2.2 and 2.4, respectively). Regarding access to the present job and later occupational mobility, a greater portion of the males reported sensing their study abroad period had been useful: 51 percent of the males as compared with 44 percent of the females referring to their present jobs; 39 percent of the males compared to 34 percent of the females commenting on occupational mobility. Here the obvious gender differences are confounded with field of study. As to present income, neither males nor females were terribly aware of any special advantages accrued as a result of their having studied abroad.

Asked about the professional application of various skills gained through study abroad, males reported more frequently than females that they used the language of the host country in conversation (59% compared with 46%) and in reading/writing (59% compared with 43%) in the job. There were slighter differences

- again primarily attributable to the distribution of graduates by field of study - with respect to travelling to the former study abroad host country and using knowledge accumulated about the country and its people.

Graduates who retrospectively estimated their academic achievement level was higher than other students in the same field reported with unusual frequency that the experiences gained through study abroad had been utilised on the job. A statistical test of the correlation between the self-assessment of academic achievement, the graduates' statements that during their study abroad they had become acquainted with new areas in the discipline, that the study abroad helped in focusing on a professional specialisation and prepared them for international jobs, showed significant correlation coefficients of 0.19 and 0.20. Just as clear were relationships between the graduates' perceived academic achievement level, and their use on the job of both language and knowledge of conditions and people in the former host country (correlations of the magnitude 0.17 to 0.20).

Table S71
Relationship Between Duration of Study Abroad Period and Internationally Oriented Work Responsibilities of European Graduates, by Field of Study
(in months of period abroad)

Internationally oriented responsibilities	Level of incidence	Business studies	Engineering	Natural science	Law	Foreign languages
			Field of study			
Using the language of your SAP host country in work-related telephone conversations, face-to-face discussions with people from that country etc.	High	19.5	12.8	7.0	18.8	8.6
	Low	16.4	12.0	6.6	11.5	6.6
Using the language of your SAP host country in writing/reading business related memoranda, reports etc.	High	19.8	12.6	7.1	18.5	8.1
	Low	16.4	12.2	6.5	12.0	7.1
Using firsthand professional knowledge related predominantly to the SAP host country	High	20.3	13.2	7.4	20.0	6.7
	Low	17.3	12.2	7.2	12.3	7.5
Using firsthand knowledge of the country and people of your SAP host country	High	19.6	13.7	8.0	16.2	7.8
	Low	17.6	12.1	6.5	13.8	7.2
Professional travel to the SAP host country	High	20.6	13.6	7.7	14.1	10.0
	Low	17.3	12.1	7.1	14.2	6.9
Professional travel to foreign countries other than the host country of your SAP	High	20.0	12.8	6.4	16.0	7.7
	Low	17.6	12.4	7.4	14.1	7.2
Using knowledge of your field of study acquired during your SAP	High	20.3	13.6	5.6	19.8	8.6
	Low	16.8	11.6	8.0	12.1	7.1

*   1 or 2 on a scale from 1 = "continuously" to 5 = "not at all"
**   3 to 5 on same scale
Source: Questionnaire for Graduates SAEP G 20 and 40 (G AUSDAU, G 513-519)

An examination of whether the duration of the study sojourn may have been linked to the extent to which graduates later used that experience in their occupations yielded the results shown in Table S71 which registers a positive impact for longer duration sojourns. Graduates who reputedly made great use in their job of the language of the host country, travelled to the host country, or used the knowledge acquired abroad about the field of study, had on average spent a twenty percent longer period studying abroad than students who reported less use of these study abroad experiences. These findings are different from the outcome noted for the 1984/85 group. The latter, shortly after returning from their sojourn, did not perceive the duration of their time abroad had significantly affected their gains from this experience. Perceptions of these gains probably do change over time, undoubtedly influenced by the quality of a graduate's international exposure as the person moves further into his or her career.

Table S72
Nationality of Spouse/Partner and Links Between Study Abroad and Career of European Graduates (in arithmetic means)

	Nationality of spouse/partner		
	Home country	SAP host country	Other country
Getting first job was facilitated by SAP experience*	2.8	2.0	2.6
Getting current (last) job was facilitated*	2.8	1.9	2.4
Job transfer/mobility was influenced by SAP experience*	3.0	2.4	2.6
Starting salary was higher due to SAP experience*	3.9	3.4	3.8
Current (last) salary was higher due to SAP experience*	3.8	3.2	3.5
Organization has contact with SAP host country**	3.0	2.0	2.5
Organization has contact with other countries**	2.3	1.9	2.3
Using the language of your SAP host country in writing/reading business related memoranda, reports, etc.**	3.0	1.5	2.6
Using firsthand professional knowledge related predominantly to the SAP host country**	2.9	1.5	2.6
Using firsthand knowledge of the country and people of your SAP host country**	3.7	1.8	2.5
Professional travel to SAP host country**	4.1	3.0	4.2
Using knowledge of your field of study acquired during your SAP**	3.3	2.3	2.5

*   Scale from 1 = "facilitated to very great extent" or "very positively influenced" or "substantially higher" to 7 = "detrimental to very great extent" or "very negatively influenced" or "substantially lower"
**   Scale from 1 = "continually" to 5 = "not at all"
Source: Questionnaire for Graduates SAEP G 33 - 40 (G VINTPART; G 451, 454, 457, 460, 463, 466, 468, 513 - 515, 517, 519)

Finally, the graduates who most frequently reported their study abroad experience had been useful in gaining employment and who had made most use of the knowledge acquired from study abroad had partners from the study abroad host country. Graduates whose partners came from other countries also reported, for some aspects, a higher utilisation of the study abroad than graduates whose partners came from the same country as themselves (see Table S72).

7.7 Benefits beyond International Employment

The benefits of study abroad during the first stages of a career are numerous, but it is not the literal content of the study or work placement which most often translates directly into specific advantages at the workplace. Rather, it is the transfer effect of certain personality characteristics, working styles and social skills that have been moulded under the influence of the study abroad which appear most rewarding during this time when young people are attempting to gain a stable hold on a job, and on a more longterm style of life in general. The study abroad appears to promote the capacity to adjust to unknown situations, to interact well with various kinds of people, to be prepared to undertake new tasks and subject oneself to new working conditions. The experience with the "unusual," the ability to react to unfamiliar conditions, and the ability to learn from comparison are among the most fundamental effects. As the graduates tell it:

"Since the subjects taught during my study period in France did not appear in any way in the first State law examination, and since, in addition, no in-depth knowledge of French or international law was demanded of me, either in the history of law or in the area of contemporary law, the study period abroad meant for me no more - but no less - than a helpful step on the way to general building and development of my personality." (German Law graduate)

"In my opinion, there is no better way to learn language and to acquire knowledge of a different culture than from firsthand experience. In this way one becomes acclimatized to one's surroundings with both active and passive learning taking place. Obviously one learns from reading and teaching, but it seems that socialisation becomes significantly important as part of the learning process. Therefore it seems relevant to say that not only are one's academic horizons broadened, but also one's perceptions change and finally the learning process becomes a dual one. In a society where life necessitates travel and international communication, this type of experience is invaluable and I would say essential not simply for the use of the individual, but for the benefit of the whole of society. As my work involves constant communication with overseas visitors, it is essential that I can understand the people with whom I am dealing, and not simply converse with them." (British Foreign Language graduate)

"Studying and living abroad for more than two years allowed me to develop greater personal independence; access to other ways of life, maturity and assurance, also in dealing with potential employers. The rest of the study abroad remains marginal and has no great significance for professional experience." (French Business Studies graduate)

"I now have a broader and deeper mind as a human being. My study abroad experience is on the 'top three' list of my life. I have gained more self-confidence and an international perspective. These facts *make* **my life, both private and at work." (Swedish Natural Science graduate)**

7.8   Long-Term Effects of Study Abroad: The Views of U.S. Graduates

In the case of the USA, telephone interviews were conducted with 76 former participants of study abroad programmes. The persons interviewed provided written information through a questionnaire on their biography, for example date of graduation, major job held since graduation, income, marital status, and experiences abroad since their study abroad period.

Initially, 158 graduates were selected from the some 23,000 former study abroad participants at the four American universities addressed in this study. At the outset, 101 individuals agreed to participate. Owing to the disparate circumstances, the final number of those replying to the written questionnaire and being interviewed lessened to 76 of these:
- 15 had gone abroad more than 20 years ago, 22 15-20 years ago, 27 10-15 years ago and 12 5-10 years ago;
- 59 percent were female.

For technical reasons persons were not interviewed who lived outside the USA at the time the interviews were conducted, though one would expect that the life courses and perspectives of those living abroad differ considerably from those remaining at home.

All individuals interviewed completed their bachelor's degree, 36 percent had a master's and 28 percent received a doctorate. 92 percent were employed at the time of the interview. Two thirds were married and ten percent of these had foreign born spouses.

The interviews showed that 59 percent of interviewees felt that their study or other significant experiences abroad had influenced their subsequent career choices and employment outcomes. This was less frequently true for individuals with only a bachelor's degree (44 percent) as well as for those in managerial and administrative types of work (43 percent). No significant difference can be observed according to age and sex.

Many interviewees were notably active in educational institutions and in cultural, economic or political organisations with international tasks.

For example, a secondary school teacher in social studies reported that he teaches international relations, world history and other global issues in two thirds of his classes. He expressed concerns about the "fundamentalist rightists attacks on global education". He pointed out that having interacted personally with people from another society

"dramatically forces you to look for the other side of the issue and you find out real quickly how ethnocentric the American press and news coverage of events are. So it kind of forces you to be a bit more openminded about the situation. That's one of the major themes in my teaching."

A university professor who had been in France during his undergraduate study of literature, explained on the one hand how his "cross-cultural repertoire" changed his attitude to literature and how he became interested in teaching in Europe and Canada. On the other hand, he pointed out that this interest led beyond those regions and eventually led him to learn Mandarin and to teach for some time in the Far East.

"I decided that I wanted something more foreign than Western Europe, something that would cut me adrift from Western civilization."

Those utilizing their international experience in major public and private organisation were almost all in the intermediate professional or managerial ranks of organisation hierarchies rather than in the senior most policy making positions. They were highly educated in a specialized field of knowledge, had pragmatic expertise in the language, behaviour norms and power structure of their foreign counterparts, and had some sophisticated understanding of the enduring traditions and critical problems of a major world region.

A graduate who had assignments in various internationally-oriented public organisations said, in reflecting on the significance of his study abroad experience for his subsequent career:

"It took me to a threshold that was very important to arrive at because of my work subsequently. And then an understanding of the people, how they think, that I couldn't have picked up without that in-depth experience at that time. That and an understanding of the French politically which has helped me in understanding the African institutions which are variants of the French system. I am interested in American international relations and I feel this specialization requires both academic background in a functional area, mine is economics, and hands-on experience which opens up opportunities. One of them by itself is not enough. More generally, it gave me an awareness of other cultures and a sensitivity to different ways of thinking and communicating, all of which is currently important to me professionally."

An attorney in an international law firm summed up his foreign experience in the following way:

"I guess I want a career and lifestyle that have international influences throughout my life. I think I always want my job to have some sort of international dimension and I always want to have friends from foreign countries. Which means that I will probably always live in a fairly large city and probably on the East Coast because those are the places more likely to have ready access to people from foreign countries. Not to mention the fact that that's where you're going to find the most ethnic restaurants and foreign films and Italian suits, and I can startle the Senegalese vendor by speaking to him in his native tongue...

And all of this is overlaid with my feeling about American politics and American foreign policy, especially with respect to developing countries. I don't want to put it into an oversimplified way of thinking that it is US versus THEM, democracy versus communism. You have to understand how local oligarchies and common people in regional areas view our policies. American policy is perceived differently abroad than it is perceived here. And you always have to look at it through a lens - a European lens, or a regional lens, or the lens of whatever country is being affected."

Some graduates emphasized the importance of their study abroad experience for their careers and life courses, even if their professions did not require complex international knowledge. A customs inspector pointed out:

"Not that I got the job because of that particular interest at all but I kept it because that was a dimension of the work experience that I love. I would not still be in the job that I'm in if it did not include that dimension. Just contact with people from other cultures is really critical to me to keep a balance and a perspective on my own self as an American and in the work I do. Although the contacts I have with people from other cultures are usually very brief, they're extremely satisfying and they're necessary to my life. I have an opportunity to have them every day.

In customs services, we have many different nationalities of people represented among the inspectors. A lot of people call upon me to explain the bothersome behavior of the French - their impoliteness, brusqueness, etc. It reminds me of when I was in France and I was constantly being called upon to justify the American point of view. I laugh and explain. It's the same thing in reverse, and I love it. And then I am also called upon to translate French documents at work."

There were a few graduates who utilized their cross-cultural skills in their present employment (or underemployment) but who, at the time of the interview, felt dissatisfied, restless, uneasy, bored or trapped in their work role because it did not give them greater opportunities for making contributions to their central values which had evolved from their transnational educational opportunities and experiences.

Also many of those who reported that they were not able to make much use of their international experience, had experienced periods in their life in which they were dissatisfied with such a limited use. At the time of the interview, they felt dissatisfied with their level of income and/or responsibility, or reported that they would ideally prefer a different life style, even if they did not feel actual frustration about their insufficient opportunity to utilize aspects related to their foreign education or experiences. In some cases, this attitude came about after various periods of work in which chances of utilizing cross-cultural competence were limited. One individual recalls the first step of such a career:

> "My uncle who was helping me fill out my résumé for a law position told me to take out any references to my interests in foreign travel and seeing foreign countries... They think you want to take more than one or two weeks' vacation and won't want to work 65-70 hours a week, day in and day out."

In summing up the findings of the interviews conducted with the former study abroad students from the USA institutions, we note similar responses to those provided by European graduates who replied to a written questionnaire. International experience is an essential qualification for a substantial proportion of them. Those making use of their cross-cultural experiences in a less complex way still regard this highly, whereby some of them look for career changes in order to put these experiences to better use. There were a few more American than European graduates stating that their interests in other cultures and societies were not highly regarded or even viewed with suspicion; also, a slightly higher proportion seemed to be stressed and dissatisfied that they were not succeeding in utilizing their international experience in a meaningful way in their professional acitivities. Regarding the latter finding, we certainly have to bear in mind that all the European graduates surveyed were still in early stages in their career and still quite hopeful regarding possible changes in the paths which their life might take, even if they were dissatisfied with their job tasks at the time of the survey. Finally, both the European and American graduates pointed out that cross-cultural experiences were important for them in reflecting upon their tasks and living conditions and in handling new situations, even if international experience and knowledge were not required as an immediate skill on their job.

Chapter 8

Determinants of Change in Students' Competence, Attitudes and Views

8.1 Basic Questions and Procedures of the Analysis

This chapter sets out the results of a statistical analysis designed to identify some of the key determinants of changes in student competences related to study abroad.

First, it is necessary to set the analysis in the context of the aims and structure of the study as a whole. The aim has not only been to measure the change in attitudes, values and competences of the students from various countries and fields of study during their sojourn; it has also attempted to identify which factors are likely to have contributed to the types of change noted. As already pointed out in the introduction, five general domains of potential factors can be discerned:

(1)   Individual characteristics of the students participating;
(2)   Characteristics of the study abroad programmes;
(3)   Programme-related outcomes of study abroad (such as the academic recognition granted for study abroad);
(4)   The students' living and study experiences connected with the actual sojourn;
(5)   Problems the participants face during the sojourn and upon returning to their home institution.

The "outcomes" of study abroad in terms of the effects on students - in other words, the dependent variables in this analysis - have been analysed in four domains:

(6)   academic;
(7)   foreign language;
(8)   cultural;
(9)   professional.

The list of potential factors, above, does not cover all areas addressed in the study. The first volume also referred to goals which underlie the study abroad programmes as well as to their administration/governance, and institutional contexts. As these cannot impinge upon the students' learning processes directly, but at most exert indirect influences through shaping characteristics of the study abroad programmes, these aspects were taken into consideration only if it was noted that the substantial influence of programme characteristics upon the competences, values and attitudes of students, appeared to be closely linked to goals, context and administration variables. This did not turn out to be the case, as shown below.

Also excluded from the analysis was students' testimony on the extent to which they were satisfied with their stay abroad and further, any recommendations they would make for changes in the programmes. These were excluded on the grounds that they could not be clearly considered impact variables, since it could not be ascertained whether students were merely referring to pleasant or unpleasant experiences; or, alternatively, basing their indications of satisfaction or recommendations for change on the nature and extent of competences they felt they had acquired during the period abroad.

Finally, it was tempting to try to establish the professional impacts of certain programme characteristics by juxtaposing programme characteristics with graduates' statements about the professional utility of their participation in a study abroad programme. This approach would have been appropriate only if it could be proved that the essential characteristics of the study abroad programmes had not changed between the time of the graduates' participation and the time the current evaluation polled the programme directors. This could not be done.

Other determinants of the approach taken in the statistical analysis included the assumption that the increase in student competences would be seen in certain, but not all, areas. Consequently, no index of overall growth was established. Rather, a broad range of individual impact variables was viewed singly, and for each one an investigation was made into the factors likely to have contributed to change. For example, what especially reduced the difficulty participants had in communicating in the language of the host country in academic settings?

Obviously, not all programmes emphasised identical goals. Some favoured bettering foreign language proficiency for "general use," whereas others encouraged students to improve in using foreign language largely for academic purposes. Some programmes aimed to promote knowledge about foreign cultures, whereas others expected considerable change in students' attitudes and values. Therefore, any measure to establish an aggregate score for the impacts of study abroad would not respect the diversity in the very intentions of the programmes.

Table S73 illustrates how any aggregate measure of the overall impacts of study abroad programmes is inappropriate. The Table provides a correlation matrix for a selection of the impact measures contained within the various areas analysed. The only significant correlations which could be observed were within individual impact areas: for example, between reading and writing proficiency in the foreign language.

In most cases, the impact of study abroad is measured in terms of the differences in (the self-assessment of) competences, values and attitudes which participants made a few weeks before and again a few weeks after the study abroad period. This measure is undoubtedly the most suitable approach, but it is not without its problems. If the impact of study abroad programmes is measured by comparing competences before and after the study abroad period, there is likely to be considerable evidence of growth if competences were very low before departure. To counterbalance this to some extent, increases of 2-4 on a five-point scale were amalgamated into one category, entitled "substantial increase".

Table S73
Correlation Matrix of Select Study Abroad Outcome Variables Concerning Participating Students (Pearson Correlation Coefficients*)

	1	2	3	4	5	6
1 Academic progress abroad	.					
2 Opinion about higher education in host country	.09	.				
3 No restraint in communicating with host country teachers	-.00	.04	.			
4 Knowledge of host country society	.07	.04	.03	.		
5 Academic competence: views and perspectives	.09	.11	-.02	.07	.	
6 Influence of study abroad programmes upon achieving post-graduation work goals	.11	.08	.11	-.04	.14	.

Source: Post-Study Abroad Questionnaire SAEP F (F 325, CP8A, L2B,VKOWHCX, VABSYX, F 955)

Another problem was that the actual basis for making assessments might have changed during the students' time abroad. Students could have raised their aspirations as to what should be regarded as a relatively high level of competence, and thereby any "actual" increase in competence could have been underestimated when measured in the particular way that was chosen. This is why it is important to confirm, as was possible in this study, that the basis in making the self-appraisals did not change substantially during the period abroad.

Finally, the impact of a study abroad programme upon the participants' various competences is not limited to the period of their actual sojourn. From the point at which they became interested in participating in a programme, students most probably began to accumulate knowledge about their intended host country. In this, the preparation provided by the programme as such is likely to have played some role as well.

In spite of these several limitations, the comparison of competences before and after the study abroad period is a superior measure of impact to a once-off mapping of competences only after the fact. A solely retrospective approach obviously cannot take into consideration the differing levels of participants' competence prior to their departure for study abroad.

The statistical analysis is confronted with typical problems of multi-level analysis since it draws primarily upon two different sources: information provided by programme directors and that elicited from students. This provides two different statistical aggregations. One is based on the level of the individual participant in a programme, and the other takes the programme as the unit of analysis. The combination of these two causes some complications. This second volume of the study focuses on the participants, not the programmes. Thus, the units aggregated in most Tables are the more than four hundred students who replied to both the Pre- and the Post-Study Abroad Questionnaires. This means that the programmes for which student numbers are high are more frequently presented. Whereas this is appropriate in principle, there is a danger that if a few large programmes engender certain effects which do not characterise the smaller programmes, the latter might be overshadowed by the former. To allow for this bias, the analysis was conducted on two different bases: the first on the number of students and the second on the number of programmes, whereby the averages of the replies of all students participating in a given programme were taken into consideration. A comparison of results derived from both procedures revealed, in fact, a relatively high degree of consistency.

There is also the issue of validity of replies with which to contend. In some cases both students and programme directors provided views on the same issues. In principle, there could be discrepancies between the views of the one group compared with the other. An example would be the extent to which the study abroad period was granted academic recognition. Another would be the nature and extent of problems participants faced abroad. In these situations, there were relatively high positive correlations.

Most of the statistical procedures were performed on the total number of students replying to both questionnaires. This procedure was based on the assumption that all aspects surveyed should have been relevant - albeit to a greater or more limited extent - for all participants. For example, it was assumed that regular communication with host country nationals would help improve knowledge about the culture and society of the host country regardless of the home country or field affiliation of the study abroad participant. It was not expected that such communication would be helpful, for example, for the French and detrimental for the German students while abroad.

There are reasons to assume, however, that differences by country or by field of study might play a role in other situations. Mandatory preparation linked to the study abroad programme might have more visible effects for students from countries in which foreign language learning in secondary school is not strongly emphasised, and a marginal effect in cases where students had studied the foreign language rather thoroughly in school. To take another example, improved academic achievement due to study abroad might have a completely different meaning in the Natural Sciences as compared with Foreign Languages. Therefore, the possible impact of home countries and fields of study was examined with the help of co-variance analyses.

Within the bounds of the current study, it was not considered possible to conduct separate analyses of the relationships between programme characteristics and impacts according to country and field of study. For separate statistical analyses of the relationships, an even larger number of programmes would have had to be involved. This was not feasible because of resource constraints. However, on the data generated for this evaluation, correlation analyses and co-variance analyses showed very few exceptions to the predominant pattern of the results, either by country or field of study.

As already emphasised, the major question for research was whether various study abroad programme features were instrumental in bringing about certain effects on participating students. An exploration of the relationships between aspects of student background (for example, parental educational background and the extent of students' international experience before the particular study abroad period under review) and outcomes of study abroad thus plays only a secondary role. These relationships are included in the analysis in order to assess whether certain programme characteristics really are influential or whether the effects perceived should be attributed to the characteristics of the "pool" of students.

The statistical measures were chosen on the assumption that there were continuous relationships to be observed: the more that particular experiences were gained, the more pronounced were certain impacts. This assumption frequently underlies such a statistical analysis, even if, strictly speaking, the data are based on ordinal scales. For some of the measures, a separate analysis was run on the "high achievers" and "low achievers" (in each case, approximately twenty percent who showed the most change and who showed the least, respectively). This analysis supported the assumption that continuous scales were appropriate.

8.2   Statistical Procedures

As a first step, a list of "central variables" was established. A selection of variables was indispensable since the overall information collected on the study abroad programmes, their participants, the study period abroad far exceeded the range that could be managed in a statistical analysis. Several content-oriented and methodological criteria were taken into account in this selection process:
- *The theoretical importance of the aspects:* For example, which changes of competence were considered to be most important in order to explore the factors leading to such changes.
- *Hypotheses about the role certain factors could play:* A decision was made, for example, to examine the role that duration of the study abroad period might play; not, however, accommodation at the home institution prior to the sojourn.
- *Similarity of measures:* In situations where, for example, most measures of change in foreign language competence turned out to be closely linked, only a few dimensions of foreign language competence were examined in looking for factors which could explain the observed changes.
- *The ability to describe aspects in suitable statistical measures.*
- *Findings of the first volume:* If it turned out that certain institutional and programme variables did not influence programme-related outcomes or the degree of problems reported by students, they were not taken up in the analysis.

The list of 58 central variables thus established is presented in Table S74. Of these, 26 variables - the dependent variables - denote competences, values and attitudes of the students, whereas the first 32 listed in the table refer to potential factors which might shape these.

In a second phase of the analysis involving simple statistical correlation procedures, a number of variables were excluded when they were shown to be un-

Table S74
List of Variables Employed in Analysing Study Abroad Outcomes with Respect to Participating Students

Variables	Source
Participants' background	
1. Age	[D111]
2. Sex	[D112]
3. Parents' educational background	[VEDPARS]
4. Parents' occupational background	[VOCUPPAR]
5. Distance between parental home and students' university	[D143]
6. Past international experience	[VINTEXPS]
7. Study abroad as reason for choice of institution/field of study	[SAPCHOICS]
8. Foreign language proficiency as motive for study abroad	[D339]
9. Cross-cultural learning and ecperience as motive for study abroad	[VMOTCULS]
10. Academic considerations as motive for study abroad	[VMOTACS]
11. Academic achievement prior to study abroad	[D227]
Characteristics and outcomes of study abroad programmes	
12. Compulsory/optional status	[C147]
13. Duration of period abroad	[C448]
14. Foreign language preparation for sojourn	[AGG 178]
15. Organisation of academic aspects abroad	[AGG174]
16. Organisation of social aspects abroad	[AGG175]
17. Extent of home-host-institution cooperation in operating study abroad programme	[VCOOP]
18. Academic recognition of studies taken abroad (programme directors' view)	[VRECOGP]
19. Home-host institution cooperation in designing study abroad programme	[AGG 173]
Participants' experiences abroad	
20. Integration within host institution	[VINHOST]
21. Knowledge about host country gained through reading	[VIREAD]
22. Knowledge about host country gained through lectures	[VORCOM]
23. Knowledge about host country gained through talking with host nationals	[F361]
24. Study abroad to broaden academic and cultural background	[VACADD]
25. Taking courses in language of host country while abroad*	[VSAPLANG]
26. Museum attandance during period od study abroad	[F331]
27. Travel during sojourn abroad	[F334]
Problems encountered by participants abroad	
28. Financial problems	[F619]
29. Academic problems	[VLERNPRO]
30. Problems with living situation/social environment abroad	[VENVPRO]
31. Problems obtaining academic recognition of work done abroad	[VACCREDG]
32. Extent to which prolongation of overall degree programme is likely	[VPROLONG]

continued table S74

Variables	Source
Academic Outcomes	
33. Academic competence: theoretical and methodological	[VABTMX]
34. Academic competence: views and perspectives	[VABSYX]
35. Academic competence: developing comparative perspectives	[VABCPX]
36. Views regarding importance of: theories and methods	[VIMPTMX]
37. Views regarding importance of: certain academic habits and approaches	[VIMPILX]
38. Views regarding importance of: interactive learning comparative	[VIMPCPX]
39. Academic progress abroad	[VACPRG]
Linguistic outcomes	
40. Proficiency in speaking host language, general	[VSPEAKX]
41. Proficiency in speaking host language, academic	[VASPEAKX]
42. Proficiency in reading host language, general	[VREADX]
43. Proficiency in listening host language, general	[VLISTX]
44. Proficiency in writing host language, general	[L1]
45. No restraint in communicating with host country students in host language	[L2A]
46. No restraint in communicating with host country teachers in host language	[L2B]
47. No restraint in communicating in host country language for daily needs	[L2C]
Cultural outcomes	
48. Knowledge of host country society	[VKNOWHCX]
49. Opinion about higher education in host country	[CP8A]
50. Opinion about host country's foreign policy	[CP8B]
51. Opinion about cultural life (e.g. art, music) in host country	[CP8C]
52. Global awareness VGLOBX]	
53. International understanding: freedom of mobility, political freedom	[VIUFREX]
54. International understanding: cosmopolitanism ("citizen of the world")	[VIUCOSX]
55. Sociability	[VHSSOCX]
56. Personal confidence	[VHSCONX]
Professional outcomes	
57. Determination of career goals	[P1]
58. Influence of study abroad programme upon achieving post-graduation work goals	[F955]

*   i.e. Other than intensive language programme especially designed for the study abroad programme

**   includes: regular class attendance, active class participation, out-of-class communication between teachers and students etc.

Source: Central Variables SAEP

related to other variables. Two examples are: first, changes in students' international orientation as measured by comparing replies to the Pre- and Post-Study Abroad Questionnaires did not show significant relationships to any of the 32 student profile, programme characteristic or experience abroad variables. It was thereby concluded that changes in international orientation were more likely influenced by completely different factors from one case to the other. Second, among the possible independent variables, the age of the students at the time of their stay abroad did not appear to explain different degrees of change in the students' competences, values and attitudes after their sojourns.

Table S75
Role of Student Background, Study Abroad Programme Characteristics, and Students' Experiences Abroad in Study Abroad Outcomes Concerning Participating Students (Pearson correlation coefficients*)

Student background programme characteristics and students' experiences	Outcomes						
	Academic progress abroad	Opinion on higher educ. in host c.	No restraint communic. w. host c. teachers	No restraint communic. host lang. daily needs	Knowledge host c. society	Academic competence: views, perspec.	Influence of study abroad on work goals
Past international experience	-.04	-.04	-.20*	-.29*	.007	-.08	.15
Importance of study abroad in choice of institution cooperation in programme	-.21	-.06	-.16	-.12	-.20*	.01	.19*
Sex	.01	-.03	-.14	-.10	-.01	-.02	-.10
Home-host institution cooperation in programme	-.15	-.16*	-.08	-.05	.01	.06	.10
Course in host country language while abroad	.12	-.25*	.28*	.26*	.10	.06	.02
Museum attendance abroad	-.02	-.23*	.06	.05	.02	.02	.01
Broaden academic, cultural background whole abroad	.30*	-.09	-.04	-.10	.07	.07	.07
Academic problems abroad	-.27*	-.18*	.12	.20*	-.11	-.06	-.02

*   Significant at .01 level
Source: Central Variables SAEP

This analysis was based on correlation matrices for all students as well as for students from each home country and each field of study. In addition, the weight of differences by country and by field of study was controlled with the help of a two-stage variance analysis. This bivariate analysis showed that only nine of the dependent variables were seemingly influenced by student background and experience factors. The finding for these variables are presented in Table S75, though two variables have been dropped since they were closely linked to certain of the remaining ones.

In a third phase of the analysis, the seven variables in table S75 for change of competences, values, and attitudes in the process of the study abroad period were subjected to a two-stage regression analysis. This permitted an examination of whether some of the student background and experience variables which seemed to play a role according to the previous steps of the analysis were spurious, for example, because they were closely linked to other variables which had stronger weight. The findings are presented in Table S76[1].

The fourth phase consisted of a more detailed analysis of the influence of study abroad programme characteristics was examined. As outlined above, two procedures were taken. First, the programmes were taken as the basis for analysis and, in this case, arithmetic means of the replies of all responding participants per programme were taken as the measures. This procedure was followed for the 34 programmes which had at least five students who replied to both the Pre- and Post-Study Abroad Questionnaire. On this basis, separate regression analyses were processed for student background variables, programme characteristics, and experiences and problems faced for each of the seven dependent variables employed at this stage.

Additionally, the statistically significant relationships which resulted from having taken the programmes as the units of analysis were subjected to a variance analysis in which the students were the units analysed. In this way, it could be examined whether the findings of the previous stage had to be attributed to the uneven number of participants in each programme. The major relationships found are reported in Table S77.

The fifth phase examined further whether each programme created a common frame of experiences and problems for the students. For this, a check was made on whether the standard deviation of replies to the various questions about experiences and problems abroad was lower among participants by each programme, than among all the surveyed students taken together. This analysis was based on the eleven programmes which had at least ten participants who replied to both the Pre- and the Post-Study Abroad Questionnaires.

---

[1]
The asterisks in Table S75 refer to significant associations. Correlation coefficients can vary from -1.00 to +1.00. To illustrate, the -1.00 would hold if all the students choosing to study abroad to improve their foreign language proficiency made little progress in this respect during their sojourns, whereas all students not reporting such a motive made substantial progress. The +1.00 would mean all students who wished to improve their foreign language proficiency abroad through the study abroad programme did accomplish this objective.

Table S76

Role of Student Background, Students' Experiences and Problems Abroad in Study Abroad Programme Outcomes Concerning Participating Students (Beta-coefficients of multiple regression analysis*)

Students' background, experiences and problems	Outcomes						
	Academic progress abroad	Opinion on higher educ. in host c.	No restraint communic. w. host c. teachers	No restraint communic. host lang. daily needs	Knowledge host c. society	Academic competence: views, perspec.	Influence of study abroad on work goals
Home-host inst. coop. in progr.							
Motive for study abroad: for. lang.							
Proximity parent home and university		.14					
Age							-.15
Past international experience			-.24	-.17			
Sex				-.31			
Parents' occupational background							
Motive for study abroad: cultural	.16						
Importance of study abroad in choice of institution/field		.16			-.20		.18
Parents' educational background							
Likelyhood degree progr. prolong.							
Financial problems							
Travel during sojourn							
Course in host c. lang. while abroad			.27	.20	.15		
Problems with living situation							
Broaden acad., cultural backgr. abroad							
Host country knowledge through natives							
Host country knowledge through reading		-.16					
Museum attendance abroad		-.21					
Academic recognition problems			.11				
Host country knowledge through lectures							
Integration in host institution	.25				.13		.23
Academic problems		-.17					

*   Only scores significant at .01 level

Source: Central Variables SAEP

Table S77
Role of Study Abroad Programme Characteristics in Study Abroad Outcomes Concerning Participating Students (Pearson correlation coefficients and beta-coefficients of multiple regression analysis*)

Programme characteristics	Academic progress abroad	Opinion on higher educ. in host c.	No restraint communic. w. host c. teachers	No restraint communic. host lang. daily needs	Knowledge host c. society	Academic competence: views, perspec.	Influence of study abroad on work goals
Extent of home-host-inst. cooperation in operating study abroad programme							.17 (.17)
Organisation of academic aspects abroad							.16
Organisation of social aspects abroad					(.10)		
Foreign language preparation for sojourn	-.14 (-.14)	-.16 (-.23)					
Compulsory/optional status		.22 (.28)		(-.21)	-.19 (-.19)		.15
Home-host institution cooperation in designing study abroad programme		.15					
Duration of period abroad				.13 (.25)			

*   Only scores significant at .05 level
( ) Beta-coefficients
Source: Central Variables SAEP

Finally, in the sixth phase, a search was made for any patterns in student background, programme characteristics and in students' experiences and problems abroad, for the approximately twenty percent of students whose competence improved most strongly overall, as well as the twenty percent whose competence improved the least. This was to see whether some factors stood out more clearly for these "extreme" cases than when the data was viewed across the average of all students surveyed.

8.3   Major Findings

As already mentioned in the description of the procedure, changes in the students' competences, values and attitudes can, only to a limited extent, be attributed to specific characteristics of the programmes, or student background, or the experiences or problems the students encountered abroad. The outcome variables which are significantly linked to some of the independent variables are:

(1)   Academic progress abroad (as compared to what the students would have expected for a corresponding study period at home);

(2)   Change in opinion about the higher education system of the study abroad programme host country;

(3)   Increase in knowledge about the culture and society of the host country;

(4)   Enhanced proficiency in listening comprehension in the language of the host country;

(5)   Enhanced speaking proficiency in the language of the host country, in academic contexts;

(6)   Less restraint in communicating with students in the host country language;

(7)   Less restraint in communication with teachers, in the host country language;

(8)   Less restraint in communication in the language of the host country in matters of daily life; and

(9)   Expectation that study abroad will contribute positively toward achieving professional goals.

On the other hand, the available data provide little if any explanation for changes in students':
- views about the importance of various teaching and learning styles;
- international orientation and most of their opinions about culture and society in the host country;
- personal and social confidence; and
- feelings about the extent to which their career goals are set.

Nor were all measures of foreign language proficiency related to the variables on student background, study abroad programme characteristics or experience and problems encountered.

Among the above mentioned nine impacts of study abroad, some significant relationships were found:

(1) On the basis of two variables regarding restraint in foreign language communication (7 and 8 on the list above), it was concluded that the ability to com-

municate in the language of the host country increased most strongly if students had already spent a considerable period of time abroad prior to their participation in the programmes under review, and then during these programmes took instruction in the host country language. Further, the students who were least restrained in communicating in the language of the host country in daily life were also those who faced the least amount of learning problems during the period abroad.

(2) Students perceived they had attained a higher level of academic progress during their study abroad period than they would have expected had they remained at home in cases where:
- cultural motives played a role in opting for participation in study abroad;
- participation in study abroad was not mandatory in the respective course programme; and
- the participants' integration at their host institution was high.

(3) Students' knowledge about the culture and society of the host country improved most if:
- the opportunity to participate in a study abroad programme had been a major consideration for their selection of field of study or the institution of higher education in which they enrolled;
- participation in the study abroad programme was not a mandatory element of the overall course programme followed at the home institution; and
- students travelled a lot during their sojourn.

(4) Changes of students' opinions about higher education in the country where they spent their study abroad period were most frequently related to other variables. They became more negative if:
- participation in the study abroad programme was not a mandatory element of the course programme at the home institution;
- students were enrolled at a home institution which was not located in the vicinity of their parents' residence;
- students' cultural experience abroad had been rather "broad" in terms of visiting museums, attending theatre, concerts, the cinema;
- students experienced learning problems during their study abroad period;
- no complete recognition of study abroad could be expected;
- prolongation of the overall course of study was likely;
- co-operation between the home and the host institution of higher education was not progressing very well; and
- foreign language preparation was limited.[2]

---

[2] One further finding was that students' opinion about their host country's higher education became more positive, if students had been enrolled at home at an institution which was relatively close to their parent's home. In other words, the students' opinion about higher education in the host country became more positive if this represented a sharper break from their prior pattern.

(5) Finally, a different pattern of factors emerges in connection with the students' assumptions upon return that the study abroad period should be helpful in achieving their professional goals. This view is frequently noted:
- for male students;
- for students for whom participation in a study abroad programme had already played a role in directing their selection of field of study or the institution in which they enrolled;
- on the part of participants in mandatory study abroad programmes;
- for students whose study abroad period was relatively highly structured with respect to regulations about courses to be taken, etc.; and
- for students who experienced a high degree of integration at the host institution.

Analysing the larger programmes, those in which the number of students replying to Pre- and Post-Study Abroad Questionnaires was ten or more, showed that the standard deviation in reports about their experiences was about three-quarters of the standard deviation for students in the entire sample. This indicates that, to some extent, study abroad programmes indeed set a frame which makes certain experiences abroad more likely than others. However, this influence is obviously not so strong that all participants have the same experience abroad. There is room left for individual differences, arising from the differences in the individual personalities involved.

To summarise the major findings, it appears that in some areas, some outcomes of study abroad are associated with particular experiences and behaviour abroad. Taking foreign language courses abroad seems to help improve foreign language competence. Travelling abroad is associated with increasing knowledge of culture and society of the host country. Facing problems while studying abroad is likely to lead to more negative assessment of higher education in the host country.

Some plausible links were also noted between characteristics of study abroad programmes and student "outcomes." Close co-operation between the home and the host institutions is associated with substantial growth in the study abroad participants' command of the host country language, their more positive opinion about higher education in the host country, as well as their expectation that the study abroad period will be useful to them in their future profession. A high degree of integration at the host institution seems to support the students' view that they gained more academically during the study abroad experience than would have been possible during a corresponding period (of study) at home.

It is especially critical to consider the differences between mandatory and voluntary participation in study abroad (as part of an overall degree programme in higher education). Students participating voluntarily seemed to have increased their knowledge substantially about culture and society in the host country. On the other hand, students participating in mandatory study abroad programmes assessed the higher education abroad more positively after the sojourn than before, and considered their stay abroad would enhance their career prospects. The latter finding can be more readily understood if one recalls that a substantial portion of the mandatory programmes are in Business Studies.

As far as student characteristics are concerned, the expression of a definite interest in studying abroad already at the point of applying to higher education and choosing a field of specialisation turns out to be important. When students who are this strongly wedded to the idea of study abroad finally do carry it out, their foreign language abilities improve substantially, their view on higher education in the host country is more positive after the sojourn, and they believe that the study abroad experience will be useful to their careers.

The most remarkable result is that altogether, differences between student characteristics, programme characteristics, students' experiences and problems abroad have relatively weak explanatory value for the different academic, foreign language, cultural and professional "outcomes." Or, looking from the opposite direction of the matrix, it is surprising that social background, academic achievement prior to study abroad, most ways of preparing for the sojourn, as well as the duration of the study abroad period, did not seem to determine the outcomes.

If one had expected striking impacts of certain elements in the study abroad programmes or of the individual participants, one would be disappointed about the results of the preceding statistical analysis. Some considerations, though, might lead to completely different conclusions. First - as the findings show - complex settings rather than single, isolated characteristics are more likely to shape academic and cultural learning outcomes, from study abroad. Second, the factors which potentially have some influence by way of impact on the students obviously vary from one programme to the next. It might well be for any one programme that support by the university administration, duration of the stay abroad or social background of the participants, have tremendous influences on the way in which students can be affected by their participation in the study abroad programmes. Viewing all the programmes together as was done in the current analysis, does tend to mask a lot of the individual variations.

Statistical analyses such as have been conducted here can only point out possible factors at play in cases for which there are substantial variations in the distribution of the elements throughout the study abroad programmes and the students analyzed. It might be that the strong, committed input of the programme directors is more essential for the success of study abroad programmes than all the other factors discussed above. The statistical analysis could not bring this out, however, because such a high level of commitment marked nearly all the programmes. Furthermore, the analysis was conducted on "success stories" in the sense that all the programmes under evaluation had been going for several years. If the history of programmes which had not survived had been included in the evaluation, it might have pointed to some other factors critical to the success of organised study abroad.

We are simply led to conclude that the successful functioning of study abroad programmes is not confined to a limited set of conditions. At the same time, there are no pat recipes for success.

Chapter 9

Conclusion

The first volume of findings from the Study Abroad Evaluation Project (see Chapter 11) closed with the reflection that the success of study abroad programmes can only be adequately assessed by giving primary consideration to the effects which participation in these programmes has on the students themselves. To demonstrate these effects on the basis of our research, has been the central purpose of this second volume, and in conclusion it would seem appropriate to draw together some of the more significant of these findings. Doing so will inevitably throw up almost as many new questions as it provides answers, but no apologies are made for this: particularly in such a comparatively sparsely researched area as study abroad, the identification of potentially rewarding avenues for further studies can be a useful function in its own right.

9.1   The Participants in Study Abroad

Before considering the various types of impact of study abroad on students and graduates which our research has revealed, it is worth recalling some of the salient features of the student population about whom we are speaking.

The overall picture to emerge is that the participants do not demonstrate many characteristics which single them out from the student population at large in their respective countries, disciplines and institutions. For example, nearly all the participants were in the typical 19-25 age range, with the British, French and American students being significantly younger than their German and Swedish counterparts. The percentage of women among study abroad participants in the programmes analyzed is also approximately the same as in the student body as a whole in the particular subjects concerned, though individual programmes did show variations from this norm.

In two respects, however, discrepancies from the profile of the general student population should be noted. First, students whose parents have completed a higher education degree or who are in more highly qualified occupations appear to constitute a higher percentage of participants in organized study abroad programmes than among the overall student population. It would be interesting to pursue this matter further both with a larger sample of students and programmes and in respect of students going abroad on an individual basis, i.e. outside the framework of organized programmes. This finding should not, however, be dramatized. Except in the French programmes, no very pronounced social selection among students participating in study abroad was revealed by our research.

Secondly - and this was a more pronounced feature than that identified above - study abroad programmes clearly also have a strong attraction for students who in various respects have *already had some international experience*: students who had themselves or whose parents or brothers and sisters had previously already spent some time abroad. 22 percent of the students interviewed had lived and in some cases worked abroad beforehand; 25 percent had attended schools or higher education institutions abroad - for the most part in short duration exchange programmes, but to some extent also for a longer period of time.

This finding should be regarded as particularly important in policy terms, for it highlights the need to consider the question of student mobility and exchange in the wider context of education as a whole. It is clear from our study that for very many students the desire to spend a period of study abroad is kindled long before higher education entry, let alone in the middle of university studies, and this is borne out by national survey data from other sources also, notably from the Federal Republic of Germany, based on much larger student samples. With the increasing incidence of cheap opportunities for youth travel, one may assume that this situation will become more rather than less pronounced in the future. If, therefore, it is the intention of policy-makers to promote increased international flows of students, at least between the countries involved in our survey, measures related to higher education should not adopted in isolation but rather form part of a more coherent and comprehensive package covering travel and study abroad opportunities for young people in general, and in particular for the purpose of going to other countries as part of school education.

As noted already in the first Volume I, the question of student motivation is clearly a factor to be taken into account when providing study abroad programmes. Our research has unequivocally shown that for the majority of participants, the prospect of being able to spend a period of study abroad had excited a powerful influence on their choice of *field of study and their home institution*. This is particularly true for some subjects which include a compulsory period of study abroad for all participants.

The desire to acquire an enhanced knowledge of foreign languages, as well as first hand experience of living in another country and thus of becoming acquainted with a country and its people are quoted as being the students' most important reasons for participating in study abroad. The expectation that participation in study abroad will contribute to improved professional and employment prospects is also emphasized as being one of the most important motives: this expectation is particularly marked among students of business. Foreign language students may well have fewer expectations with regard to employment prospects; they do, however, expect that study abroad will markedly improve their academic performance and their grades. Other motivations appear to play a general subordinate role, and only a minority of students in our survey decided to embark upon study abroad with the express desire of becoming acquainted with either subject matter or methods of teaching and learning which they would be unlikely to come across at their own institution.

These findings with regard to student motivation are interesting in their own right, but their interest is both heightened and relativized when seen in the context of the expectations which the staff members responsible for the programmes

place in the study abroad experience (see Volume I), and when they are compared with the outcomes of study abroad on the students (see later sections of the
present Chapter).

9.2 Students' Experiences and Problems Abroad, and their overall Assessment of the Study Abroad Period

The first Volume of the report looked at a number of the organizational features
of study abroad programmes, and the student surveys conducted in the framework
of the Study Abroad Evaluation Project enabled researchers *inter alia* to assess
the extent to which these factors were utilized in practice by the students and were
considered effective by them. One such feature distinguishing participation in a
study abroad programme from more individual forms of mobility, is that more
specific arrangements are made at the host institution for the *supervision and support*
of students. In fact about 90 percent of students report respectively that this
kind of assistance was given with regard to the search for accommodation and
other practical matters, as well as academic questions and cultural and leisure activities.
More than two-thirds received support with regard to learning about the
country and its language, making contacts and becoming acquainted with their
particular region. The majority of students said they were satisfied with the kind
of support given in this regard.

Study abroad clearly provides a very good opportunity of getting to know the
host country, its inhabitants, their way of life, mentality and culture. Conversations
with inhabitants are considered by the participating students to be the most frequent *source of information* on the host country; alongside this, newspapers and
magazines, radio and television also play an important role. Visits to museums,
concerts, cinema, etc. are undertaken more often than they were previously at the
home institution. Opportunities to travel within the host country are also made
use of exhaustively - however more so by Swedish and American students, who
had less previous experience of travel abroad, than by British, French and German students.

It is interesting that on the basis of our data, it would appear that people whom
students meet *outside* the higher education institution in the host country are just
as important as host country *students* when it comes to getting to know the host
country. The type of accommodation which students have during their stay abroad
appears to play a significant role in this regard: for those living in student halls of
residence, which more students do while abroad than at home, students of the
host country are the most important contact partners; for those who are accommodated elsewhere people they meet outside the higher education institution are
often rated as being important in reaching an understanding of the host country.

After their return almost all students say that *study abroad* was particularly
valuable in two respects : in improving their knowledge of foreign languages and
in enabling them to become acquainted with people in a foreign country. At this
point those aspects reappear which were the focus of their highest expectations
before the study abroad period.

However, whereas in terms of students' expectations of study abroad, as we have seen in the previous section of this chapter, academic advantages of such study were of subordinate importance, it is worth recording that on return from abroad students also saw *this* aspect of their experience as having been very worthwhile: **more than half of the students reported that it had been a valuable academic experience to be confronted with different subject matter and with different teaching and learning methods** at their host institution, compared with those at their institution back home. And leaving aside the students' own value judgement as to whether or not this process had been *worthwhile*, the *extent* to which the students are exposed to a changed learning environment as a contrast to their course of studies at their home institution is clearly very extensive indeed: no fewer than 69 percent of the students report that while abroad they attended lectures involving topics and areas of specialization not offered by their home institution. Similarly 60 percent experienced other methods of teaching and learning and 23 percent made use of laboratory, computer or other facilities not available in that form at home. 59 percent chose courses with a view to broadening their academic background and roughly one quarter developed a new area of specialization or changed their academic specialization.

Indeed, our research revealed that students were highly sensitized towards differences in the academic learning climate at their respective home and host institutions. A differentiated picture emerges from their perception of institutions in the various host countries concerned, but one feature stands out as common to students from all five countries, namely the **great importance attached to the opportunities for out-of-class contacts between students, and also between students and staff.** Study abroad programme planners will be well advised to keep this consideration strongly in mind when preparing such programmes in the future.

Asked which was the most positive experience of their stay abroad the majority of students mention personal contacts: hospitality, interesting conversations, readiness to help, joint activities with foreign students and - this is emphasized by many students who spent their study period abroad in the USA or Great Britain - close contact between teachers and students. **The great importance attached by students to integration into the life of the host country** becomes apparent in that their most common complaint, given a list of various potential *difficulties*, was that too much time was spent with students or other people from one's own country. Activities to encourage integration at the host institution would therefore appear to be a key area requiring programme directors' attention.

Students' experiences related to *academic study during their stay abroad* naturally depend in many respects upon the requirements of the study abroad programme (whether lectures are prescribed to a large extent in advance, or are left up to the student's individual choice; whether lectures are selected with a view to learning as far as possible the same topics as would have been covered at home or conversely to experience contrasts, and so on). Comparing statements made by students who participated in the same programmes, however, it becomes clear that **study abroad experience is not narrowly pre-formed by the particular programme but that, in most cases, plenty of room for individual experiences exists.**

As indicated in our analysis of study abroad programme structures in Volume I, a large proportion of the programmes in business studies, and some of those in engineering and foreign languages, provided their participants with compulsory or optional **work placement experience in industry** as a separate phase during the study period abroad. In overall terms, one quarter of all the students in the survey carried out such a placement (no American students were involved), and the experience **was rated very highly** indeed. Participants saw such placements as providing an invaluable opportunity of becoming acquainted, in a non academic context, with industrial reality and the language, inhabitants and life-styles of the host country. Between two thirds and three quarters of those surveyed from each country were of the opinion that they had in this way enhanced their chances of employment, prepared themselves for internationally orientated job tasks and improved their prospects of obtaining a job involving interesting assignments. In most cases, the supervision provided by the higher education institutions in and both host and home country was considered minimal and inadequate; supervision provided by the company involved, on the other hand, was seldom criticized. Not all experiences tallied with expectations, but 66 percent of all participants are of the opinion that the work placement period abroad was an even more valuable experience for them that their period of academic study abroad.

Comparatively few programmes provide re-integration support mechanisms for students returning from abroad, and the findings from the student surveys corroborate programme directors' perception: **very few students refer to problems of re-integration on their return** (or mention that they have availed themselves of the opportunity of utilizing support mechanisms such as special guidance and counselling services, where these exist).

One problem does, however, clearly raise itself in this regard, namely that of the academic credit or recognition provided for study abroad on students' return. Thus only 46 percent of German and 52 percent of British students as against 74-78 percent of students from the other three countries involved were granted full academic recognition for study abroad by their home institution on their return. (It should be remembered, however, that many students, particularly from Germany, whose studies were granted recognition only partially or not at all had not requested such recognition either.) 45 percent of the students - ranging from 62 percent of German to only 18 percent of French students - expect that their studies will be prolonged as a result of study abroad. The desire for better recognition of study abroad is also one of the suggestions made by students in reply to the general question as to how study abroad can be improved (other respondents reported that they would like to see improvements in preparation for study abroad or with regard to teaching and the study situation abroad).

The conclusion is therefore justified that the programme directors' highly positive perception of the situation concerning academic recognition arrangements is not fully shared by the students. Since the award of appropriate recognition is so central to the raison d'être of organized study abroad programmes of the type with which our research has been concerned, this is certainly a consideration to which great importance should be attached by future programme planners.

From the overall assessment of the problems which students had encountered in respect of their study abroad period, however, overall assessment of the difficulties in adjusting to the different teaching and learning methods encountered abroad and problems of finding appropriate accommodation (around one-fifth of all students encountered such problems) were most frequently mentioned. There are obviously eloquent messages here for programme-planning in the years ahead, and the accommodation problem may be expected to become particularly acute if the numbers of students involved in study abroad are boosted by the advent of large-scale funding schemes. Financial problems (cited by one student in eight) and problems with the academic level of courses abroad (one in eleven) were the next most frequently mentioned problem areas, whereas language problems (one in twenty) were on the whole satisfactorily tackled.

In conclusion to this recapitulation of students' experiences during the study period abroad, and their perception of its usefulness, we must however recall that students' overall assessment of their study (and work placement) phase spent in another country is overwhelmingly positive. No fewer than 95 percent of all participants reported that they were satisfied with this experience despite the various problems which many of them had to overcome.

9.3   Academic Outcomes of Study Abroad

Already in the preceding section we have noted the remarkable extent to which students become exposed to a different teaching and learning situation while abroad, and the generally very positive way in which they regard the value of this experience. Results from the Before/After survey serve to confirm these impressions.

Even before embarking on study abroad students considered their *academic competences* - acquaintance with theories and methods, scientific reflection, interactive learning, systematic working and studying under pressure - on the whole in a positive light. It is therefore not surprising that in only very few of the total of 19 categories opinions were significantly more positive after study abroad than before. However, **where changes are discernible, they are clearly linked to the study abroad experience**. Thus students felt they had improved with regard to knowledge of the state of research abroad and to developing comparative perspectives, as well as to establishing what were the most important aspects of their study course.

There are also clear indications that study abroad sharpens students' awareness of learning processes and increases their motivation to learn scientific methods generally, since after studying abroad, a high proportion of students rated the importance of many methods of academic thought and work more highly than they had before. The majority of students surveyed place a higher value on extra-curricular communication between teachers and students as a mode of learning and as a means of furthering their general intellectual development, after the study abroad period than they did previously. Similarly, the practical application of knowledge and the acquisition of knowledge from other disciplines are clearly considered to be more important after a period of study abroad than beforehand.

These interesting insights into the effects of foreign study on academic success go hand in hand with remarkable findings with regard to students' perception of the way in which study abroad affects their actual *performance* in academic terms. **More than half of the students reported that their academic performance abroad had been actually better than they would have predicted for themselves at their home institution (23% even reported considerably better performance),** and a further quarter felt that their attainment level was approximately equal at home and abroad. Only the remaining quarter felt that they had experienced a curtailment of academic performance while abroad (only 7% saw the negative difference as being considerable). Considering that learning in a foreign language, different day to day living conditions, other methods of learning etc. do not make attaining even the same degree of academic success abroad as at home appear self-evident, these findings may be regarded as an indicator of the remarkable academic success of the study abroad programmes analyzed. Further research into this aspect of the impact of study abroad would certainly be valuable, and should be extended to cover the question of the possible impact of study abroad on students' academic performance upon their return to their home institution.

9.4 Foreign Language Outcomes of Study Abroad

In assessing the impact of study abroad on students' competence in the host country language, it should be noted in the case of our research that the students participating in the study abroad programmes under review already rated their foreign language competence relatively highly even before their departure. 90 percent, for example, felt able to buy clothing in a department store; 72 percent believed they could understand a lecture given in a foreign language. But **even from this high starting point, foreign language proficiency rose considerably during the study abroad period** : only four percent said after their return that they were still unable to follow lectures in the foreign language concerned.

Students' self-assessments before and after study abroad regarding the extent of their mastery of the language of the host country make it clear that increases in their foreign language proficiency in various dimensions proceed more or less hand in hand; there are, for example, very few students who are of the opinion that their reading ability is very high or improved markedly, and who feel on the other hand that their speaking ability remained relatively poor or stagnated while they were abroad.

In summarizing their language competence upon return, students on the whole considered their academically related *listening and reading* comprehension to be better than with regard to general everyday areas. On the other hand they are of the opinion that they can *speak* the language of the host country better in general everyday situations than within the framework of their studies. In general Swedish students regarded their proficiency in the language of the host country (in their case, however, this was always an English-speaking country) both before and after study abroad in the most positive, American students in the most negative light. German students had a lower opinion of their knowledge of the respective language of the host country before the study abroad period than had British and French students. This difference had for the most part been cancelled out after the study abroad period.

Students of foreign languages generally rated their foreign language competence less highly than did those in other subject areas. At first sight this appears surprising; however, it is possible that students in this field tend to judge their foreign language competence by particularly high standards compared with students in other fields.

Only eight percent of the students reported with regard to their present foreign language competence that at the end of the study abroad period they felt the language barrier to be a distinctly limiting past factor on their academic conversations with teachers. At the beginning of the period of study abroad on the other hand - this was their retrospective judgement - 62 percent had felt restricted. It is clear from various sources of information that on their return from a period abroad of the type under review in the present Project less than ten percent of students believe their foreign language ability to be insufficient to allow them to follow lectures successfully abroad.

9.5   Cultural Outcomes of Study Abroad

Participants in study abroad appear in many respects to acquire through study abroad a high level of information on the politics, the society and the culture of the host country. For example, before the study abroad period only 37 percent were convinced that they were well acquainted with the political system and institutions of the host country; this was true of 63 percent on their return. Similarly, interest in other countries and in general international relations in general also rose significantly.

On the other hand, *opinions* on politics, society and culture of the host country changed on average only in very few respects : the higher education system of the host country as well as that country's treatment of recently arrived immigrant groups are generally judged in a rather more negative light after the study abroad period. Students' perception of politics, society and culture in their own country on average remained the same. A more detailed analysis of assessments made makes it clear that general stereotypes, in as far as they existed among some students with regard to specific countries - for example among some British students with regard to Germany or some European students with regard to the USA - give way to more differentiated opinions which differ significantly from one area to the next : on average cultural life in France, the media in Great Britain, German customs and traditions, social structures in Sweden, and American universities are judged in the most positive light, while opinions diverge on the politics of the respective countries.

Participants in study abroad were already internationally oriented to a large degree before the actual study abroad period. This is made clear by the answers they gave to questions regarding their attitudes to other people and societies, their desire to become more closely acquainted with other countries, their respect for other countries, their readiness to judge their own country critically, their belief in the need for close international cooperation and concern for world-wide political developments. Not surprisingly, therefore, only very slight changes could be detected after the study abroad period, though critical attitudes towards the students' own country and their desire for international peace did increase slightly.

Students from European Community countries undertaking study periods in another EC Member State in the framework of the study abroad programmes analyzed, are on the whole strongly in favour of cooperation within the Community. 96 percent of the French and German students (though only 69% of those from the UK) felt that the Community should be strengthened. Similarly, 80 percent of the French and German students (as against 69% of their British counterparts) expressed the view that more emphasis should be placed on European cooperation in the fields of education and culture. Again, however, there is on average scarcely any difference between attitudes before and after the study abroad period.

Finally, the extent to which experience gained through living for a time in another culture and through close contact with people of another culture brings about changes in students' *self-appraisal* was examined. However, it did not prove possible with the investigative instruments chosen to substantiate this finding by quantatitive data analysis: a comparison of the replies to a self perception test administered before and during the study abroad period revealed on average no significant difference in respect of the dimensions chosen, namely social self-awareness and personal self-awareness. In reply to a general question, a substantial number of students were of the opinion that study abroad had made a significant impression on the development of their personality, and this perception tallies with the views expressed repeatedly and convincingly by the programme directors.

9.6 The Importance of Study Abroad in Employment and Career Terms

In the framework of the Study Abroad Evaluation Project, a survey was carried out among former students from the four European countries concerned, who graduated between 1980 and 1984 and who had previously participated in one of the study abroad programmes under review. 458 responses were received, and both the high rate of return and the findings to which the responses gave rise were remarkable.

In all, two-thirds of the respondents reported that study abroad had been helpful (43%) or even very helpful (23%) in finding their first job. Graduates also mention the positive effects of study abroad on occupational mobility: many reported that they had subsequently been transferred to positions in which there was a more pronounced international orientation.

Furthermore, it emerges from our findings that graduates who report that study abroad prepared them for assuming international tasks also have a **relatively high salary**; the same is true of those graduates who say that they use the language of the host country in the direct exercise of their professional duties and who are able to bring the occupational experience gained during the study abroad period to bear on their jobs. Our data was not, however, adequate to demonstrate a positive effect of the study abroad period on the salary levels of graduates right across the board.

More than half of the (European) graduates report that the organizations in which they are employed have business connections with the study abroad host country (53%), and that they themselves use the language of the host country in oral (54%) and written (53%) communication in a professional context. 54 percent state that the experience they gained of the country and its people during study abroad benefits them professionally. This is the case for graduates in all fields of study investigated and approximately to the same extent for men and women. 39 percent even report that they *use the specialized knowledge acquired during the study abroad period in their occupation*; this does, however, apply more to business and engineering graduates than to law graduates or graduates of natural science or foreign language subjects.

In their private lives, too, the former participants in the study abroad programmes under review reported a strong international orientation : 14 percent of them had foreign partners when the survey was carried out, in almost half of all cases from the study abroad host country. These particular graduates also show a statistically much higher incidence of employment in occupations with an international character than other former study abroad participants.

Looking back some years after completing their studies, graduates *assess the outcomes and effects of study abroad* in many respects similarly to students a few weeks after their return. However, graduates consider the contribution of study abroad towards understanding their own country to be somewhat greater than do students; conversely they see study abroad as being significantly less important with regard to becoming acquainted with other teaching methods and subject matter aspects of their studies.

Closing remarks made by graduates with regard to the importance of study abroad in employment and career terms (in response to an open question inviting them to make any other comments which they might consider relevant) include several different examples of activities in which knowledge of other countries, proficiency in foreign languages and other dimensions of first-hand international qualification play an important role.

However, it also becomes clear that **a considerable number of graduates - especially those who had studied law or foreign language subjects, but also some graduates in business, engineering and natural sciences - are disappointed not to have found occupations with a pronounced international dimension, however though even in these cases the graduates' judgement of study abroad is predominantly positive. In some cases there is reference to the impact of study abroad on other competences and spheres of life.**

Above all, however - and this is also true both for graduates in occupations which have a direct international dimension and those which have not - **emphasis is laid on other effects of study abroad upon personality, work style and social competences which are of more general importance professionally than on impacts directly attributable to job-related knowledge during study abroad: study abroad seems to promote the ability to adjust to unfamiliar situations, to deal with different kinds of people, to be prepared to take on new duties and new working conditions, to get to know previously unknown subject matters, to manage in unaccustomed circumstances and to learn from comparisons - attributes which are clearly important both professionally and socially and whose significance extends far beyond the specific framework of internationally oriented jobs.**

9.7 Concluding remarks

The many questionnaires, interviews and other research methods utilized during the Study Abroad Evaluation Project have, as may be seen from the present student-oriented volume and its partner volume relating to the structure and dynamics of the study abroad programmes themselves, given rise to a multiplicity of findings, including a whole range of demonstrable impacts of study abroad programmes on those who participate.

In the course of this research, a systematic effort was made not only to identify and chart the incidence of such outcomes, but also to ascertain what specific factors gave rise to them: the extent, for example, to which academic, foreign language, cultural and professional outcomes are attributable to experiences made and problems encountered during the study abroad period, or to characteristics of the study abroad programmes concerned or to the individual profile characteristics of the students themselves, was analyzed.

Additional research, including in-depth case studies, will be needed in future years to pursue this line of investigation further, but our own analysis has enabled us to draw certain conclusions based on the sample of study abroad programmes under review.

From our research, it emerged that *in some areas experiences and modes of behaviour during the period of study abroad lead to corresponding outcomes* : students who take foreign language courses abroad demonstrate above average increases in foreign language competence; students who travelled widely acquired particularly extensive knowledge of the culture and society of the host country; those who had learning difficulties abroad judged the higher education system of the host country in a more negative light after the study abroad period than before.

A number of plausible correlations between the characteristics of study abroad programmes and their outcomes for the participants are also discernible : for example close cooperation between the home institution and the partner institution abroad leads to a more significant increase in knowledge of foreign languages, to a more positive assessment of the higher education system of the host country and to higher expectations with regard to the occupational utility of study abroad.

Students participating in programmes for which a period of study abroad is not obligatory report particularly often high academic achievement and a considerable increase in their knowledge of the culture and the society of the host country. This is probably attributable in large part to the fact that in some study abroad programmes of this type students opting for study abroad tend to represent a highly selected group in terms of their motivation and academic competence. Furthermore, these programmes generally attach fewer formal requirements to the study period abroad. Conversely, participants in obligatory programmes, while judging the higher education system of the host country more positively on their return, also report somewhat more problems regarding academic achievement while abroad; in this connection the fact that obligatory programmes are more ambitious with regard to curricular integration may be an important factor.

With regard to the impact of students' individual background and motivations on study abroad outcomes, it should in particular be pointed out that students who had already laid great importance on participation in study abroad when choosing their higher education institution or their particular subject report significant improvement in their knowledge of foreign languages, judge the higher education system of the host country more positively on their return and have a high opinion of the occupational utility of study abroad. A greater proportion of male students than female students expect to derive professional utility from study abroad.

It is nevertheless worthy of note that the statistical analysis carried out reveals only *relatively few significant correlations* between students' individual profiles, programme characteristics and general experience gained from a stay abroad on the one hand, and academic, foreign language, cultural and professional outcomes on the other. For example, the importance placed by students on academic learning, the extent of their international orientation, any enhancement of personal and social confidence as well as the development of definite ideas with regard to professional goals cannot consistently be traced back to specific factors. Nor, conversely, does it appear that differences in social background, academic achievements before the stay abroad, the majority of aspects related to the preparation of study abroad or the length of the study abroad programme may be adduced as a consistent explanation for variations in the outcomes of study abroad.

The apparently small number of clear statistical correlations is probably attributable to a number of factors. First, and above all, it must be recognized that the outcomes of phases of learning cannot usually be explained by individual factors but are more the result of complex conditions : different factors may therefore be decisive for the success of programmes in each case. Secondly, despite their seeming diversity in structural and institutional terms, the programmes selected for analysis in fact demonstrate a high degree of uniformity in respect of various elements which, it may be assumed, can have a particularly significant impact on their success or failure : for example, many of the programmes are characterized by an enormous commitment of the programme directors, and all programmes investigated involved a period of several months abroad.

On the basis of our analysis it is therefore not possible to identify specific "recipes for success". This itself, however, is a most important finding, implying as it does that programmes operating in very different circumstances and demonstrating very different characteristics can be successful: when it comes to any organized study abroad programmes, all roads lead to Rome.